Practical JSF in Java EE 8

Web Applications in Java
for the Enterprise

Michael Müller

Apress®

Practical JSF in Java EE 8: Web Applications in Java for the Enterprise

Michael Müller
Brühl, Nordrhein-Westfalen, Germany

ISBN-13 (pbk): 978-1-4842-3029-9   ISBN-13 (electronic): 978-1-4842-3030-5
https://doi.org/10.1007/978-1-4842-3030-5

Library of Congress Control Number: 2018941459

Managing Director, Apress Media LLC: Welmoed Spahr
Acquisitions Editor: Steve Anglin
Development Editor: Matthew Moodie
Coordinating Editor: Mark Powers

Cover designed by eStudioCalamar

Cover image designed by Freepik (www.freepik.com)

Distributed to the book trade worldwide by Springer Science+Business Media New York, 233 Spring Street, 6th Floor, New York, NY 10013. Phone 1-800-SPRINGER, fax (201) 348-4505, e-mail orders-ny@springer-sbm.com, or visit www.springeronline.com. Apress Media, LLC is a California LLC and the sole member (owner) is Springer Science + Business Media Finance Inc (SSBM Finance Inc). SSBM Finance Inc is a **Delaware** corporation.

For information on translations, please e-mail rights@apress.com, or visit http://www.apress.com/rights-permissions.

Apress titles may be purchased in bulk for academic, corporate, or promotional use. eBook versions and licenses are also available for most titles. For more information, reference our Print and eBook Bulk Sales web page at www.apress.com/bulk-sales.

Any source code or other supplementary material referenced by the author in this book is available to readers on GitHub via the book's product page, located at www.apress.com/9781484230299. For more detailed information, please visit www.apress.com/source-code.

Printed on acid-free paper

To my wife Claudia and my kids:

*Thank you for your patience during night-writing
and other long sessions.*

I love you.

Table of Contents

About the Author

Michael Müller is an IT professional with more than 30 years of experience, including about 25 years in the healthcare sector. During this time, he has worked in different areas, especially project and product management, consulting, and software development. He gained international knowledge not only by targeting international markets but also by leading external teams (from Eastern Europe and India).

Currently he is the head of software development at the German DRG institute (`http://inek.org`). In this role, he is responsible for web applications and other Java and .NET projects. Web projects are preferably built with Java technologies such as JSF with the help of supporting languages like JavaScript.

Michael is a professional JSF user and a member of the JSR 344 and JSR 372 (JSF) expert groups. Due to his community activities, he was invited to join the NetBeans Dream Team and became a member in January 2016. You may contact him through his blog `blog.mueller-bruehl.de`. Follow him on Twitter at `@muellermi`.

About the Technical Reviewer

Manuel Jordan Elera is an autodidactic developer and researcher who enjoys learning new technologies for his own experiments and creating new integrations.

Manuel won the 2010 Springy Award: Community Champion and Spring Champion 2013. In his little free time, he reads the Bible and composes music on his guitar. Manuel is known as `dr_pompeii`. He has tech reviewed numerous books for Apress, including *Pro Spring Messaging* (2017), *Pro Spring*, 4th Edition (2014), *Practical Spring LDAP* (2013), *Pro JPA 2*, Second Edition (2013), and *Pro Spring Security* (2013).

You can read his 13 detailed tutorials about many Spring technologies and contact him through his blog at `www.manueljordanelera.blogspot.com`. Follow him on Twitter at `@dr_pompeii`.

Acknowledgments

All content unless otherwise mentioned is written by me. But a couple of people provided me feedback, helped with wording, or did a technical review on TinyCalculator and/or Books. Besides the people who are mentioned below, a special thank you to John Wright, who also provided a couple of comments. And a special thank you to all the other people who provided a mostly one-time feedback. All of you helped to improve this book.

Pratap Chatterjee is a software engineer who has worked with enterprise application software development for over 20 years, mainly in the telecommunication industry in England with BT and T-Mobile UK as programmer, designer, developer, and team leader with Java and web technologies. Currently Pratap lives in Sweden with his wife and two sons. He's working for Karolinska Institutet, one of the world's leading medical universities. Pratap enjoys programming, and in his role as a programmer developer, he has written applications that help in the publication of doctoral courses and admission of students by the university. Pratap has also reviewed technical articles and recently reviewed *Grails in Action*, 2nd Edition (Manning, 2014), by Glen Smith and Peter Ledbrook.

Constantin Marian Alin is a passionate Java developer focused on developing web/desktop applications using the latest Java technologies. Beside daily work and learning, in the past few years he has written and published articles for the Developer. com and DZone communities. Currently, he's focused on developing RIA/SPA applications for the GIS field by integrating the power of Java frameworks like JavaServer Faces, PrimeFaces, AngularJS, Bootstrap, RESTful, EJB, JPA, and more with the GIS specialized software, such as ArcGIS, OpenLayers, GeoServer, Google Maps, and others.

Anghel Leonard is a senior Java developer with more than 13 years of experience in Java SE, Java EE, and related frameworks. He's written and published more than 50 articles about Java technologies and more than 500 tips and tricks for many websites dedicated to programming. In addition, he's written books including *Pro Java 7 NIO.2* (Apress), *Pro Hibernate and MongoDB* (Apress), *Tehnologii XML XML în Java* (Albastra), *Jboss Tools 3 Developer's Guide* (Packt Publishing), *JSF 2.0 Cookbook* (Packt), *JSF 2.0 Cookbook: LITE* (Packt), *Mastering JavaServer Faces 2.2* (Packt).

ACKNOWLEDGMENTS

Currently, Anghel is developing web applications using the latest Java technologies on the market (EJB 3.0, CDI, Spring, JSF, Struts, Hibernate, and so on). For the past two years, he's focused on developing rich Internet applications for geographic information systems.

Special thanks to the reviewers of this edition, **Manual Jordan Elera** and **Mathew Moodie**, who provided input to refine and enhance this book.

Preface

Developing web applications with Java and JavaServer Faces (JSF) had been a great pleasure (and success) to me for a couple of years when I realized first wanted to write a book about JSF in late 2010. I got in touch with some German publishers with the goal of writing around 200–250 pages about this subject, nothing more. "No thanks, too special" was one answer. The other: "Great. Add some more pages, another thousand, and write about the whole Java Enterprise Edition. Keep JSF smaller than 200 pages." Frustrating answers.

So, I started to blog about JSF in early 2011. And I became a member of the JSF 2.2 (JSR 344) Expert Group. Unlike most of the other volunteers, I wasn't a JSF implementer, but an expert JSF user. I became a member of the JSF 2.3 (JSR 372) Expert Group too. I'm still an expert JSF user, but I started to code a bit within the JSF sources. If I'm accepted as an expert group member for JSF's next version, whatever it may be called after the transition to the Eclipse Foundation, I want to contribute code.

My tutorial on web development with JSF is still the most popular part of my blog (blog.mueller-bruehl.de), and I never gave up my intention to write a book about this subject. Over time, I switched from blogging in German to writing about development in mostly English. And that German publisher would be happy to learn that I now write about related Java EE stuff also.

With the articles of my blog as a solid foundation, I started to write my book, *Web Development with Java and JSF*, which I first published myself in 2014 using Leanpub (www.leanpub.com/jsf). It became a kind of living book. The first version only covered the fundamentals. Every reader who purchased it was able to download later updates. Thus, the book grew up.

In 2016 Apress first asked me to publish the book as is. I declined, because I wanted to add more stuff. When they asked me again in 2017, the book had reached such a stage that I agreed. Of course, there is still more to write about, but for every book you need to make a final decision on content.

Today, you hold in your hands an enhanced edition of my former book. It follows the same approach, combining theoretical background with practical development. The title *Practical JSF in Java EE 8* is a clue that it's not only about JSF — you can't use this UI technology in isolation. Rather, it's embedded in a full stack of technologies we know as the Java Enterprise Edition (Java EE). Java EE 8 was released on September 21, 2017, and Oracle has begun its donation of Java EE to the Eclipse Foundation. Even if future versions will be called Jakarta EE, the latest version still is Java EE 8 with JSF 2.3. Because this book is about practical development, it concentrates on applications, not on the latest features. Although all applications in this book operate with Java EE 8, most of the apps might be realized with Java EE 7, which is still state-of-the-art in most enterprise environments. Only those functions that rely on newer Java EE features need the appropriate version — the last application described in this book, Alumni, takes advantage of such new features.

In a sense, this book teaches you to develop Java EE applications with JSF as user interface. It's a book for Java enthusiasts. Knowledge about web technologies is helpful, but not required. For developers who aren't familiar with HTML, CSS, and other stuff, I've added some introductory chapters in the appendixes.

Enjoy!

—Michael Müller

PART I

TinyCalculator

CHAPTER 1

TinyCalculator

TinyCalculator is the first and simplest application discussed in this book. It's nothing more than a simple calculator for basic arithmetic. But it is useful to show some fundamental concepts of web applications with Java and JSF.

As a kind of appetizer, and unlike how I'll handle the other applications, I'll first show you the whole application, with a little explanation afterwards. Then, as a kind of restart, I talk about the foundations of web applications and explain TinyCalculator and different approaches.

You can access the source code for TinyCalculator by clicking the Download Source Code button at `www.apress.com/9781484230299`. You can also find the source code at `http://webdevelopment-java.info`.

Creating the Application

A web application with Java and JSF uses an application server to run. Don't be afraid—your IDE usually deals with that. Later on, I'll discuss that in more detail. We'll start with the application.

For this book, I had to decide which IDE to use in the tutorial parts. NetBeans, either the Java EE or All edition, comes with GlassFish. At the time of writing, the direct link to the download page is `https://netbeans.org/downloads/index.html`. Because NetBeans has been donated to Apache, this location may change. If that link isn't available anymore, refer to `https://apache.netbeans.org`. Just install it, and no further configuration is needed to start with simple applications. It's quite easy.

Many of this book's basic examples are based on NetBeans 8 (English), which is bundled with GlassFish 4. GlassFish 4 is the reference implementation of Java EE 7, which is fine for TinyCalculator. To enable the brand new Java EE 8 features, you need GlassFish 5 or any other Java EE 8–compliant server, once available. GlassFish 5 will be

© Michael Müller 2018
M. Müller, *Practical JSF in Java EE 8*, https://doi.org/10.1007/978-1-4842-3030-5_1

bundled with NetBeans 9. Since the first donation (IDE) is still in progress, and Java EE is part of the second Java EE 8 donation, this may be a lengthy process. I'll describe how to update to Java EE 8 just after TinyCalculator's explanation.

All applications in this book are built with Apache Maven (`http://maven.apache.org`), which is bundled with NetBeans. The Maven application structure is almost independent from the IDE. Thus, you may use any IDE of your choice (see also Chapter 2). Depending on your IDE, you may open Maven projects directly (for example, with NetBeans) or you may need to perform a simple import (for example, with Eclipse).

As a novice to JSF or Java EE, you may not have created any Java-based web application before. So, I'll start this one from scratch in the form of a step-by-step tutorial. Unlike in future chapters, I'll cover the whole application here without detailed explanation, and then we'll catch up after the tutorial:

1.   Launch NetBeans.

2.   From the File menu, choose New Project. NetBeans displays the New Project wizard, as shown in Figure 1-1.

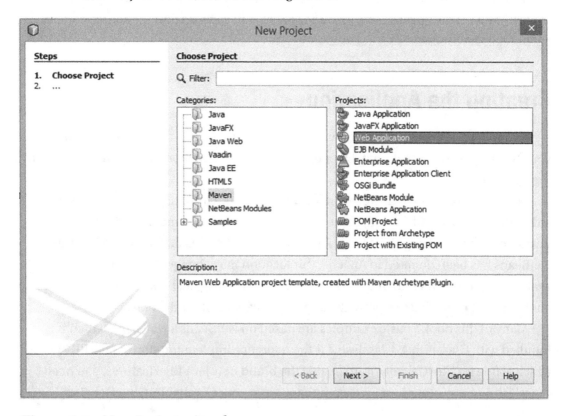

Figure 1-1. *New Project wizard*

3. Click the category Maven, click Web Application, and then click Next. NetBeans displays the New Web Application wizard, as shown in Figure 1-2.

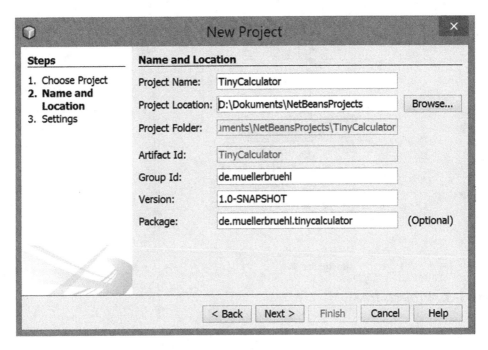

Figure 1-2. *New Web Application wizard*

4. For the Project Name, enter **TinyCalculator**. You may adapt the other fields as desired, or just keep them unchanged. It's good practice to set the Group Id to the reverse notation of your domain. Click Next, keep the settings in the next dialog unchanged, and click Finish.

NetBeans creates a skeleton of a new web application for you and displays it within the projects tree, as shown in Figure 1-3.

Figure 1-3. *Projects tree*

5. Right-click (secondary click) TinyCalculator in the projects tree and choose Properties from the context menu. The Project Properties screen appears, as shown in Figure 1-4.

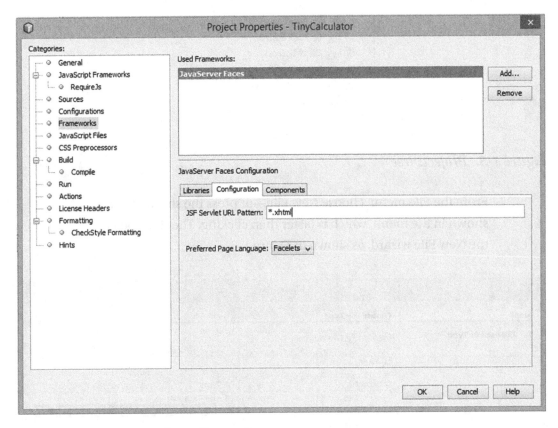

***Figure 1-4.** Framework configuration*

6. Choose the Frameworks category. Choose JavaServer Faces and click the Add button. Click the Configuration tab and change the contents of the JSF Servlet URL Pattern box to ***.xhtml**. Click OK.

    While adding JSF to your project, NetBeans creates a web page called index.xhtml within the web pages, keeping the formerly created index.html file.

7. On the projects tree open the Web Pages node (if it's not already open), as shown in Figure 1-5. Select index.html and delete it.

Figure 1-5. *Projects tree*

From the File menu, choose New File—or press the shortcut key shown in the menu, which is faster than clicking. The IDE opens the New File wizard, as shown in Figure 1-6.

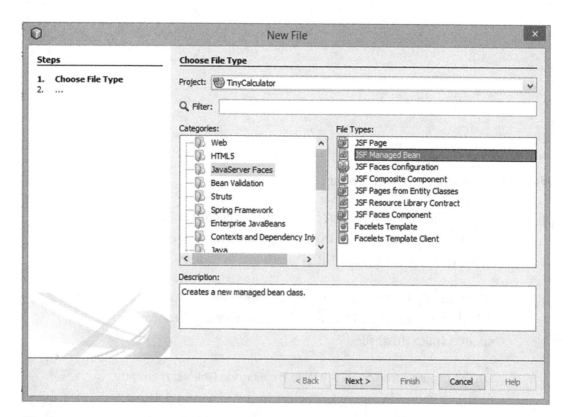

Figure 1-6. *New File wizard*

8. Choose the category JavaServer Faces and then choose JSF
    Managed Bean. Click Next.

The New JSF Managed Bean window appears, as shown in Figure 1-7.

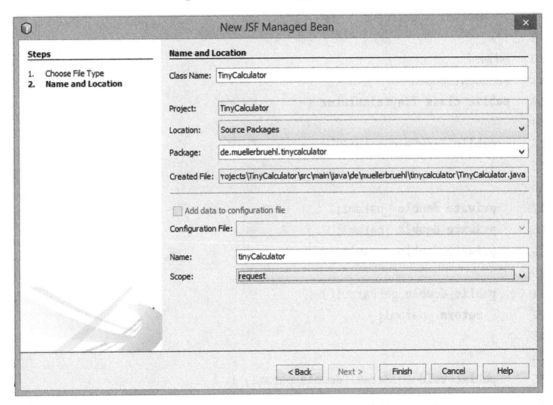

Figure 1-7. *New JSF Managed Bean*

9. Enter **TinyCalculator** as the Class Name and from Scope select
    request. Click Finish.

NetBeans creates and opens a Java class file named
TinyCalculator.

10. Now, edit this class. Key in or paste the code shown in Listing 1-1.

Listing 1-1. Editing the TinyCalculator Class File

```
1    package de.muellerbruehl.tinycalculator;
2
3    import javax.inject.Named;
```

```
 4    import javax.enterprise.context.RequestScoped;
 5
 6    /**
 7     *
 8     * @author mmueller
 9     */
10    @Named
11    @RequestScoped
12    public class TinyCalculator {
13
14      public TinyCalculator() {
15      }
16
17      private double _param1;
18      private double _param2;
19      private double _result;
20
21      public double getParam1() {
22        return _param1;
23      }
24
25      public void setParam1(double param1) {
26        _param1 = param1;
27      }
28
29      public double getParam2() {
30        return _param2;
31      }
32
33      public void setParam2(double param2) {
34        _param2 = param2;
35      }
36
37      public double getResult() {
38        return _result;
39      }
```

```
40
41    public void setResult(double result) {
42        _result = result;
43    }
44
45    public String add(){
46        _result = _param1 + _param2;
47        return "";
48    }
49
50    public String subtract(){
51        _result = _param1 - _param2;
52        return "";
53    }
54
55    public String multiply(){
56        _result = _param1 * _param2;
57        return "";
58    }
59
60    public String divide(){
61        _result = _param1 / _param2;
62        return "";
63    }
64 }
```

You may notice the underscores indicating the fields. This usage differs slightly from the Java naming conventions. If you're interested in why I'm doing it this way, see Appendix D.

11. Open the index.xhtml page in the editor and change it to the following:

```
1  <?xml version='1.0' encoding='UTF-8' ?>
2  <!DOCTYPE html>
3  <html xmlns="http://www.w3.org/1999/xhtml"
4      xmlns:h="http://xmlns.jcp.org/jsf/html">
5    <h:head>
```

```
6        <title>TinyCalculator</title>
7      </h:head>
8      <h:body>
9        <h1>TinyCalculator</h1>
10       <h:form>
11         <div>
12           <h:outputLabel value="Param1: "/>
13           <h:inputText value="#{tinyCalculator.param1}"/>
14         </div>
15         <div>
16           <h:outputLabel value="Param2: "/>
17           <h:inputText value="#{tinyCalculator.param2}"/>
18         </div>
19         <div>
20           <h:commandButton value="Add"
21                             action="#{tinyCalculator.add}"/>
22           <h:commandButton value="Subtract"
23                             action="#{tinyCalculator.subtract}"/>
24           <h:commandButton value="Multiply"
25                             action="#{tinyCalculator.multiply}"/>
26           <h:commandButton value="Divide"
27                             action="#{tinyCalculator.divide}"/>
28         </div>
29         <div>
30           <h:outputLabel value="Result: "/>
31           <h:outputText value="#{tinyCalculator.result}"/>
32         </div>
33       </h:form>
34     </h:body>
35   </html>
```

12. Run the project by clicking Run ➤ Run Project (TinyCalculator).

   If your application server isn't running yet, NetBeans will start
   your GlassFish application server—and your browser, too. It will
   display the TinyCalculator, as shown in Figure 1-8.

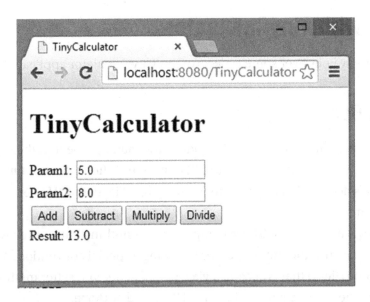

Figure 1-8. *TinyCalculator in action*

13. Take a big breath—soon you'll get an explanation of what has happened so far.

NETBEANS CODE COMPLETION

As you might expect, a good Java IDE will assist you in creating code. There's no need to type in the whole source code. For example, you can simply type three attributes and let NetBeans create the getters and setters for you. NetBeans will create the code by the aid of the Insert Code menu. Open the context menu (right-click within the source and choose the appropriate menu or press Alt+Insert. Describing all the features of an IDE is far beyond scope of this book, but you can check NetBeans help, which is available online via the Help menu.

Note   For this step-by-step tutorial, I added the whole source code. In future listings, I'll usually omit imports, simple getters and setters, and more for brevity. If you're missing an import, press Alt+Shift+I, and NetBeans will add the imports. Other IDEs offer a similar shortcut. Also, usually I'll mix code examples along with detailed information.

Working with TinyCalculator

This section briefly goes over some aspects of the TinyCalculator application.

Managed Beans

I assume, for you as a Java developer, the code of the managed bean is the most familiar part of the TinyCalculator application. In JSF, developers often talk about *managed beans*, and that's how NetBeans called them in its New File dialog. However, this term isn't really accurate.

A *Java bean* is a reusable software component. It's nothing but a pure Java class with a no-argument constructor and properties following a special convention. A *property* is a private attribute (field) that is accessed via a pair of getter and setter methods. These methods follow the naming convention of setName and getName.

From the abstract perspective of object-oriented programming, the state of an object is held by attributes. An *attribute* is a variable that can have any modifier, such as private, protected, public, static, and so on. The term *attribute* is widely used and can imply nearly everything. Although it's the correct term to describe the state of an object, in Java other terms are often used (which might also be called differently in other languages). In this book, I mostly use the following:

- A *field* is a private (or sometimes protected) instance variable.

- A *property* is a field that is exposed by a pair of getter and setter.

JavaServer Faces is designed to run both in Enterprise Java Beans (EJB) containers as well as in servlet containers. Both are called *application servers*. Whereas the first one contains a full or partial stack (besides the full platform, only one profile, the *web profile,* is defined) of Java EE technologies, including servlet, the latter only serves servlets. Thus, other Java EE technologies, like Contexts and Dependency Injection (CDI), are not available in servlet containers. Some widely known examples of EJB containers are GlassFish and WildFly. Examples of servlet containers include Tomcat and Jetty.

If JSF runs on a pure servlet container, JSF manages so-called *backing beans*. Such a bean will be annotated as @ManagedBean, and that's where the term *managed bean* originates. Starting with Java EE 6/JSF 2.0, developers could use CDI *named beans* too, which is today's recommended technology. In TinyCalculator, we use a CDI named bean. Such a bean is annotated by @Named. The current version, JSF 2.3, deprecated the old JSF managed beans. If you want to use CDI managed beans, you either need to use an EJB container like GlassFish or add the CDI framework to the servlet container. A named or managed bean might be accessed by its name.

The second annotation, @RequestScoped, declares the bean's lifetime—with every request from your browser, an instance of this class is created and destroyed by the termination of the request. A longer lifetime might be declared by @SessionScoped (providing one instance of the bean per user session), @ApplicationScoped (one instance during the application's lifetime), and more. I'll talk more about this later in the book.

In the example, we used a CDI named bean, as in Listing 1-2.

Listing 1-2. CDI Annotation for a Request Scoped Bean

```
1    import javax.inject.Named;
2    import javax.enterprise.context.RequestScoped;
3
4    @Named
5    @RequestScoped
6    public class TinyCalculator {...}
```

A JSF managed bean, on the other hand, would be declared as in Listing 1-3.

Listing 1-3. JSF Annotation for a Request Scoped Bean (Do Not Use)

```
1    import javax.faces.bean.ManagedBean;
2    import javax.faces.bean.RequestScoped;
3
4    @ManagedBean
5    @RequestScoped
6    public class TinyCalculator {...}
```

Caution   Always use the annotations for named/managed beans in conjunction with the appropriate scope annotations—for example, both JSF annotations or both CDI annotations. In particular, a named bean with JSF scope would result in a runtime error.

Although you can't mix these annotations within a single bean, it is possible to use both types (named and managed) beans within one application. That might be useful for migrating older applications that used JSF managed beans. It's possible to add new features by implementing them as CDI named beans while keeping the existing beans. Then, over time, the existing beans might be changed to named beans too.

But why should you prefer CDI named beans over JSF managed beans? As their name suggests, JSF managed beans are developed especially for and dedicated only to JSF.

CDI (Contexts and Dependency Injection) is relatively new to Java EE and has made it into EE 6. It allows the container to "inject" appropriate objects into your object. These objects may not be known at compile time, and the dependencies will be resolved at runtime. This allows loose coupling of objects. One essential part of this solution is a general naming concept.

Because CDI named beans may be used in different Java EE technologies, JSF itself slowly migrates to CDI, which sometimes replaces the proprietary solution. JSF 2.3 at last simply allows to inject JSF-related objects into places where it had been very tricky before to access these values. The migration to CDI is mostly complete for this version.

Note   As of JSF 2.3 (Java EE 8), JSF managed beans (@ManagedBean) became deprecated.

But is CDI available in pure servlet containers like Apache Tomcat? No, but JSF isn't available either until you deploy the JSF library to enable it. Similarly, you may add CDI to a servlet container: just provide a CDI implementation—for example, Weld (`http://repo1.maven.org/maven2/org/jboss/weld/servlet/weld-servlet/`). In the case of Tomcat, there is a simpler solution: Use TomEE (`http://tomee.apache.org/index.html`), which is Tomcat bundled with Java EE technologies, implementing the Java EE Web Profile.

BEAN PASSIVATION

If the bean's lifetime is expanded to more than one request, the server still has to manage this object, even though the next request may take a while or will never occur. The latter is mitigated by a session timeout. Until then, the bean is alive. Where there is a lot of traffic, this memory consumption may cause problems.

To avoid memory problems, or for other reasons, depending on the implementation, the container might *passivate* a bean: the object is persisted somewhere, such as to disk, and during the next request, when needed, is restored into memory (*activated*).

To enable this feature, the bean must implement the *Serializable* interface.

PREVIEWING SCOPES

I discuss scopes in detail later in this book. But to give you an initial feeling about scopes, you may perform a little task.

1. Add a logger and log the construction of the TinyCalculator class:

```
1   private static final Logger LOGGER = Logger.getLogger("TinyCalculator");
2   public TinyCalculator() {
3       LOGGER .log(Level.INFO, "ctor TinyCalculator");
4   }
```

2. Launch the application and watch the NetBeans console window.

3. Perform some calculations and then close and reopen the browser and application.

4. Perform some more calculations.

5. Now exchange the @RequestScoped annotation for @SessionScoped, and then for @ApplicationScoped, and perform the same operations.

6. Observe the different output.

Did you observe the message "ctor TinyCalculator" printed to the console (*ctor* is an abbreviation of *constructor*)? You'll also find the message in the log. It appeared once for every request when using the @RequestScoped annotation. Using @SessionScoped, this message appears for a new session (such as after closing and relaunching the browser) only. Using @ApplicationScoped, the message appeared only for the first call to the bean after the app had been launched.

The calculation methods may look quite strange. These are not functions returning the calculated value, but methods returning a string and perform the calculation by changing the status of the result variable. The simple reason is that the calculation is called within the

17

action of the appropriate button. Such an action performs a page navigation. Returning an empty string or null keeps the browser "staying" on the current page. In fact, this page will be reloaded (I cover page navigation in detail later in the book). Using JSF 2.2 or later, such a function might be declared as void, alternatively.

The Page

I don't want to anticipate the detailed explanation coming up in the next chapters. I just want to point out that the page will be rendered as HTML and sent to the browser. If you're familiar with HTML, you would recognize only some HTML elements. JSF's former intention was to provide the programmer a kind of known interface, hiding away that HTML stuff. Because of that, JSF offers a set of its own tags, which are included in the page and are replaced before sending the page to the browser. These tags are regular XML tags, assigned to appropriate namespaces:

```
1    <h:outputLabel value="Param1: "/>
2    <h:inputText value="#{tinyCalculator.param1}"/>
```

This is a label with a value (text) of "Param1:" followed by a text element. The value of the text element is retrieved from and sent back to our bean. #{...} denotes the Expression Language (EL), which is used to glue parts of the user interface to the managed bean. tinyCalculator refers to our bean—by default, the EL uses the bean name with a lowercase first letter, followed by dot notation and referring methods. In the case of properties, this establishes a two-way communication with the getter/setter pair. Name refers to getName and setName (omitting the get and set prefixes). Thus, the text element reads and writes the property:

```
1    <h:commandButton value="Add" action="#{tinyCalculator.add}"/>
```

In the case of the buttons, each action defines one of the calculating methods.

Note   Starting with JSF 2.2, an alternative approach was introduced, reducing the JSF-specific tags and using more pure HTML. This is known as *HTML-friendly markup* or more often *HTML5-friendly markup*, even though it is not HTML5 specific.

The Relationship Between Code and View

The rough relationship between browser view, page definition, and managed bean should be understandable from the explanation. But a picture, like Figure 1-9, is worth a thousand words.

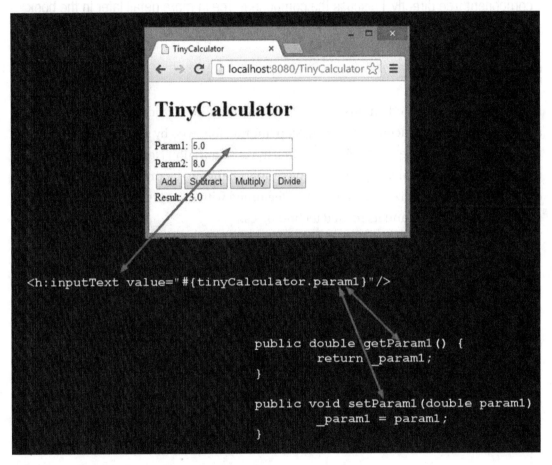

Figure 1-9. *Rough relationship between code and view*

The tag `<inputText ...>` represents a text field in the browser. Its values are bound to a getter/setter pair of the bean. When JSF renders the page, it calls the getter to retrieve the value for the input field. And after clicking an operation button, the content of the page is sent to the server (using an HTTP POST under the hood). JSF transfers the data into the model (our bean) by using the setter.

Note   The simplified presentation shown earlier is useful for an initial understanding of JSF, but it ignores one important fact: the component tree. When processing a request, all JSF components are held within a tree data structure. Depending on enhanced features of your application, it may be useful to access or manipulate this component tree directly. I discuss the component tree in more detail later in the book.

Summary

In this chapter we created our first small JSF application. To provide a quick result, this application was introduced as a step-by-step tutorial, followed by a brief discussion.

There is much more to explain, including the configuration NetBeans built for us under the hood and which we modified by simply changing the project's properties. This chapter is just an appetizer—a quick start. Beginning with the next chapter, I'll discuss the foundations of JSF and its related technologies.

CHAPTER 2

Foundations

For web development, a few different technologies are used. This chapter discusses the basics of some of those and mentions other important technologies, including the following:

- Web applications

- Hypertext Transfer Protocol (HTTP)

- Hypertext Markup Language (HTML)

- Cascading Style Sheets (CSS)

- JavaScript

- Java

- Maven

- Selenium and Arquillian

- Servlets

- Deployment

Web Applications

When I use the term *web application* in this book, I'm going by the following definition:

A web application is a client-server application interacting dynamically with the user via a web browser.

Thus, we are talking about distinct parts: the client, presenting the user interface, and the server, executing the main part of the application. The client is linked to the server via the Internet. The application logic may be organized in layers and split between client and server. To get a more responsive user experience, some bits are

21

© Michael Müller 2018
M. Müller, *Practical JSF in Java EE 8*, https://doi.org/10.1007/978-1-4842-3030-5_2

executed on the client side. Unlike an application using a specially programmed client, a common web browser is used to display the presentation layer. That means we can't manage every detail. Instead, we have to rely on the browser's functionality, which mainly is to retrieve and display such content as HTML pages. An HTML page doesn't only include text information, but images, media files, and more. Besides the content, the browser needs to handle the layout and, optionally, execute script code. We send all this stuff to the browser, but we can't control all of its behavior.

A simple web server, only delivering static pages, is not a web application for the purposes of this book. But by using a standard web browser, a web application might be used on any platform for which a (modern) browser is available. A web browser is connected to a web server via HTTP. Because of that, a web application has to deal with some of the restrictions of this protocol, as described in the next section.

HTTP

The Hypertext Transfer Protocol is a logical transport layer (*application protocol*), acting on a stack of other layers, down to the physical transport layer. Usually HTTP is used atop TCP/IP. As the name suggests, it was primarily designed to distribute hypertext information. As such, it is the foundation of the World Wide Web.

HTTP is a stateless request-response protocol. A server is listening for a request and sends back a response, as illustrated in Figure 2-1. Then the communication terminates.

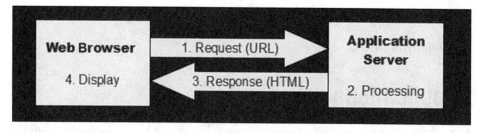

Figure 2-1. *HTTP request-response cycle*

The simplified illustration in Figure 2-1 shows a typical request-response cycle as triggered by the user when retrieving a page. In fact, the response is an HTTP response, composed of a message header and body, that might carry information other than HTML, such as JSON, XML, or something else.

Any subsequent request acts independently of the prior ones. This kind of protocol affects the way a web application works with its clients. To proceed with a user session of the application, a session management needs to be implemented on top of HTTP. The goal of this session management is to remember the current state of the application. Either the server needs to store application's state somewhere and provides key information to the client, or the server transfers the complete state information to the client.

For the latter approach, there's nothing to remember on the server side. Any status might be restored by the information the client provides during a subsequent request. Such an approach keeps memory consumption on the server lean. Sending lots of information over the web has some important drawbacks. Latency will slow down the application. Another drawback involves security. If the network transport isn't secured by a protocol like Transport Layer Security (TLS), then the information sent might be read by unauthorized persons. Saving the whole state to the client avoids "sticky" sessions: the next request might be processed by a different server behind a load balancer.

The first approach just mentioned is to keep all information on the server and send only an identifier to the client. Such an identifier is called a *session id*. Common possible ways to convey a session id are by using a hidden field or sending an HTTP cookie. If the server holds the state, the session needs to be continued by the same server unless you implement a solution to share this state information between different servers. For example, the app state might be saved within a shared key-value store and can be restored by any server that receives the session id. In practice, a modern server might serve a few dozens or a hundred thousand sessions per day. So, in many scenarios, such "sticky" sessions won't matter.

SESSION HIJACKING

Due to the nature of the HTTP, the server needs information like the session id to determine how to proceed. If an unauthorized person (such as a cracker—meaning *criminal hacker*) captures this information, they could take over the session. That's called *session hijacking*. JSF offers some additional features to secure your application.

Luckily, session management is implemented by the Java environment. Within servlet/JSF configuration, it's possible to choose between client or server state.

During a request, HTTP addresses a Uniform Resource Identifier (URI). Additionally, it tells the server which HTTP method to use. This is often called a *verb*. The most interesting methods for use with JSF are GET and POST.

URI, URL, URN

Some people say a Uniform Resource Identifier (URI) is commonly used in the context of REST (short for *REpresentational State Transfer,* discussed in Chapter 24), and a web page is addressed by something called a Uniform Resource Locator (URL). But indeed, a URI might be either a URL or a Uniform Resource Name (URN). You can read more about URNs at www.ietf.org/rfc/rfc3986.txt.

Addressing web pages as well as addressing a resource according to the REST programming style deals with locations, not with names. Thus, in both contexts we use URLs. And because any URL is a URI, I use URI in this book.

GET queries information from the server by use of a URI. Additional parameters might be appended to the URI—for example, http://it-rezension.de/Books/books.xhtml?catId=2. That addresses the server found at it-rezension.de, and within that, the application and page Books/books.xhtml. A parameter catId=2 is appended.

With a POST request, information is sent to the server within the body of the request—for example, a web form (HTML) contains some input fields and a submit button. Hitting this button initiates a POST request.

Within the context of REST, the methods (verbs) PUT and DELETE are important too. The idea behind REST is to assign defined actions to the verbs. Although this book is about JSF, and a pure JSF application won't use REST, the Alumni application I describe in Chapter 24 is not a monolithic application. Rather, it takes advantage of a service with an API that follows the REST concept.

HTML

HTML is used to describe the content of a web page. Like XML, HTML is derived from the Standard Generalized Markup Language (SGML).

As a Java developer, I assume you're familiar with XML. Like XML, HTML uses tags to structure the content of a page. Within XML you may define any tag of your choice and assign any meaning to it. Unlike XML, HTML tags are predefined and have special relevance. For example, <head> denotes the header of a HTML file, <p> denotes a paragraph, and so forth. Thus, HTML is not extensible in the sense that XML is.

TAG GUESSING

In one way, HTML is less restrictive than XML: missing closing tags aren't flagged as errors but are automatically closed. Browsers try to handle overlapping tags. Some people praise this behavior because it means writing less markup, takes less work, less data is transferred, and pages load faster (but will a few less characters really make a page load faster?).

Different browsers may handle missing or interlaced tags in a different way, and guessing how to complete the missing parts sometimes results in dangerous code. (Check out *The Tangled Web* by Michael Zalewski (No Starch Press, 2011) for more on that.) To avoid this bunch of problems, I advise you to use XHTML, a variant of HTML redefined on XML. XML requests that you close every opened tag. Besides avoiding the problem just mentioned, this enforces well-formed documents that might be processed by XML tools if administrable.

An HTML document starts with a <DOCTYPE>, followed by exactly one <HTML> tag. Then <HEAD> and <BODY> tags might be included. In the case of XHTML, the <DOCTYPE> is preceded by the XML version, as shown in Listing 2-1.

Listing 2-1. Sample HTML Page with Form

```
1   <?xml version='1.0' encoding='UTF-8' ?>
2   <!DOCTYPE html>
3   <html>
4       <head>
5           <title>TinyCalculator</title>
6       </head>
7       <body>
8           <h1>TinyCalculator</h1>
9           <form>
10              <div>
```

```
11                        <label>Param1: </label>
12                        <input type="text" value="0.0" />
13                    </div>
14                </form>
15            </body>
16        </html>
```

You can read more about HTML, including a commented list of important tags, in Appendix A.

CSS

HTML provides some little tags for styling the page with emphasis, italics, and more. Cascading Style Sheets (CSS) were developed as a much more powerful design tool. As a rule of thumb, you should separate layout from content. Thus, don't use the HTML styling tags. Use CSS exclusively for the layout of a page.

By using CSS, it's possible to address an element and assign layout information within curly braces, as shown in Listing 2-2.

Listing 2-2. Sample CSS Statements

```
1    h1 {
2        font-size: 2em;
3    }
4
5    h2 {
6        font-size: 1.5em;
7        font-style: italic;
8    }
```

Listing 2-2 demonstrates how to apply layout information to the HTML header tags. In line 1, we address header 1 (h1). The statement in line 1 affects the font size, which is set to 2em. This is a *relative* size, which is double the standard size (whatever is defined as standard—for example, by the browser's setting or another CSS statement). Lines 5 to 8 define a smaller header with italic style. As you can see, a couple of layout directives, each terminated by a semicolon, might be placed within the curly braces. In this sense, CSS equals Java programming.

In the preceding example, HTML tag names are used to address HTML elements. Often, we need to apply variable styles to different tags of the same name. To address the correct element we either need to build a kind of path by mentioning different tags (for example, `div div` to address a `div` within a `div`) or we assign a class or an id to the HTML element and use that for addressing. These addressing elements might be combined to define complex paths. Such an addressing element is called a *selector*. Certain rules exist to avoid ambiguity.

With CSS, you may influence not only the layout of an element, but its position and visibility also. The layout information might differ depending on the output device or screen size. Combining all these features, we might create a *responsive web design*: the layout is changed and adjusted by the size of the browser window.

Chapter 10 discusses using CSS in a web application. I'll show you how to create a responsive design with CSS. You may observe its behavior by opening Books (available at `https://it-rezension.de`) with different devices or simulate this by changing the size of your browser window.

Today, a couple of libraries exist that offer you aid for designing your web application. One popular library is Bootstrap (`https://getbootstrap.com`), which doesn't rest upon CCS only but on JavaScript too, and more.

As with HTML, I don't want to bore readers who are familiar with CSS. I provide an introduction to CSS in Appendix B.

JavaScript

JavaScript is the programming language of the client side. Almost every modern browser has implemented a JavaScript interpreter or a just-in-time (JIT) compiler. Microsoft introduced VB Script some years ago, but JavaScript has emerged as the language of choice, and it's well understood by the Microsoft browser too.

Note   JavaScript was created by Netscape and became standardized by the European Computer Manufacturer's Association. Thus, its official name is ECMAScript. *JavaScript* is the name of Netscape's implementation of ECMAScript, whereas Microsoft's implementation is officially called *JScript*. JavaScript is commonly used as synonym for ECMAScript, and I do that in this book.

JAVASCRIPT AND JAVA

JavaScript is neither Java nor derived from Java! Previously it was called *LiveScript*, but was soon renamed. It is a full-fledged programming language and is used for server programming, too (http://nodejs.org).

Java 8 comes bundled with a JavaScript interpreter written in Java called *Nashorn*. It's capable of accessing Java classes, and this enables running and testing portions of Java code without the need to compile. That's especially useful when discovering new libraries or testing some new Java constructs. You'll find an example of interpreting Java code by the aid of Nashorn at my blog: https://blog.mueller-bruehl.de/netbeans/interactive-java-using-nashorn-part-i/.

Even better, Java's current version 9 includes the Java Shell (JShell), which realizes a real read-eval-print loop (REPL). You can read more about that also on my blog, at https://blog.mueller-bruehl.de/netbeans/interactive-java-with-jshell/.

JavaScript is used to enhance client behavior or to initiate partial requests (AJAX). JSF hides JavaScript behind its AJAX tag. Sometimes it's useful to develop a bit of JavaScript code. As a Java developer, it should be no problem for you to follow the simple examples described in this book, such as the one shown in Listing 2-3.

Listing 2-3. JavaScript Example: Showing a Message

```
1    alert("The information has been saved");
```

Unlike Java, JavaScript is not a typed language. Thus you may assign an integer to a variable and later on replace its value with a string.

Java

Java is the main technical foundation for programming web applications in this book. I assume you're familiar with Java SE.

All web applications discussed in this book are built using Java EE. The Java EE platform is built as a JSR (Java Specification Request, Java EE 7: JSR 342, Java EE 8: JSR 366). That's an umbrella specification describing a complete architecture built up from a mass of technologies, each defined by its own JSR. Throughout this book I'll introduce most of those technologies.

Maven

For professional Java development, you need a build tool. Lots of developers never care about their build tool because it's configured by their favorite IDE. Others know their build tool perfectly and like to tune every detail.

For still other developers, there are three popular tools in the Java world: Apache Ant (`http://ant.apache.org`), which acts more imperatively, Gradle (`https://gradle.org`), and Apache Maven (`http://maven.apache.org`), which follows a more declarative approach. Apache's website calls Maven a "software project management and comprehension tool." Popular IDEs, like NetBeans, have built-in support for both tools. Nevertheless, whichever tool you prefer, Ant-based projects often use a configuration that's specific to the IDE you use, whereas Maven projects follow a stricter convention, thus becoming mostly independent of the IDE. NetBeans, for example, is capable of opening Maven projects directly. Other IDEs (like Eclipse) offer an input feature for Maven-based projects.

To ensure the most compatibility with your favorite IDE, all applications discussed in this book are built with Maven.

Selenium and Arquillian

Selenium (`http://docs.seleniumhq.org`) automates browsers. Besides macro recording and replay, such automation may be fully controlled from within a Java application—for example, by a test. Doing so enables GUI testing of web applications.

Testing beans or other components that are managed by a container can be a hassle. Arquillian (`http://arquillian.org`) allows testing of the interesting parts of a web application within a container. It fully integrates with test frameworks like JUnit.

Although this book doesn't focus on unit testing or test-driven development, I will discuss some simple test scenarios with both tools.

Servlet

A *servlet* is a Java class hosted in a servlet container that dynamically processes requests and constructs responses. This class must conform to the Java Servlet API. Like other Java EE components, it's specified by the *Java Community Process* (JCP). The servlet

version included in Java EE 7 is JSR 340: Java Servlet 3.1 Specification (https://
jcp.org/en/jsr/detail?id=340), respectively JSR 369 (https://jcp.org/en/
jsr/detail?id=369): Java Servlet 4.0 in the case of Java EE 8. (JSR is short for Java
Specification Request.)

Although a servlet theoretically might respond to any request, the Java EE
implementation responds to HTTP requests only. Thus, I use the term *servlet* as a
synonym for *HTTP servlet*. The servlet's lifecycle is maintained by the container. The web
client (the browser) interacts with the servlet by request/response, as described in the
section "HTTP." A servlet is a class extending the abstract class javax.servlet.http.
HttpServlet. In most common scenarios, at least two methods, doGet and doPost, will
be overwritten to implement specific behavior and send back the response. These two
methods refer to the appropriate HTTP methods GET and POST.

A servlet is invoked by a client's request to a specific path (of the URI). By using the
simple annotation @WebServlet("/path"), this might be defined. While discussing JSF
configuration, I'll talk about configuring servlets by a configuration file (web.xml). JSF
itself is implemented as servlet (FacesServlet).

If you enhance the TinyCalculator by NetBeans 8's Add Servlet wizard (New file ➤
Web ➤ Servlet) and provide Hello as the name, NetBeans generates the code shown in
Listing 2-4.

Listing 2-4. Programmatically Generating an HTML Page by a Servlet

```
1    [imports omitted]
2
3    @WebServlet(name = "Hello", urlPatterns = {"/Hello"})
4    public class Hello extends HttpServlet {
5
6        /**
7         * Processes requests for both HTTP <code>GET</code>
8         * and <code>POST</code> methods.
9         *
10        * @param request servlet request
11        * @param response servlet response
12        * @throws ServletException if a servlet-specific error occurs
13        * @throws IOException if an I/O error occurs
14        */
```

```
15   protected void processRequest(HttpServletRequest request,
16           HttpServletResponse response)
17           throws ServletException, IOException {
18       response.setContentType("text/html;charset=UTF-8");
19       try (PrintWriter out = response.getWriter()) {
20           /* TODO output your page here.
21               You may use following sample code. */
22           out.println("<!DOCTYPE html>");
23           out.println("<html>");
24           out.println("<head>");
25           out.println("<title>Servlet Hello</title>");
26           out.println("</head>");
27           out.println("<body>");
28           out.println("<h1>Servlet Hello at "
29               + request.getContextPath() + "</h1>");
30           out.println("</body>");
31           out.println("</html>");
32       }
33   }
34
35   /**
36    * Handles the HTTP <code>GET</code> method.
37    *
38    * @param request servlet request
39    * @param response servlet response
40    * @throws ServletException if a servlet-specific error occurs
41    * @throws IOException if an I/O error occurs
42    */
43   @Override
44   protected void doGet(HttpServletRequest request,
45           HttpServletResponse response)
46           throws ServletException, IOException {
47       processRequest(request, response);
48   }
49
```

```
50        /**
51         * Handles the HTTP <code>POST</code> method.
52         *
53         * @param request servlet request
54         * @param response servlet response
55         * @throws ServletException if a servlet-specific error occurs
56         * @throws IOException if an I/O error occurs
57         */
58        @Override
59        protected void doPost(HttpServletRequest request,
60                HttpServletResponse response)
61                throws ServletException, IOException {
62            processRequest(request, response);
63        }
64
65        [...code omitted ...]
66    }
```

If you start this application and complete the URI with /Hello, you can verify the servlet responding to your request, as shown in Figure 2-2.

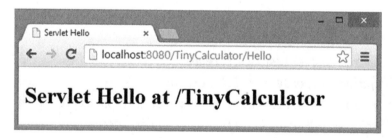

Figure 2-2. *Hello servlet in action*

As mentioned, we need to override the doGet and doPost methods. This is where we usually put our code to react on the HTTP methods. If there's no difference between handling a GET or a POST request, both methods might delegate to a common handler. That's how NetBeans generates this skeleton file. This common handler is the processRequest method (lines 15ff). This skeleton responds with a web page. All HTML tags are written to the output stream by Java instructions. Beside literal HTML code,

NetBeans inserted a method call to this output: `request.getContextPath()`, which refers to the context path of the current application. The context path is the first part of the URI after server and port. It's the place the application lives. In Figure 2-2, this is the `"/TinyCalculator"` output. We'll use this method again for a service we use in Chapter 24.

Writing HTML code directly inside Java code is not a good approach for anything beyond a trivial example. One way is to separate the HTML page from the Java code using Java Server Pages (JSP). The page is stored on its own with embedded JSP tags and is compiled into a servlet at a later time. Even though still active, pure JSP might be considered as ancestor of JSF. In fact, the early versions of JSF used JSP for the view definition.

Deployment

All servlets, including JSF, run within a servlet container. When we launched TinyCalculator, NetBeans automatically started GlassFish (if not already running) and deployed the application to the application server.

If we want to install an application to a production server, we may add this server to the NetBeans environment (or to your favorite IDE) and let the IDE perform the deployment to the production system. If, for some reason, it's not possible to use the IDE for deployment, you might deploy the application by yourself. This process depends on the application server you use.

In the case of GlassFish, you can either deploy at the command line using the `asadmin` command or use your browser to log in to the administrator console. GlassFish offers an Application menu intended to deploy, undeploy, start an application, and more. Last but not least, you may use Maven to deploy the application automatically subsequent to the build process.

Summary

This chapter introduced the technical foundations of web applications as developed during this book: HTTP, HTML, CSS, JavaScript, Java, Maven, Selenium and Arquillian, servlets, and deployment. Selected technologies were briefly explained, and others were just mentioned. I skipped over discussing Java EE and JSF, which are not part of the foundations but are the main subjects of this book.

For readers unfamiliar with the browser parts of this technology stack, this book offers additional information about HTML in Appendix A and CSS in Appendix B.

CHAPTER 3

JavaServer Faces

Whereas JavaServer Pages (JSP) is used to define pages, which are compiled to servlets, JavaServer Faces (JSF) is a complete web MVC (Model-View-Controller) framework. Interestingly, it is implemented as a servlet itself.

Here is a short excerpt of the specification:

- Makes it easy to construct a UI from a set of reusable UI components

- Simplifies migration of application data to and from the UI

- Helps manage UI state across server requests

- Provides a simple model for wiring client-generated events to server-side application code

- Allows custom UI components to be easily built and reused

JSF is intended to handle component status across multiple requests. It can be used to process complex forms, even if they span multiple pages. It provides a strongly typed event model for events created on the client side and implements powerful page navigation.

JSF defined by a series of JSRs:

- 2004 JSR 127 JavaServer Faces

- 2006 JSR 252 JavaServer Faces 1.2

- 2009 JSR 314 JavaServer Faces 2.0

- 2010ff JavaServer Faces 2.1, maintenance release of JSF 2.0

- 2013 JSR 344 JavaServer Faces 2.2

- 2016 JSR 372 JavaServer Faces 2.3

© Michael Müller 2018
M. Müller, *Practical JSF in Java EE 8*, https://doi.org/10.1007/978-1-4842-3030-5_3

If you're interested in JSF's full history, including which feature was introduced with which version, you may want to read the appropriate JSRs. But be warned: a specification is a mostly abstract defining document—it's neither an introduction nor a practical guide.

A former JSF intention was to hide away HTML and provide the programmer a familiar programming concept with event processing. Beginning with JSF 2.2, you may use mostly JSF tags, or create predominantly HTML documents, flavored with some JSF-specific attributes.

In this book, we'll start with the first (traditional) approach, using specific tags. Later on, we'll work with HTML-friendly markup, which might be a good choice if you're familiar with HTML. As you'll see, both styles have specific advantages.

View Definition Language

JSF uses an exchangeable View Definition Language (VDL) to define the user interface. Currently, JSF supports JSP and Facelets.

JSP was used from the first version on. Since the JSF lifecycle differs a bit from the JSP lifecycle, Jacob Hookom developed an alternative VDL called *Facelets* that integrates perfectly with JSF. Facelets became the standard VDL with JSF 2.0. All major new features from this version on, such as templating, composite components, and more, are only available for Facelets. Even though JSP is still supported for compatibility, you may treat it as deprecated.

All applications in this book are built with Facelets.

Web vs. Traditional Application

In a traditional application, the application itself is usually responsible for the presentation. Even if you use a special display server such as the X Window System, it's still controlled by the application.

But in a web application, the data is passed to a browser, which takes care of the presentation. To do this, the server packs the content to be displayed into a format that the browser understands—for example, into an HTML or XHTML document. In addition, the server may provide some layout information in the form of Cascading Style Sheets (CSS). Everything else is up to the browser. Just as there are different browsers, the representation also can be different. The continuous development of standards fortunately ensures a gradual convergence. But if the user uses their own browser configuration, the presentation again might be different.

Not only does a web application delegate the output to a client-side browser, the application normally doesn't become active by itself! Only when the user requests a page via the browser does the application become active on the server, perform some operations, and deliver the content to the browser. Depending on the user's input, the content of a page might be changed without navigating to a new URL. This (apparently) active change of content may feel to the user as initiated actively by the server side. In fact, this kind of processing is often done by a small background request with the aid of Asynchronous JavaScript and XML (AJAX).

Besides (X)HTML and CSS, we've touched on another browser-side technology: JavaScript. The browser requests some data in between using JavaScript and exchanges parts of the browser content, known as the Document Object Model (DOM). In JSF terminology, this is done by partial processing and/or partial rendering. This kind of magic gives the impression that the server updates the screen, even though in reality it's the client that makes the request to the server for information (client-side pull). A real *push*, meaning that the server actively changes the representation, is a little more complex. The response to the client is artificially delayed in order to transmit more information later on, when new information arises on the server side. Or you may use newer technologies like WebSockets. WebSockets requires more explanation and will be discussed later in this book.

In a traditional application, the program usually responds immediately to a user input. In a web application, the program only detects user input when a new page or (usually in conjunction with AJAX) partial new data is requested. By this time, entries can already be made in various fields. It's not hard to imagine that the application has to handle this in a different way. At this point, JSF supports the programmer and raises corresponding events on the server for each entry, so that the programming model is not entirely different from the one developers often use.

Another difference: a web application usually runs in an execution environment that provides a number of services. Such a runtime environment is denoted as a *container*. In the case of JSF, it's a so-called servlet container. This points to the underlying technology of the servlets. Even when developing with JSF, the direct use of servlets may sometimes be appropriate, so it can't hurt if you familiarize yourself with servlet technology.

The servlet container provides the application with interfaces to other services. It's part of an application or web server. Many servers principally comprise a container, and then the container and application server concepts are often used interchangeably. In fact, a server can host multiple containers. For example, GlassFish does not only host a servlet container but an EJB container too. In the following section, we'll first look at the application server from the outside.

Now, when a user wants to use the web application, in his browser he calls the application URI. The client makes a request to the HTTP server. This recognizes, depending on the URI, that it must not simply deliver a static page to the browser. So the server forwards the request over the container to the web application, which in this case is the JSF servlet in conjunction with the user code, and there it's processed. The output is generated as an (X)HTML document, which is sent to the browser, where it's displayed. The process is illustrated in Figure 3-1.

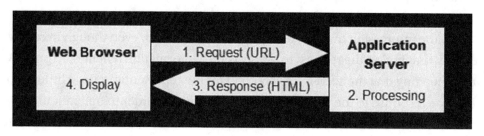

Figure 3-1. *HTTP request-response cycle*

Technically speaking, the response is HTTP, which may contain information other than HTML. For example, the response might be an image embedded within an HTML page. Thus, many programmers think of an HTML response. Figure 3-1 shows this simplified view.

From this perspective, we consider the application server to be a *black box*. What happens inside it is interesting. Recall briefly the previous applications—here you've defined a JSF page. We used Facelets as the page language. Besides HTML, every Facelets page definition contains some JSF-specific tags, such as <h:inputText>. Within the browser, we provided the URI of such a page. Stepping forward in the application, this URI won't be provided by the user (by typing in the URI) but by the application itself.

The server determines the page to be rendered based on the URI, parses its contents, and resolves the tags. In the simplest case, the tags are replaced by appropriate data, and the resulting page is sent to the browser. This is only half of the truth. The browser indeed could have displayed the data of the application before. So JSF first checks whether there's already a session. If so, the component tree—the logical representation of the view model—is restored. Entries are validated, and the data model is updated. In total, JSF has six different phases for step 2 in Figure 3-1.

Let's dig a bit deeper and take a brief look inside processing and the JSF lifecycle.

JSF Lifecycle Overview

The JSF lifecycle consists of six phases, illustrated in Figure 3-2:

1. Restore view

2. Apply request values

3. Process validations

4. Update model values

5. Invoke application

6. Render response

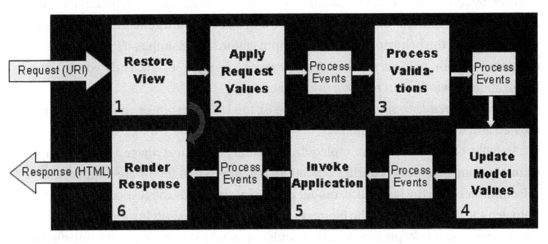

Figure 3-2. *JSF lifecycle*

Figure 3-2 shows the six main phases and some smaller boxes in between indicating event processing. The arrows show the sequential processing, indicating the normal flow. It may differ for a new page, as indicated by the curved arrow. Between some phases, events (of the preceding phase) are processed. As an exceptional result of this processing (not shown in the figure), you may leave the sequential flow.

When a request encounters the server, at first the component tree is restored. If it's a request for a new page, there is no existing component tree. Thus, there is nothing to restore, but to create a new component tree. In this case, phases 2 through 5 are useless and will be skipped. The server simply renders the response and sends it back to the client.

In phase 2, the incoming values will be applied to the components within the tree. I'll explain the component tree soon—for now, just imagine the tree as an in-memory representation of each JSF tag of the page.

The *process validations* phase (phase 3) will validate and convert the data. Imagine there's an input field for a person's age. In the browser, the user might enter any text, and that incoming string must be converted into a number. Then the valid range is checked—for example, from 0 up to 120 years.

Once the values are converted and validated, the model values will be updated in phase 4. This is when the incoming values will be assigned to the model's—for example, a managed bean's properties.

In phase 5, JSF will invoke the application by calling the appropriate events, such as change value events, action events, and more. In a traditional application, these events are fired by screen components like buttons, icons, menu items, and so on. In a web application, the browser only sends requests, and all events are generated on the server side to emulate the behavior of a non-web application. For example, if JSF detects a different value for an input element, it generates a "changed" event. Thus, you as the application developer can react on this event.

During the *render response* phase (phase 6), the HTTP response, mostly HTML is created and then sent to the client.

Usually, only if a phase is completed successfully is the next phase acted on. For example, if an error occurs during validation, the phases that follow are skipped, and JSF continues with the last phase, render response, and sends the response to the client. Between the main phases in the figure, you can see *process events* boxes. During such a process event you may programmatically quit the usual workflow and continue directly with the render response phase. For a complete picture, we need to add arrows pointing from each process events box to phase 6. Such a bypassing of the normal workflow might be initiated by an exception. Depending on the kind of exception, JSF generates messages that are sent back to the client. Even more, but less often used, you can terminate the whole lifecycle during process events.

As a consequence, if, for example, a single input field fails during validation, none of the other fields will be pushed to the model. This "all or none" approach helps to get mostly consistent data. But sometimes it may be worthwhile to receive partial data, even if some other parts of the data are erroneous. To achieve that, JSF offers an `immediate` attribute, which might be set to `true` to alter this behavior for the appropriate UI element.

This has been a short overview about the JSF lifecycle. We'll dig deeper into it while discussing diverse aspects of the example applications.

JSF Namespaces and Tags

So far, I've discussed JSF tags without much explanation. Tags like `<h:inputText ...>` or `<h:commandButton>` sound more familiar to a Java developer (for example, compare with Swing: `JTextField` or `JButton`) than the HTML equivalents `<input type="text">` or `<input type="button">` and are mostly self-explanatory. In fact, JSF was designed to present Java developers with an abstraction similar to known technologies, including powerful event processing.

But the browser displays HTML pages, and that's what must be sent from the server to it. As shown in the section about servlets, HTML tags can be embedded into Java code by writing out a series of HTML statements. The JSF way is to separate page from code and at the same time offer an abstraction using tags from the JSF tag library. The tags are included in the HTML pages in XML style.

The tags shown so far belong to the Standard JSF Component Library. To declare `inputText` as belonging to that library and not to any other, it's prefixed with `h:`. This prefix is defined as an alias of the `http://xmlns.jcp.org/jsf/html` namespace, which indicates the library. `xmlns:h="http://xmlns.jcp.org/jsf/html"` is a pure XML namespace declaration. Although the URI is specific to the library, you can choose your own prefixes, but I suggest using the recommended aliases.

A namespace is used to avoid naming conflicts. In XML, you may define your own `<h1>` tag. In XHTML, you must distinguish between your tag and the standard head 1 tag. You need to define a new namespace and an alias. To use your `h1` tag, you need to prefix the tag with the alias—for example, `<my:h1>`. Read more on this at `https://en.wikipedia.org/wiki/XML_namespace` or `www.w3schools.com/xml/xml:namespaces.asp`.

Tip   Prior to JSF 2.2, the standard namespace was `java.sun.com/jsf` instead of the current one, `xmlns.jcp.org/jsf`. For compatibility, the old namespace can still be used. I recommend using the new (`xmlns.jcp.org`) specification only. The former one might become deprecated.

The Standard JSF Component Library consists of a few parts, as shown in Table 3-1.

Table 3-1. *Standard JSF Component Library Parts*

URI	Prefix	Name
http://xmlns.jcp.org/jsf	jsf:	Pass-through elements
http://xmlns.jcp.org/jsf/core	f:	Core library, not specific to HTML
http://xmlns.jcp.org/jsf/html	h:	HTML library
http://xmlns.jcp.org/jsf/facelets/	ui:	Facelet Templating tag library
http://xmlns.jcp.org/jsf/composite	cc:	Composite Component tag library
http://xmlns.jcp.org/jsf/passthrough	p:	Pass-through attributes

Note   PrimeFaces, a popular way to extend JSF, used the `p:` prefix long before JSF was extended by pass-through attributes. To avoid conflicts if you use both, you have to choose a different prefix for one of them. Developers with an existing codebase often keep the `p:` prefix and use something like `pt:` for the pass-through attributes.

As the namespace suggests, the next libraries aren't part of the Standard JSF Component Library, but remain from JSP times. It offers some useful tags that are used in this book. (The first versions of JSF were built upon JSP, which is a slightly older technology that you still can use outside the JSF context, too. Thus, these libraries aren't related to JSF itself, but might be used within JSF.)

Starting with JSF 2.0, Facelets became the preferred VDL, and most of the improvements in this and newer versions are available for Facelets only. Only the core and HTML library are available for pages built with JSP. On the other hand, the JSP Standard Tag Library offers useful tags, shown in Table 3-2, that are used in this book's applications.

Table 3-2. *JSP Standard Tag Library Tags*

URI	Prefix	Name
http://xmlns.jcp.org/jsp/jstl/core	c:	JSP Standard Tag Library (JSTL)
http://xmlns.jcp.org/jsp/jstl/functions	fn:	JSTL functions

In Appendix C, you'll find an overview of all the tags with short descriptions. A full description is available online at https://docs.oracle.com/javaee/7/javaserver-faces-2-2/vdldocs-facelets/toc.htm. If you prefer a printed reference, check out *JavaServer Faces 2.0*, by Ed Burns and Chris Schalk (McGraw-Hill, 2010).

Component Tree

When processing a request, JSF searches for the requested page and scans its content. Apart from pure HTML, the page can contain special tags, like <h:inputText value="..."/>. As I explain in Chapter 5, an element is enhanced by a special XML namespace, which indicates handling by JSF. All those UI elements will be collected into a tree data structure. This is the *component tree* that's built up or restored in the restore view phase.

Listing 3-1 shows a reduced page.

Listing 3-1. Reduced Page Example

```
1    <?xml version='1.0' encoding='UTF-8' ?>
2    <!DOCTYPE html>
3    <html xmlns="http://www.w3.org/1999/xhtml"
4         xmlns:h="http://xmlns.jcp.org/jsf/html">
5      <h:head>
6         <h:outputLabel value="Demo"/>
7      </h:head>
8      <h:body>
9         <h:form>
10            <h:outputLabel value="Param1: "/>
11            <h:inputText value="#{tinyCalculator.param1}"/>
12         </h:form>
13      </h:body>
14    </html>
```

In the restore view phase, JSF will build a component tree like the one shown in Listing 3-2 (which is a simplified presentation).

Listing 3-2. Simplified Component Tree

```
1                  [UIViewRoot]
2                      |
3   [UIOutput (Head)] --|-- [UIOutput (Body)]
4       |                   |
5   [HtmlOutputLabel]          [HtmlForm]
6                             |
7            [HtmlOutputLabel] --|-- [HtmlInputText]
```

As you can see, the root of this tree (always) is UIViewRoot. Below that, you'll find two siblings representing the head and body of that page, and below that, the other elements nested within that page.

In this example, all elements with the special tags of the jsf/html namespace (prefixed by h:) show up in the component tree (Listing 3-3). If you omit this namespace, these elements will be treated as pure HTML and won't be included in the component tree.

Listing 3-3. Reduced Page Example with Fewer JSF Prefixes

```
1    <?xml version='1.0' encoding='UTF-8' ?>
2    <!DOCTYPE html>
3    <html xmlns="http://www.w3.org/1999/xhtml"
4          xmlns:h="http://xmlns.jcp.org/jsf/html">
5       <head>
6           Demo
7       </head>
8       <body>
9          <form>
10             <h:outputLabel value="Param1: "/>
11             <h:inputText value="#{tinyCalculator.param1}"/>
12         </form>
13       </body>
14    </html>
```

And Listing 3-4 is the simplified tree resulting from the page.

Listing 3-4. Component Tree of HTML Page with Standard (non-JSF) Tags

```
1                [UIViewRoot]
2                     |
3    [HtmlOutputLabel] --|-- [HtmlInputText]
```

This seems to be a much simpler tree, doesn't it? So, should you prefer those simple forms? It depends. Sometimes it's helpful to traverse the component tree. Traversing a slim tree may be easier and/or faster, but in the first version, all elements were represented by tags, which are handled by JSF. If you replace the render engine, these tags might be rendered in a different way, while the second version mixes tags and pure HTML. Thus, it can be used only with an HTML renderer. Because JSF is commonly used for (X)HTML pages, that's not a really big drawback. A couple of JSF elements, like commandLink, need to be embedded within a JSF managed form.

Note   JSF is designed to work independently from HTML. Thus, somebody might create a different render engine—for example, to render a PDF from the tags. But I don't know any other render engine than HTML.

Again, if you prefer purer HTML, to keep the component tree small, you should prefer HTML-friendly markup.

Some elements, like buttons, can only invoke an action if embedded in a form, which is included in the component tree. So you should always prefer to declare the form with a JSF tag, as shown in the earlier example, or with HTML-friendly markup.

As mentioned, the trees here are simplified. Performing the following exercise, you'll notice some UIInstructions. These contain the other (HTML) elements to hold the whole page.

TRAVERSING THE COMPONENT TREE

1. Add a button to the TinyCalculator with the following code:

```
value="Print component tree" action="#{tinyCalculator.printTree}".
```

2. Launch the application.

3.   Click the button and observe the output.

If you like, you can replace the simple output method `logElement` by an exchangeable algorithm, such as by using Strategy or Visitor pattern. See Listing 3-5.

Listing 3-5. Simple `print` Function for the Component Tree

```java
/**
 * printTree might be used within an action of a button
 * As required for an action, it returns a String
 * @return ""
 */
public String printTree() {
    UIViewRoot root = FacesContext.getCurrentInstance().getViewRoot();
    printTree(root, 0);
    return "";
}

private void printTree(UIComponent element, int level) {
    logElement(level, element);
    for (UIComponent child : element.getChildren()) {
        printTree(child, level + 1);
    }
}

private void logElement(int level, UIComponent element) {
    String out = "";
    for (int i = 0; i < level; i++) {
        out += "----";
    }
    out += element.getClass().getSimpleName()
            + " - " + element.getFamily()
            + " - " + element.getRendererType();
    _logger.log(Level.INFO, out);
}
```

Note   JSF offers a tag for debugging (don't forget the appropriate namespace): `<ui:debug hotkey="1"/>`. If a page containing this tag is displayed in your browser, press Ctrl+Shift+1 to get some useful information such as component tree, variables, and view state. Replace the 1 with any key of your choice. If the key attribute is omitted, it defaults to d. Depending on your browser and installed add-ons, this default key might be used for something else.

Navigation

Navigation is an essential part of applications. In a desktop application, you might open a dialog by clicking a menu option or selecting a register tab. In a web application, we always deal with pages. Although we might provide the user a look and feel, like having a tab control, everything is still a page.

The standard navigation element of HTML is a link. But within a JSF application, navigation might also be triggered by a button click. Prior to JSF 2.0, navigation rules had to be defined within the `faces-config.xml` file (see Chapter 6 for more).

Navigation might be defined like this:

```
1    <navigation-rule>
2        <from-view-id>/index.xhtml</from-view-id>
3        <navigation-case>
4            <from-outcome>add</from-outcome>
5            <to-view-id>/index.xhtml</to-view-id>
6        </navigation-case>
7    </navigation-rule>
```

Let's assume there's an Add button on the page. This button is assigned to a method, which returns the string add. If, starting on page index.xhtml, the button is clicked, then the page index.xhtml should be opened next. In this case, it's simply the same page—and that's exactly what we've done with TinyCalculator.

But our example was simpler. There was no navigation rule defined. Starting with JSF 2.0, the outcome of an action method might directly be used as the next URL. Thus, our add method simply returns index.xhtml to navigate to this page. Or even simpler, it returns an empty string (or null) to stay on the page. This feature is called *internal navigation* (or *implicit navigation*). But *external navigation*, which is defined by XML, is still allowed and will overwrite the internal navigation rules.

In the example applications in this book, we'll mostly use internal navigation.

Summary

JSF has been developed in the open process of Java Specification Requests (JSRs). The latest version is JSF 2.3. JSF supports two different view definition languages: JSP (JavaServer Pages) and Facelets. Because new features are available for Facelets only, this book mostly omits JSP in favor of Facelets.

One challenge of web development is the stateless behavior of the underlying HTTP protocol. Although mostly hidden by JSF, a minimum level of knowledge is helpful. JSF tackles this challenge by its lifecycle phases. JSF offers a couple of namespaces and tags to describe the pages (views) of an application and builds up a component tree of these elements when processing a request. Navigation between web pages might been defined externally (via XML config files) or internally. This book mostly uses internal navigation.

CHAPTER 4

Expression Language

Building the TinyCalculator, we used some special expressions, beginning within the delimiters #{ and }. These expressions, always using the form #{expr}, are defined by the Expression Language (EL). JSR 341: Expression Language 3.0 is part of Java EE 8 (read about it at `https://jcp.org/en/jsr/detail?id=341`). The same release had been part of Java EE 7.

Unified Expression Language

Originally the Expression Language was defined for JSP using the form of ${expr} (with a leading $). Then JSF introduced a slightly different syntax. The main intention was to support the higher level JSF lifecycle. This JSF EL used a leading ' for an expression, as we did in TinyCalculator.

Beginning with Java EE 5, JSP EL and JSF EL became unified. Hence, you may sometimes read about the Unified Expression Language. Although the expressions are unified now, both format conventions (the leading $ and leading #) are supported, even if the leading character still indicates slightly different behavior if using JSP as VDL. ${expr} (with expr being short for expression) is evaluated at page compile time (*immediate expression*), whereas #{expr} is evaluated at runtime (*deferred expression*). Remember, a JSP is compiled to a servlet. And JSP is still supported as VDL for JSF. Using the modern Facelets VDL, the page definition is always interpreted at runtime. There is no compile time. So, you may replace all expressions within the TinyCalulator example to use the ${expr} form and it won't make a difference. All the examples in this book use the #{expr} form.

Also in EL, you may read about *value expressions* and *method expressions*. What's the difference? Let's recap some expressions from the TinyCalculator: #{tinyCalculator.param1} is a value expression, whereas #{tinyCalculator.add} is a method expression. In these simple examples, we can't see any syntactic difference. To identify which is which,

© Michael Müller 2018
M. Müller, *Practical JSF in Java EE 8*, https://doi.org/10.1007/978-1-4842-3030-5_4

you need to know the context. Java conventions may help you: param1 is a subject, and add is a verb. Java methods shall start with a verb and may continue with something else. In case of properties, the verbs are get and set, followed by a name (the subject). And, as shortly explained for the TinyCalculator example, #{tinyCalculator.param1} is a kind of two-way binding, omitting get and set.

Note   A bit more generally, we may say #{myBean.myProperty} is a value expression, whereas #{myBean.myMethod} is a method expression.

The part before the first dot (or as used in other examples, the first opening square bracket) is called the *base*, whereas the part after is called a *property*—or in case of a method expression, a *method*. In this example, the base is a bean. As explained later, the base also might be a variable or an implicit object.

In the common case of referring to a bean, the name of the bean (if not defined to be something else, the bean's classname—you may define a different name within the @Named annotation, such as @Named("myBaseName")) is used for the base, but with a lowercase first letter.

If needed, the property is broken into smaller parts by using the common dot syntax. invoice.customer.street refers to the street of the customer object within an invoice. Within pure Java, it might look like Listing 4-1.

Listing 4-1. Java Equivalent to EL invoice.customer.street

```
1    Invoice invoice = ...;
2    ...
3    String street = invoice.getCustomer().getStreet();
4    ...
5    invoice.getCustomer().setStreet(newValue);
```

For a method expression, parentheses might be used #{tinyCalculator.add()} or omitted, as shown earlier. If the method called by EL has parameters, you need to add the parentheses.

Value Expression

So far, we've discussed a very common form of a value expression—to get or set values.

To retrieve values, a value expression is an expression that delivers a value as its result. It's possible to calculate this value, and the result might be of any type. In this section, we'll dig into this a little.

Operators

The EL offers a couple of operators that are well known to you as a Java developer. I won't explain them, I'll just list them. As a specific feature, some operators may be noted as short textual abbreviations, to avoid conflicts that might occur by using characters that might be escaped within HTML. This alternate notation is listed within square brackets:

- +, -, *, / [div], % [mod]
- < [lt], <= [le], == [eq], >= [ge], > [gt], != [ne]
- && [and], || [or], ! [not]
- cond ? expr1 : expr2
- instanceof, empty (test for empty string, collection, map, and so on)
- += (string concatenation)
- = (assignment), ; (semicolon), () (parentheses)
- Lambdas and streams

Lambdas and streams are available in Java SE 8, but in EL 3.0 running on Java 7, you can use them with the same syntax. As discussed later, this cool feature is useful for a couple of tasks.

A simple + is just an arithmetic operator, whereas += is a string concatenation. To demonstrate, let's misuse the TinyCalculator result variable (remember, a double). Because EL is independent from JSF components, it is possible to insert EL expressions anywhere in a page. Insert them, without the line numbers, just before the </h:form> tag, as shown in Listing 4-2, and run the application.

Listing 4-2. EL Demonstration

```
 1    <br/>
 2    #{tinyCalculator.result = 10}
 3    <br/>
 4    #{tinyCalculator.result = tinyCalculator.result + 10}
 5    <br/>
 6    #{tinyCalculator.result}
 7    <br/>
 8    #{tinyCalculator.result = 10}
 9    <br/>
10    #{tinyCalculator.result += 10}
11    <br/>
12    #{tinyCalculator.result}
```

Here's a little explanation of Listing 4-2:

- *Line 1*: <br/> is the (X)HTML tag for a line break. Without this, all output would have been concatenated.

- *Line 2*: This is an assignment of the value 10 to the bean property result (more precisely, the result is assigned by the setter setResult). Simultaneously, the evaluated expression value is displayed. Because the result is of type double, 10.0 is displayed.

- *Line 4*: Adds 10 to the result, and displays 20.0. The right-hand term calls the getter, and the left-hand side (of the equal sign) calls the appropriate setter.

- *Line 6*: Just verifies the assignment. Displays 20.0.

- *Line 8*: In line 8, we reset the result's value to 10 (as we did in line 2).

- *Line 10*: A Java developer might assume the same result as in line 4, but this isn't an arithmetic operator. It's a string concatenation. It appends the 10 to the existing value and displays 10.010.

- *Line 12*: Because line 10 is a string concatenation and the result is of type double, the result of the concatenation could not be assigned. Instead, JSF threw an exception. We may use the <h:message> tag to display the exception's message. Here we concentrate on EL, not JSF tags. The result is still 10.0.

Dot and Square Bracket

In a Java object, you may dig down to details by using dot syntax. As seen already, the same applies to the EL:

```
1   invoice.customer.street
```

Alternatively, a square bracket syntax will do the same:

```
1   invoice.customer["street"]
```

Square brackets are also used to access members of maps.

Method Expression

Method expressions invoke public, non-static methods. If the method has no parameters, the parentheses may be omitted:

```
action="#{tinyCalculator.add}"
```

produces the same result as

```
action="#{tinyCalculator.add()}"
```

Unlike older versions, you may pass parameters to method expressions.

Depending on the component, JSF expects either a value expression or a method expression. For example, in an action attribute, JSF expects a method expression, so `<h:commandButton value="Divide" action="#{tinyCalculator.param1}"/>` would cause an error.

Implicit Objects

The base might be a bean, a variable (discussed later in this book), or an implicit object. An *implicit* object is managed by the container. Table 4-1 provides a short overview.

Table 4-1. *Implicit Objects*

Implicit Object	Description
application	Refers to the ApplicationContext of the ServletContext. This is different from the JSF Application object!
applicationScope	A map of data stored in the application scope. For example, application scoped beans are stored within this map.
cc	The top-level JSF Composite Component that is currently processed.
component	This implicit object refers to the currently processed UIComponent.
cookie	A map of cookies in the HTTP set-cookie header.
facesContext	Provides access to the current FacesContext.
flash	Provides access to the so called flash object. This is an object which is stored by JSF for a short time only, till the next request.
flowScope	Similar to applicationScope, but for flow scope.
header	This refers to a map of HTTP headers for the current request.
headerValues	A map of HTTP headers for the current request. Each value is an array String[] of all values for the key.
initParam	A map containing the init parameter of the current application.
param	A map of all parameters associated with the current request.
paramValues	As before, with each value represented asman array String[] of all values for the key.
request	The current ServletRequest.
requestScope	Similar to applicationScope, but for request scope.
resource	A map of resources (javax.faces.application. ResourceHandler).
session	The current HttpSession.
sessionScope	Similar to applicationScope, but for session scope.
view	The current UIViewRoot.
viewScope	Similar to applicationScope, but for view scope.

Summary

The Expression Language (EL) is the glue between the page (presentation) and the code. It consists of expressions that get or set a value (value expressions) as well as method calls (method expressions). Both operate on Java beans, variables, or implicit objects. The EL is placed within the marker #{...} nearly anywhere within a page definition. It might be used within a JSF tag as well as for the pure HTML part.

CHAPTER 5

HTML-Friendly Markup

In the early days of JSF, most developers knew Java, but not HTML. The JSF tags are designed to provide a view description without any need for a deep HTML knowledge. Times have changed, and today many developers are familiar with HTML. So, why not define a page by its target language, HTML? That's what HTML-friendly markup is for.

HTML-friendly markup is one of the features introduced with JSF 2.2. HTML5-friendly markup, or more precisely, *pass-through elements* and *pass-through attributes*, were introduced to support additional features of HTML5. For example, you can add a pass-through attribute to add microdata or other new HTML5 features.

Personally, I prefer to omit the 5, because this feature works well with other HTML versions, too. The problem with calling it *HTML5-friendly* is that people assume a feature is HTML5-specific when it's not.

HTML-Friendly TinyCalculator

Let's rework the TinyCalculator application. Just to recap, Listing 5-1 shows the original page with traditional JSF tags.

Listing 5-1. TinyCalculator with JSF Tags

```
1   <?xml version='1.0' encoding='UTF-8' ?>
2   <!DOCTYPE html>
3   <html xmlns="http://www.w3.org/1999/xhtml"
4         xmlns:h="http://xmlns.jcp.org/jsf/html">
5     <h:head>
6         <title>TinyCalculator</title>
7     </h:head>
8     <h:body>
9         <h1>TinyCalculator</h1>
```

© Michael Müller 2018
M. Müller, *Practical JSF in Java EE 8*, https://doi.org/10.1007/978-1-4842-3030-5_5

```
10          <h:form>
11              <div>
12                  <h:outputLabel value="Param1: "/>
13                  <h:inputText value="#{tinyCalculator.param1}"/>
14              </div>
15              <div>
16                  <h:outputLabel value="Param2: "/>
17                  <h:inputText value="#{tinyCalculator.param2}"/>
18              </div>
19              <div>
20                  <h:commandButton value="Add"
21                                   action="#{tinyCalculator.add}"/>
22                  <h:commandButton value="Subtract"
23                                   action="#{tinyCalculator.subtract}"/>
24                  <h:commandButton value="Multiply"
25                                   action="#{tinyCalculator.multiply}"/>
26                  <h:commandButton value="Divide"
27                                   action="#{tinyCalculator.divide}"/>
28              </div>
29              <div>
30                  <h:outputLabel value="Result: "/>
31                  <h:outputText value="#{tinyCalculator.result}"/>
32              </div>
33          </h:form>
34      </h:body>
35  </html>
```

Listing 5-2 shows a version that's closer to pure HTML.

Listing 5-2. TinyCalculator in HTML-Friendly Style

```
1   <?xml version='1.0' encoding='UTF-8' ?>
2   <!DOCTYPE html>
3   <html xmlns="http://www.w3.org/1999/xhtml"
4         xmlns:jsf="http://xmlns.jcp.org/jsf">
5       <head>
6           <title>TinyCalculator</title>
```

```
7        </head>
8        <body>
9            <h1>TinyCalculator</h1>
10           <form jsf:id="calc">
11               <div>
12                   Param1: <input type="text"
13                               jsf:value="#{tinyCalculator.param1}"/>
14               </div>
15               <div>
16                   Param2: <input type="text"
17                               jsf:value="#{tinyCalculator.param2}"/>
18               </div>
19               <div>
20                   <input type="submit" value="Add"
21                           jsf:action="#{tinyCalculator.add}"/>
22                   <input type="submit" value="Subtract"
23                           jsf:action="#{tinyCalculator.subtract}"/>
24                   <!-- or, using the button element: -->
25                   <button jsf:action="#{tinyCalculator.multiply()}">
26                       Multiply
27                   </button>
28                   <button jsf:action="#{tinyCalculator.divide()}">
29                       Divide
30                   </button>
31               </div>
32               <div>
33                   Result: #{tinyCalculator.result}
34               </div>
35           </form>
36       </body>
37   </html>
```

Let's take a closer look. At the beginning of this page, you'll find the XML namespace definition xmlns:jsf="http://xmlns.jcp.org/jsf". In this definition, the prefix jsf: refers to that special namespace. Now, if JSF finds an element with any attribute of it prefixed with that namespace alias, it treats the element as one that JSF will handle. JSF tries to map such elements to well-known elements, as if they used the traditional JSF tags. For example, `"input type=submit"` will be handled the same way as `h:inputText`. Any unknown element is treated as a pass-through element and rendered as is. Both kinds of elements will be collected into the component tree.

HTML-friendly markup has been available since JSF 2.2. We'll use JSF tags for the Books application (Part II) and partially switch to a more HTML-friendly style by developing Alumni (Part IV). You may choose one of these styles, depending on whether you like to use HTML or prefer to hide most of the HTML stuff. Technically, it's no problem to mix the styles as you like, but usually your code will read better if you use it in a consistent way.

Summary

HTML-friendly markup is a page style that is far closer to pure HTML than JSF tags. Only attributes that have to be processed by JSF will be marked by a special prefix, while the rest of the page will be coded using HTML.

HTML-friendly markup also means passing HTML attributes that can't be processed by JSF directly to the browser. The pass-through attributes discussed here might be used to add HTML attributes to JSF tags, which will be rendered as is. Thus, JSF tags might be enriched with any attribute, even if it's unknown to JSF.

CHAPTER 6

Configuration Files

When we created TinyCalculator, NetBeans generated some config files. Depending on the application, these files or some others are used by Java EE to configure its behavior. This chapter provides an overview of these configuration files.

pom.xml

POM stands for Project Object Model. This file is related to Maven, which is, as mentioned before, beyond this book's scope. I can only explain the most important content to convey information about libraries used in the projects. This will enable you to include these libraries in the build tool of your choice.

Thus, I'll only list snippets of the POM—like Listing 6-1, which is part of the TinyCalculator project. The POM is located in the root folder of each project.

Listing 6-1. Dependency within Maven POM

```
1   ...
2   <dependency>
3       <groupId>javax</groupId>
4       <artifactId>javaee-web-api</artifactId>
5       <version>7.0</version>
6       <scope>provided</scope>
7   </dependency>
8   ...
```

Consider line 5 of listing 6-1: I suggested downloading the NetBeans Java EE bundle. As the time of this writing, NetBeans 8.2 is still the latest released version. It's bundled with GlassFish 4.1, a Java EE 7-compliant server. Thus the version I showed earlier is still 7.

© Michael Müller 2018
M. Müller, *Practical JSF in Java EE 8*, https://doi.org/10.1007/978-1-4842-3030-5_6

Before moving on with the next application (called Books), I'll show you how to update the server. For Java EE 8, you need to provide 8.0 for the version number.

web.xml

web.xml is the servlet *deployment descriptor* file. JSF itself is implemented by Java servlet technology.

This configuration file is located in the ProjectRoot/src/main/webapp/WEB-INF folder. Within NetBeans' project tree, you'll find it in the Web Pages/WEB-INF folder. Web pages is an alias for the appropriate folder.

Listing 6-2 shows the web.xml file of TinyCalculator.

Listing 6-2. web.xml

```
1    <?xml version="1.0" encoding="UTF-8"?>
2    <web-app version="3.1"
3        xmlns="http://xmlns.jcp.org/xml/ns/javaee"
4        xmlns:xsi="http://www.w3.org/2001/XMLSchema-instance"
5        xsi:schemaLocation="http://xmlns.jcp.org/xml/ns/javaee
6        http://xmlns.jcp.org/xml/ns/javaee/web-app_3_1.xsd">
7
8        <context-param>
9            <param-name>javax.faces.PROJECT_STAGE</param-name>
10           <param-value>Development</param-value>
11       </context-param>
12
13       <servlet>
14           <servlet-name>Faces Servlet</servlet-name>
15           <servlet-class>javax.faces.webapp.FacesServlet</servlet-class>
16           <load-on-startup>1</load-on-startup>
17       </servlet>
18
```

```
19        <servlet-mapping>
20            <servlet-name>Faces Servlet</servlet-name>
21            <url-pattern>*.xhtml</url-pattern>
22        </servlet-mapping>
23
24        <session-config>
25            <session-timeout>
26                30
27            </session-timeout>
28        </session-config>
29
30        <welcome-file-list>
31            <welcome-file>index.xhtml</welcome-file>
32        </welcome-file-list>
33    </web-app>
```

The header with its version and namespaces is of the Java EE 7 version,
which defines Servlets 3.1. A lot of Java EE 8 apps still use the same descriptor file.
The Java EE 8 descriptor differs only in the versioning (using 4.0 instead of 3.1 in line 2,
and web-app_4_0.xsd in line 6). This version 4 refers to Servlets 4.0. Sadly, GlassFish 5.0
(and 5.0.1 beta) doesn't resolve some backing beans properly with the new version. You
may either use the old descriptor format, which is fine for most Java EE 8 features, or you
need to install a different app server, like Payara. I'll show you how before moving on to
the Books app.

Table 6-1 describes some important elements of the descriptor file.

Table 6-1. *Descriptor File*

Element	Description
context-param	Defines a parameter, composed of a name-value pair. The param `javax.faces.PROJECT_STAGE` is used to distinguish between `Development` and `Production`. Within the development stage, JSF offers some debugging aid, like automated messages. This feature will display all JSF messages that aren't displayed by an appropriate message element.
servlet	Defines a name and the startup order for a servlet class. This order is needed in case of dependencies if more than one servlet is defined.
servlet-mapping	Maps a URL pattern to a servlet, which is defined by this name. In the case of TinyCalculator, no special context is defined, thus the application runs within the context `//Server:port/TinyCalculator/...`. Within this context, all URLs ending with `.xhtml` are handled by the application.
session-config	Config settings for the session context. Here, one sub-element for the session timeout (in minutes) is defined. Remember, a client might stop sending requests at any time, often without terminating the app. So a timeout is very important!
welcome-file-list	Defines one or more welcome files. Within this tag, the developer needs to place a `welcome-file` tag for every welcome file. Beginning with the first entry, the server searches the URI `http(s)://server:port/appContext/welcomeFile` until it finds an appropriate file to display. A welcome file may contain a path within the app. If no welcome file is defined, GlassFish searches for `index.html`.

The `web.xml` file is used for a lot more settings. I discuss some of these later when they're used for the applications, such as security settings for the Alumni app.

faces-config.xml

So far, there is no `faces-config.xml` in TinyCalculator. But this file is needed for a couple of configurations, so I cover it when discussing the particular applications. Books, for example, uses localized property files that are configured by the `faces-config.xml` file. Or, as mentioned in Chapter 5, this configuration might be used to overwrite navigation rules.

beans.xml

Starting with Java EE 6, Contexts and Dependency Injection (CDI) became part of the Java Enterprise Edition. In those early days, CDI needed to be enabled by the beans.xml file, shown in Listing 6-3. For this purpose, beans.xml might be completely empty or just contain the XML namepace declaration.

Listing 6-3. beans.xml

```
1    <?xml version="1.0" encoding="UTF-8"?>
2    <beans xmlns="http://xmlns.jcp.org/xml/ns/javaee"
3           xmlns:xsi="http://www.w3.org/2001/XMLSchema-instance"
4           xsi:schemaLocation="http://xmlns.jcp.org/xml/ns/javaee
5           http://xmlns.jcp.org/xml/ns/javaee/beans_1_1.xsd"
6           bean-discovery-mode="annotated">
7    </beans>
```

Starting with Java EE 7, CDI is enabled by default, so you usually don't need this file in Java EE 8. You may use it to control the bean discovery mode, which isn't covered in this book.

I just mention this file for completeness, but you may face a situation where you still need to develop for a Java EE 6 environment.

persistence.xml

This file, located in the projectRoot/src/main/resources/META-INFfolder, is used to configure the Java Persistence API. We'll need it to store information in a database. It's first used and discussed in Chapter 12.

glassfish-resources.xml

As its name suggests, this is a vendor-specific configuration file. The projects in this book are developed with GlassFish, so you'll find glassfish-resources.xml in this book. This file describes resources like JDBC connections.

Depending on the application server you use, your configuration may slightly differ. Usually it should be no problem to transfer the content for use in your environment.

I discuss the settings of this file in Chapter 10's discussion of the Books application, which uses the Java Persistence API to store data.

glassfish-web.xml

So far, there's no `glassfish-web.xml` file in the TinyCalculator project. In an earlier section, I discussed the context path. By default, this context is the same as the project name. But let's suppose we want to change that:

1. Using NetBeans, open the TinyCalculator project.

2. Open the project properties by right-clicking the project in the project tree and choosing Properties.

3. Click the Run category and change the context path to `Calculator`.

4. Click OK.

NetBeans creates a `glassfish-web.xml` file, located in the `WEB-INF` folder. Alternatively, this file might be created with a (text) editor, as shown in Listing 6-4.

Listing 6-4. `glassfish-web.xml`

```
1   <?xml version="1.0" encoding="UTF-8"?>
2   <!DOCTYPE glassfish-web-app PUBLIC
3   "-//GlassFish.org//DTD GlassFish Application Server 3.1 Servlet 3.0//EN"
4   "http://glassfish.org/dtds/glassfish-web-app_3_0-1.dtd">
5   <glassfish-web-app error-url="">
6
7       <context-root>/Calculator</context-root>
8
9       <!-- omitted other context for brevity-->
10  </glassfish-web-app>
```

For brevity, I've omitted some config information. With `context-root`, the default context path is overwritten.

The `glassfish-web.xml` is needed for a couple of other configurations. I'll cover those when discussing the particular applications.

Note   In existing projects, you may find a `sun-web.xml` file. This is an alternative (older) name for the same configuration done with `glassfish-web.xml`.

Other Files

Depending on the project, other configuration files may be present—for example, `settings.xml` pointing to a nonstandard local Maven repository path or `nb-configuration.xml`. These two files are managed by NetBeans, and usually we'll keep them untouched.

I'll describe these other files when they're first used.

Summary

This chapter provided an overview about some common configuration files used for Java EE development. Most of these files are discussed in more detail in the context of the application discussions throughout this book.

CHAPTER 7

Testing with Selenium

This book focuses on web development, not *test-driven development* (TDD). Of course, it's good practice to write tests for each kind of application, whether you follow the TDD paradigm or write your unit tests just after your production code. But if a test for each piece of code described in this book were added, the book would probably double in size. There are good books on unit testing available, and I introduce some of the tools in this book, but I can't cover much unit testing in this book.

Developing web applications with Java and JSF, you'll face some unfamiliar problems compared to Java SE applications: the user interface (UI) is presented by third-party software, the browser. And most of the business logic and persistence is managed by a container. So, we have some additional environment that needs to be considered for a couple of tests.

The first problem, UI presentation within a browser, is tackled by Selenium.

Selenium Overview

What is Selenium? A look at the Selenium website (`http://docs.selenium.org`) provides this answer: "*Selenium automates browsers.* That's it! What you do with that power is entirely up to you. Primarily, it is for automating web applications for testing purposes, but is certainly not limited to just that. Boring web-based administration tasks can (and should!) also be automated as well."

Selenium is available in two versions:

- Selenium IDE

- Selenium WebDriver

The Selenium IDE comes with a macro recorder. You can start recording, call a web page, perform some operations, stop recording, and then replay these actions again and again. That might be useful to log in to an application and navigate to the page of

© Michael Müller 2018
M. Müller, *Practical JSF in Java EE 8*, https://doi.org/10.1007/978-1-4842-3030-5_7

interest. Then you may perform manual steps for testing a new feature. Or you define a piece of work that's repeated in an "endless" loop to perform a stress test.

Selenium WebDriver is a driver you can use in your Java program. Different drivers for popular web browsers are available. By the power of this driver, it's possible to automate the browser with a self-written application. So far, Selenium can be used within a testing framework like JUnit.

With both versions, it's possible to define which pages to load and which UI components to control, and to read values from these components.

Preparing TinyCalculator

During the test, the Selenium WebDriver has to address the UI components. This might be done with various addressing schemes—for example, by name, by type, by id, or by path. Addressing elements is a topic for Cascading Style Sheets (CSS) too, which we haven't discussed so far. Because the id of an HTML element has to be unique, the simplest way (without knowing the other addressing schemes) is to use this id.

JSF assigns an id to every element under its control. Such an auto-generated id will be something ugly like `j_idt18`. The number depends on the element's position and will change if elements are added or removed. To get a more readable and predictable id, Listing 7-1 enriches TinyCalculator with ids by adding `id="..."`.

Listing 7-1. TinyCalculator: More Readable Ids

```
1    [everything outside form omitted for brevity]
2
3    <h:form id="form">
4        <div>
5            <h:outputLabel value="Param1: "/>
6            <h:inputText id="param1" value="#{tinyCalculator.param1}"/>
7        </div>
8        <div>
9            <h:outputLabel value="Param2: "/>
10           <h:inputText id="param2" value="#{tinyCalculator.param2}"/>
11       </div>
12       <div>
```

```
13          <h:commandButton id="add" value="Add"
14                           action="#{tinyCalculator.add}"/>
15          <h:commandButton id="sub" value="Subtract"
16                           action="#{tinyCalculator.subtract}"/>
17          <h:commandButton id="mul" value="Multiply"
18                           action="#{tinyCalculator.multiply}"/>
19          <h:commandButton id="div" value="Divide"
20                           action="#{tinyCalculator.divide}"/>
21      </div>
22      <div>
23          <h:outputLabel value="Result: "/>
24          <h:outputText id="result" value="#{tinyCalculator.result}"/>
25      </div>
26  </h:form>
```

To claim that an id must be unique is only half of the truth. Like a Java variable, its name has to be unique within its scope, or (a bit simplified) within a nesting level. If we use the same id within a different scope, we can use a path built up by this id to get a unique addressing scheme.

To address parameter 1, we may use param1 within the same scope. This will be fine when we start to AJAXify an application (covered later in this book). Or we use the complete path form:param1. Here, *form* is the id we assigned to the containing element (the form). Suppose we assign an id to a div element (for example, <div jsf:id="div1">. Now, if we have two divs, each containing an element with the id="param1", we may address them by form:div1:param1 and form:div2:param1.

Using Selenium to test TinyCalculator, we need the complete path form:param1 to address this element.

Creating the Test

Using Maven, a test is usually created within the project under test and placed in the folder test, which is a sibling to the main folder below src. Without further configuration, Maven will execute the tests during compile time.

Selenium automates browsers. The application, which is displayed within the browser, has to run at the same time. Thus we can't use the standard test invocation of Maven. We need to run the test at the application's runtime. One solution would be to create a separate project to run the tests on TinyCalculator. Another approach is to exclude the Selenium tests during compile time. We can reach this goal by configuring the Maven Surefire plugin. If we want to perform the tests, we need to launch the application first and then advise our IDE to run the tests.

We need to distinguish between tests. To see which tests should be executed by the Maven plugin during runtime and which tests should be started at runtime, I created a package called selenium for the Selenium tests, shown in Figure 7-1.

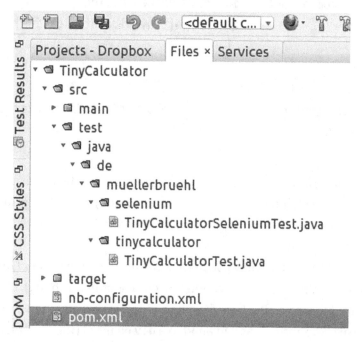

Figure 7-1. *TinyCalculator's directory structure*

For the tests, I'm using JUnit 5. Unlike JUnit 4, this version is built up by different modules. So, we need to define a couple of dependencies, which may look a bit unfamiliar to you if you've only used JUnit 4 so far. To follow the project, Listing 7-2 shows the complete POM. I'll only explain some details that are important with respect to the Selenium tests. If you need additional info on JUnit 5, please refer to the JUnit 5 user guide at http://junit.org/junit5/docs/current/user-guide/.

Listing 7-2. pom.xml

```
1  <?xml version="1.0" encoding="UTF-8"?>
2  <project xmlns="http://maven.apache.org/POM/4.0.0"
3           xmlns:xsi="http://www.w3.org/2001/XMLSchema-instance"
```

```
 4        xsi:schemaLocation="http://maven.apache.org/POM/4.0.0
 5        http://maven.apache.org/xsd/maven-4.0.0.xsd">
 6    <modelVersion>4.0.0</modelVersion>
 7
 8    <groupId>de.muellerbruehl</groupId>
 9    <artifactId>TinyCalculator</artifactId>
10    <version>1.0-SNAPSHOT</version>
11    <packaging>war</packaging>
12
13    <name>TinyCalculator</name>
14
15    <properties>
16      <java.version>1.8</java.version>
17      <project.build.sourceEncoding>UTF-8</project.build.sourceEncoding>
18    </properties>
19
20    <build>
21      <plugins>
22        <plugin>
23          <groupId>org.apache.maven.plugins</groupId>
24          <artifactId>maven-compiler-plugin</artifactId>
25          <version>3.7.0</version>
26          <configuration>
27            <source>${java.version}</source>
28            <target>${java.version}</target>
29          </configuration>
30        </plugin>
31
32        <plugin>
33          <groupId>org.apache.maven.plugins</groupId>
34          <artifactId>maven-war-plugin</artifactId>
35          <version>3.2.0</version>
36        </plugin>
37
38        <plugin>
39          <groupId>org.apache.maven.plugins</groupId>
```

```
40              <artifactId>maven-surefire-plugin</artifactId>
41              <version>2.19.1</version> <!-- 2.20.1 fails! -->
42              <configuration>
43                <excludes>
44                  <exclude>de.muellerbruehl.selenium.*</exclude>
45                </excludes>
46              </configuration>
47
48              <dependencies>
49                <dependency>
50                  <groupId>org.junit.platform</groupId>
51                  <artifactId>junit-platform-surefire-provider</artifactId>
52                  <version>1.0.2</version>
53                </dependency>
54
55                <dependency>
56                  <groupId>org.junit.jupiter</groupId>
57                  <artifactId>junit-jupiter-engine</artifactId>
58                  <version>5.0.2</version>
59                </dependency>
60              </dependencies>
61            </plugin>
62
63        </plugins>
64      </build>
65
66    <dependencies>
67      <dependency>
68        <groupId>org.glassfish</groupId>
69        <artifactId>javax.faces</artifactId>
70        <version>2.3.3</version> <!-- 2.2.19 if using GlassFish 4.1 -->
71      </dependency>
72
73      <dependency>
74        <groupId>org.seleniumhq.selenium</groupId>
75        <artifactId>selenium-firefox-driver</artifactId>
```

```
76        <version>3.8.1</version>
77        <scope>test</scope>
78      </dependency>
79
80      <dependency>
81        <groupId>javax</groupId>
82        <artifactId>javaee-web-api</artifactId>
83        <version>8.0</version> <!-- 7.0 if using GlassFish 4.1 -->
84        <scope>provided</scope>
85      </dependency>
86
87      <dependency>
88        <groupId>org.junit.jupiter</groupId>
89        <artifactId>junit-jupiter-api</artifactId>
90        <version>5.0.2</version>
91        <scope>test</scope>
92      </dependency>
93
94      <dependency>
95        <groupId>org.junit.jupiter</groupId>
96        <artifactId>junit-jupiter-engine</artifactId>
97        <version>5.0.2</version>
98        <scope>test</scope>
99      </dependency>
101
102     <dependency>
103       <groupId>org.junit.platform</groupId>
104       <artifactId>junit-platform-runner</artifactId>
105       <version>1.0.2</version>
106       <scope>test</scope>
107     </dependency>
108   </dependencies>
109 </project>
```

Unlike before, this POM is created for a Java EE 8-compliant server. If you're still using GlassFish 4.1 (as we assumed before), you need to adopt lines 70 and 83 (as stated in their comments).

Now take a look at lines 42–46: here we exclude the Selenium tests to prevent them from being executed during compile time. If you're not familiar with the Maven Surefire plugin, have a look at `http://maven.apache.org/surefire/maven-surefire-plugin/index.html`.

Lines 73–78 show how to add Selenium to the project. Adding the driver implicitly adds other dependencies, like the Selenium API itself. Other drivers for Android, Chrome, IE, IPhone, Safari, and more are also available. The driver is the part on the Selenium side to control the browser. Usually you have to install one or more components on the browser side, which enable control of the browser by the driver. In case of Firefox, we additionally need the gecko driver, which you can obtain from `https://github.com/mozilla/geckodriver/releases`.

As explained before, the POM includes dependencies to JUnit 5. Although Selenium neither depends on JUnit nor needs it to run, we use the JUnit infrastructure to run the tests.

Listing 7-3 adds a test class to the TinyCalculator project.

Listing 7-3. Sample Unit Test for Browser Automation with Selenium

```
1   public class TinyCalculatorTest {
2       private static WebDriver _driver;
3
4       @BeforeClass
5       public static void setUpClass() {
6           _driver = new FirefoxDriver();
7       }
8
9       @AfterClass
10      public static void tearDownClass() {
11          _driver.quit();
12      }
13
14      @Before
15      public void setUp() {
16          _driver.get("http://localhost:8080/TinyCalculator/index.xhtml");
17          setValue("form:param1", "6");
18          setValue("form:param2", "4");
19      }
20
```

```
21      private void setValue(String id, String value){
22          WebElement element = _driver.findElement(By.id(id));
23          element.clear();
24          element.sendKeys(value);
25      }
26
27      @Test
28      public void testAdd() {
29          _driver.findElement(By.id("form:add")).click();
30          String text = _driver.findElement(By.id("form:result")).
            getText();
31          assertThat(text, equalTo("10.0"));
32      }
33
34      @Test
35      public void testSubstract() {
36          _driver.findElement(By.id("form:sub")).click();
37          String text = _driver.findElement(By.id("form:result")).
            getText();
38          assertThat(text, equalTo("2.0"));
39      }
40
41      @Test
42      public void testMultiply() {
43          _driver.findElement(By.id("form:mul")).click();
44          String text = _driver.findElement(By.id("form:result")).
            getText();
45          assertThat(text, equalTo("24.0"));
46      }
47
48      @Test
49      public void testDivide() {
50          _driver.findElement(By.id("form:div")).click();
51          String text = _driver.findElement(By.id("form:result")).
            getText();
52          assertThat(text, equalTo("1.5"));
```

```
53        }
54    }
 1  package de.muellerbruehl.selenium;
 2
 3  import org.junit.jupiter.api.AfterAll;
 4  import static org.junit.jupiter.api.Assertions.assertEquals;
 5  import org.junit.jupiter.api.BeforeAll;
 6  import org.junit.jupiter.api.BeforeEach;
 7  import org.junit.jupiter.api.Test;
 8  import org.openqa.selenium.By;
 9  import org.openqa.selenium.WebDriver;
10  import org.openqa.selenium.WebElement;
11  import org.openqa.selenium.firefox.FirefoxDriver;
12
13  public class TinyCalculatorSeleniumTest {
14
15    private static WebDriver _driver;
16
17    @BeforeAll
18    public static void setUpClass() {
19      System.setProperty("webdriver.gecko.driver", "/home/mmueller/.
         local/geckodriver");
20      _driver = new FirefoxDriver();
21    }
22
23    @AfterAll
24    public static void tearDownClass() {
25      _driver.quit();
26    }
27
28    @BeforeEach
29    public void setUp() {
30      _driver.get("http://localhost:8080/TinyCalculator/index.xhtml");
31      setValue("form:param1", "6");
32      setValue("form:param2", "4");
33    }
```

78

```
34
35    private void setValue(String id, String value) {
36      WebElement element = _driver.findElement(By.id(id));
37      element.clear();
38      element.sendKeys(value);
39    }
40
41    @Test
42    public void testAdd() {
43      _driver.findElement(By.id("form:add")).click();
44      String text = _driver.findElement(By.id("form:result")).getText();
45      assertEquals("10.0", text);
46    }
47
48    @Test
49    public void testSubstract() {
50      _driver.findElement(By.id("form:sub")).click();
51      String text = _driver.findElement(By.id("form:result")).getText();
52      assertEquals("2.0", text);
53    }
54
55    @Test
56    public void testMultiply() {
57      _driver.findElement(By.id("form:mul")).click();
58      String text = _driver.findElement(By.id("form:result")).getText();
59      assertEquals("24.0", text);
60    }
61
62    @Test
63    public void testDivide() {
64      _driver.findElement(By.id("form:div")).click();
65      String text = _driver.findElement(By.id("form:result")).getText();
66      assertEquals("1.5", text);
67    }
68  }
```

Here are some notes on that long listing:

- In `setUpClass`, a new driver object is instantiated. In line 19 we need to define the path to the gecko driver you downloaded. As a result of this method, a browser window will open.

- Before every test (the method `setUp`), the TinyCalculator page is opened. The parameters are set to the values 6 and 4.

- There are four tests for the basic arithmetic supported by TinyCalculator. Each test clicks the appropriate button and checks the result.

- At last, in `tearDownClass`, the driver is quit. This closes the browser window.

As you may have noticed, the basic use of Selenium is quite simple. You navigate to the URL of your choice, locate elements, and perform actions:

```
WebElement element = _driver.findElement(By.id(id));
```

The `findElement` method expects a parameter of type By, which is defined as an abstract class. `By.id` invokes a static factory method that creates a concrete type of By:

```
public static By id(final String id){...}
```

By contains several factory methods to create an instance of By, which you may use to select an element. Besides `By.id`, you might use `By.name`, `By.linkText`, `By.tagName`, and more. Thus, it provides you with various ways to locate the element of interest.

To set up our tests, we have to locate the input parameters and enter some values. `sendKeys` emulates a user's input. Because we reuse the running browser window, it's essential to clear the input fields beforehand. Otherwise, the new text would be appended. On the other side, it's possible to read text from a field, with `String text = _driver.findElement(By.id("form:result")).getText();`.

Unit Test without Selenium

With our Selenium-based test, we checked the GUI and by this the underlying model. Isn't it a rule of thumb to test the model separately with a unit test? Of course, and in case of TinyCalculator, that's no problem. Listing 7-4 shows a simple test (within the TinyCalculator project).

Listing 7-4. Unit Test for the Calculator Model

```java
public class TinyCalculatorTest {

    TinyCalculator _calculator;

    @BeforeEach
    public void setUp() {
        _calculator = new TinyCalculator();
        _calculator.setParam1(6);
        _calculator.setParam2(4);
    }

    @Test
    public void testAdd() {
        _calculator.add();
        assertEquals("10.0", text);
    }

    @Test
    public void testSubtract() {
        _calculator.subtract();
        assertEquals("2.0", text);
    }

    @Test
    public void testMultiply() {
        _calculator.multiply();
        assertEquals("24.0", text);
    }

    @Test
    public void testDivide() {
        _calculator.divide();
        assertEquals("1.5", text);
    }
}
```

This tests the model without the overhead of the GUI. So, shouldn't you prefer a unit test over a test with Selenium? It depends.

Consider a named bean using injection. I'll discuss Contexts and Dependency Injection (CDI) later in this book, but let me say just one thing now: instead of creating an object manually, we want the container to do this job and provide us a reference to an object by "injecting" it to our class. You can't write a simple test for such a class. You have to either mock the object reference or use a tool like Arquillian to provide an injecting infrastructure for your tests. Instead of including compile-time tests in your application, you treat your application as a black box and perform tests at runtime from the "outside." That's what Selenium is for.

Summary

Selenium is a tool for automating browsers. As such, it can be used to perform black box testing of your application. Luckily, it's easy to use because this chapter could only provide a small peek at Selenium, which is much more powerful than these simple tests could show. Selenium can take automated snapshots, control remote browsers, and more. Besides black box testing of your application, you can use Selenium to test the GUI within different types of browsers. Standardization moves on, but there are still differences between the browser models. Thus, an application running well in one browser may show unexpected behavior in another browser or system.

The intention of this chapter is simply to act as a kick-start for Selenium. Because this book is about JSF and Java EE, I don't have room to discuss it further. But remember it for your testing scenarios of your web applications.

CHAPTER 8

TinyCalculator Recap

So far, we've discussed TinyCalculator, a small application developed for educational purposes. Using this application as an example, we've taken a short tour of some technical foundations, including the following:

- HTTP

- HTML

- CSS

- JavaScript

- Java

- Maven

We discussed a sample servlet, the technology that implements JSF. Then we went on and looked at JSF itself, including these areas:

- View definition language

- JSF lifecycle

- JSF component libraries

- Component tree

- JSF markup versus HTML-friendly markup

I introduced some essential configuration files used for JSF, Java EE, and GlassFish. Last but not least, we went over black box or GUI testing with Selenium.

We've looked at the JSF environment as a big picture. Next, we'll move on to bigger applications and dig deeper into the various aspects of web development with Java and JSF.

The source code for TinyCalculator is available from `www.apress.com/book/9781484230299`.

83

© Michael Müller 2018
M. Müller, *Practical JSF in Java EE 8*, https://doi.org/10.1007/978-1-4842-3030-5_8

PART II

Books

CHAPTER 9

Preparing for Java EE 8

So far, we've used NetBeans 8.2 with the bundled Glassfish 4.1 (the latest version at the time of writing). Java EE 7 was sufficient for TinyCalculator and the technical foundations, but now it's time set up an Java EE 8-compliant environment.

Current Evolution

In the past, new releases of NetBeans have been in sync with new releases of the core Java language as well as Java EE. But things change. Oracle donated NetBeans to the Apache foundation (`http://netbeans.apache.org`), and the next Java EE release, formerly known as Java EE 9, will be developed under the umbrella of the Eclipse foundation. (You can read the announcement at `https://blogs.oracle.com/theaquarium/ee4j-eclipse-enterprise-for-java` and its update at `https://blogs.oracle.com/theaquarium/opening-up-ee-update`.) Its new name is Jakarta EE.

The transition of NetBeans from Oracle to Apache is an ongoing process. Instead of releasing new versions for Java 9 and for Java EE 8, the process has stuck on clearing license information. As a result, this great IDE is available as a beta version at the time of writing, but sadly without the Java EE 8 features. The Java EE stuff will be part of a second donation from Oracle. That's why you still get NetBeans 8.2 as the latest release, which includes Java EE out of the box.

Luckily it's not a big problem to update the application server and prepare NetBeans for Java EE 8 development. I hope that by the time this book is in your hands, NetBeans will be available for Java EE 8 to prevent this upgrade step. I'm going to provide some updated information on my blog, when available.

However, knowing how to update parts of the environment is always helpful.

© Michael Müller 2018
M. Müller, *Practical JSF in Java EE 8*, https://doi.org/10.1007/978-1-4842-3030-5_9

Upgrade the Application Server

Although Oracle stopped its commercial support for GlassFish, this application server still is used for the Java EE 8 reference implementation (RI). GlassFish 5 is available for download at https://javaee.github.io/glassfish/download. Just download the GlassFish 5 full platform and unzip the file to any folder on your computer.

In NetBeans, click Tools ➤ Servers ➤ Add Server. NetBeans starts a wizard to add a new server. From the available server types, choose GlassFish Server and enter the name **GlassFish Server 5** (or any other name of your choice), as shown in Figure 9-1.

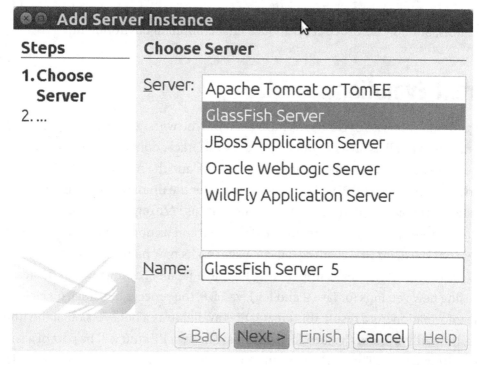

Figure 9-1. *Add new server*

Click Next.

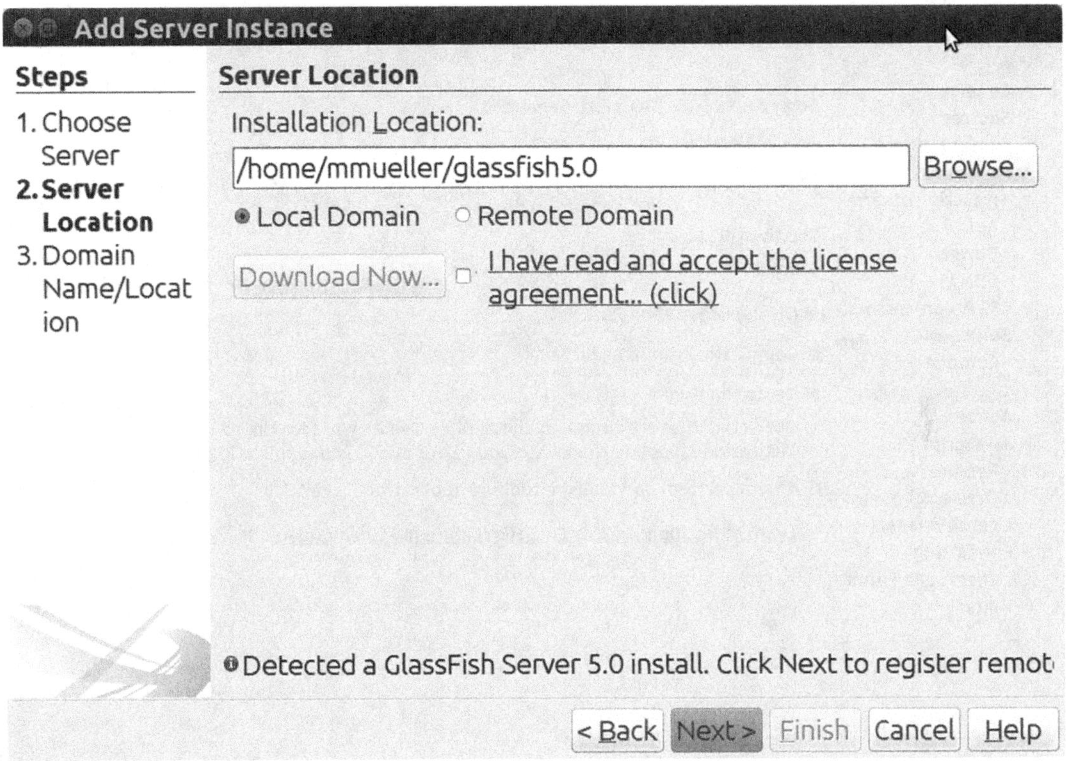

Figure 9-2. *Define the server location*

Type in your installation location or browse to the newly created folder containing the downloaded server. If everything is okay, NetBeans displays that it detected the server. Again, click Next > (All shown in Figure 9-2). In this last screen of this wizard (not shown here), NetBeans asks for the domain. Leave this dialog untouched and click Finish. NetBeans adds the newly defined server to its repository. Now right-click onto the newly created project within the Projects tree view and choose Properties. In the project properties (Figure 9-3), you can now choose this new server: right-click the project name in the Projects tree and choose Properties.

Click Run. On the right you can now select the new server, as shown in Figure 9-3. Because NetBeans doesn't know about Java EE 8, leave the Java EE Version box set to *Java EE 7 Web*. Remember, we'll define the Java EE version in the project's POM.

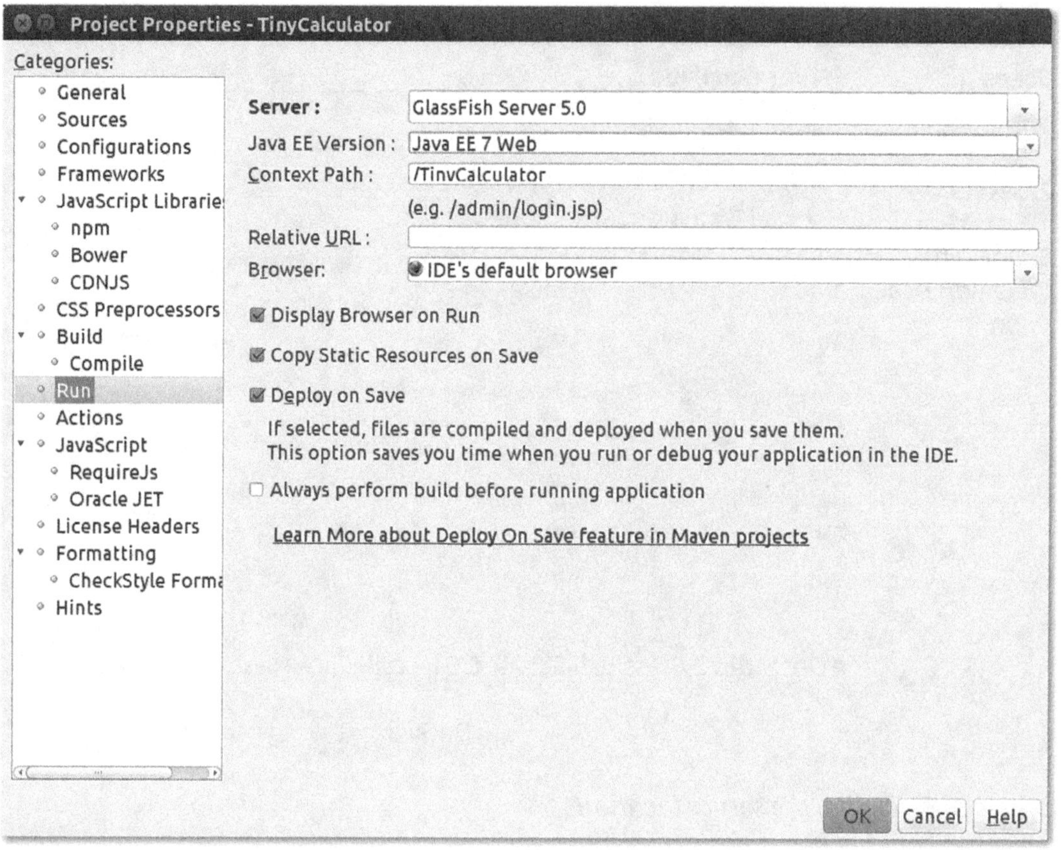

Figure 9-3. *Project properties*

Payara Server

After Oracle stopped its commercial support for GlassFish, the Payara server came to life. This server is derived from GlassFish and adds frequent support to this project. A free version is available as well as a version with commercial support. Because it's directly derived from GlassFish, you can use it instead. As a direct replacement, download your version from `www.payara.fish`. At the time of writing, Payara 5 is available as beta version (`www.payara.fish/upstream_builds`). Once you've downloaded it, follow the same installation steps described for GlassFish in the preceding paragraph.

As I write, both GlassFish 5.0 and 5.0.1 betas have problems accessing CDI backing beans for JSF if using Servlet 4. If you'd like to use GlassFish 5, you need to provide Servlet version 3.1 in the `web.xml` configuration (see Chapter 6). It's possible that this problem will be solved by the time you read this book.

There's no such problem if you use Payara 5, so I use this server for the next applications.

Summary

The current version of NetBeans doesn't support Java EE 8 out of the box. To prepare for Java EE 8 development, you need to upgrade the application server to a Java EE 8-compliant version. This short chapter showed how to perform this upgrade.

CHAPTER 10

Introducing the Books Application

Books is an application to help manage and list book reviews. This part covers the following:

- JSF templating

- Using CSS in a web application

- Persisting data with the Java Persistence API (JPA)

- Injecting beans with Context and Dependency Injection (CDI)

- Working with lists and tables

- Working with text resources

- Internationalization and localization

- Language switcher

- Validation

Books Requirements

The intent of the Books application is to present to the user an overview of book reviews penned by an author. For each book, reviews that are either external or published with this application may be linked. This might be a link to an external online source (such as a different website) or simply to some information about a printed medium where the review is published. The user can list books by category and can search. There are quite a few requirements, which can be put out as small user stories:

© Michael Müller 2018
M. Müller, *Practical JSF in Java EE 8*, https://doi.org/10.1007/978-1-4842-3030-5_10

- As a review author, I would like to enter information about a book

- As a review author, I would like to enter a review

- As a review author, I want to maintain basic data like categories

- As a user, I would like to read book-information and reviews

- As a user, I would like to search for books by title, author, and ISBN

- As a user, I would like to list books by category

- As a user, I would like to retrieve and choose from lists of all books and all reviews

- As a user, I would like to choose my preferred language, if available

All features available to the user use the same look and feel—that is, the navigation will stay on the same place whether a book or a review is currently displayed. The admin look and feel differs to visualize the different domain. The admin pages have a different background color to indicate the admin section. To achieve that, JSF templating is used. Later on, in the chapters in part IV, "Alumni," I'll discuss approaches to change the look and feel according to the user's choice.

Every book will be displayed in a table with the following information:

- Title

- Subtitle

- Author(s)

- Publisher

- Year

- Language

- ISBN

- Short descriptive text

- Cover image

- Reference to external and or internal review(s)

- Reference to category or categories

Although most information like title, author, publisher, and more will remain the same for every language, other information, such as the short descriptive text and categories, may be displayed in different languages. The current live version of Books supports English and German. This isn't a technical restriction—it's only limited by translation capabilities.

Beside books, the Books application displays reviews. This structure is simple:

- The book the review refers to

- The language of the review

- The review content

The application automatically adapts to different display sizes (thanks to *responsive design*).

Although the requirements are pretty simple, this application demonstrates a lot of techniques. Books is not a demo application only and is live on my website at `http://it-rezension.de`.

Because the application's data is well structured and homogeneous, it fits well with a SQL database. Books uses the JPA to access the database.

The look and feel and the adoption to various display sizes is realized by using Cascading Style Sheets (CSS).

You can see the live version of Books on my website. By the way, you might use it as a bibliography in addition to this book.

Development Order

Now—where to start? With a prototype of the GUI that can be provided to the customer for further review? In many projects, that might be the option of choice. Some dialogs might be sketched first, including some navigation buttons to show the planned behavior of the software. These prototypes might be built by using presentation software or directly implemented with the target language (here, Java with JSF). The latter method conveys a better feeling to the customer.

Or should we model the big picture and the activity by drawing UML or other diagrams? Or design the data model (for example, with an entity diagram) first?

In practice, you'll see all these approaches and many more. Which one is the best way to start a project depends on the project properties and the personal preferences of those involved.

The following procedure is what we call the waterfall model:

1. Collect and write down all requirements

2. Design and document the overall software architecture

3. Write down all planned functionality in detail

4. Program everything

5. Test the whole system

6. Write the user documentation and deliver it

That seems an elaborate method. And by the time the system is delivered, the requirements may have changed or some function may behave differently than how the customer expected (if the customer had a clear view about what to expect). A lesson: the waterfall method mostly fails. Agile methods are preferable. The Agile Manifesto (read it at http://agilemanifesto.org) was a milestone in this movement.

Chop the project into pieces that are iterative and implemented in increments. For each iteration, we need a short planning session. A piece of software is developed or refined and tested and—very important—delivered to the customer, or at least to an internal substitute of the customer. Thus, a short feedback loop can be included in the development process. The customer gets a quick overview of the software. Requirement changes can be incorporated quickly. Many agile people don't like the comparison, but in agile, within each iteration the development in fact follows something similar to the waterfall model, though a (very) small waterfall with a short feedback loop.

As a result of an iterative process, the development order might be changed due to influencing factors. And the detailed order becomes a bit less important because after every iteration, or sometimes within it, a correction might be applied.

For data-driven applications like Books (which mostly presents data stored somewhere to the user), I prefer to create dialog boxes as soon as possible. Because the first dialog should present a bit of the future look and feel to the user, we need an overall layout, a kind of frame where the dialog will be embedded.

What data should be used for this dialog? It depends on the size of the project, the number of people involved, their experience, and more. In any case, a good starting point is the data model. Depending on the team structure, the dialog can use this model and mock away any persistence. Database specialists might connect the data model via a service layer to the database.

Mocking data may be useful for testing or if different persons implement different parts for one feature (for example, the database part, service part, or presentation part). To present the work in progress to the user, some real data handling often suits better. As we'll see after implementing a first dialog in the next chapter, the service layer to access the data can be generalized and reused. So, it's no problem to work with persisted data for each dialog from the very beginning.

In case of Books, the data structure isn't difficult to design—we start with the data model and database access and then create the dialog that uses this data. Working iteratively, this procedure is similarly repeated for every dialog.

Because for the first dialog no service layer exists, we fill fake persistence one time. To make things clearer as you learn, activities may sometimes slightly differ from practical development.

CREATING THE BOOKS PROJECT

To start programming Books, we need to create our project. The project creation steps are the same ones explained in Chapter 1, so I assume you're able to create the project without further assistance (or reread that first chapter if necessary).

1. Using NetBeans or your favorite IDE, create a new Maven web project named Books.

2. Add the JSF framework to your project.

3. As long as NetBeans doesn't support Java EE 8 out of the box, you need to slightly update some generated files—notably pom.xml and web.xml (see Chapter 6 for more).

Summary

This chapter outlined the main features and requirements of the Books application and discussed some aspects of iterative development. In the next chapter, we'll start with a first dialog box, mocking away persistence. To begin that chapter, you should have created a fresh web application.

CHAPTER 11

Starting the Books App

Let's recap the steps for the first dialog:

1. Sketch and implement a preliminary overall layout

2. Design the data model for the first dialog

3. Implement the first dialog

4. Add persistence

Page Layout

For the first step, we have to answer an essential question: which devices will future users of the application use? Preferably a desktop or laptop computer? Or mostly a mobile device? Or any of those?

The screen layout for a small screen usually must differ from the layout for a large screen. For Books, we'll assume the user wants to access the application from a personal computer as well as from a smartphone. That means we need a flexible design that fits all sizes by dynamically changing the size of some elements and/or reordering the element positions. In other words, it needs to be *responsive*. How to create such a responsive design is the topic of Chapter 19.

To prepare a responsive design, we split the screen layout into logical groups—for example, main content and navigation. On a desktop screen, both groups might be arranged side by side, whereas for a mobile device they might be arranged vertically. Or the navigation might be hidden and displayed only on demand. For mobile devices, the content of each group might also be reduced.

Although starting out "mobile first" is popular, I assume my readers are Java developers. In that role, you usually use a desktop or laptop computer with a screen resolution of at least 1280 pixels horizontally. Thus, we'll start with a design for that kind of device.

© Michael Müller 2018
M. Müller, *Practical JSF in Java EE 8*, https://doi.org/10.1007/978-1-4842-3030-5_11

Besides the main content and navigation, Books will have a headline and a footer. The layout is sketched in Figure 11-1.

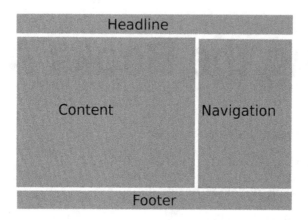

Figure 11-1. *Overall desktop screen layout of Books*

For development, I use screens with a horizontal size of 1680, 1920, and 2560 pixels. Have you ever read a document in the browser with text lines extended to those sizes? It's a mess. So, we want to restrict the horizontal size of our layout and center it in the browser window. We'll replace the white space outside with it a nice picture. Note that this approach also reduces the gap to small (mobile) devices, which need to be covered by this responsive design too.

HTML Structure

First we need to create a page. NetBeans created the page index.xhtml, which can be used and renamed. This page will contain four sections for the different areas and one container element (`div id="wrapper"`), containing the four parts mentioned earlier, which is used to limit the width of the whole page.

Before HTML5, usually a `div` was used for this purpose. Every `div` became its own id. Because this approach is still widely used, Listing 11-1 demonstrates such a page.

Listing 11-1. Rough Page Structure by `div` Elements

```
1    <?xml version='1.0' encoding='UTF-8' ?>
2    <!DOCTYPE html>
3    <html xmlns="http://www.w3.org/1999/xhtml"
4          xmlns:h="http://xmlns.jcp.org/jsf/html">
```

```
5    <h:head>
6      <title>Books</title>
7    </h:head>
8    <h:body>
9      <div id="wrapper">
10       <div id="header">
11         <h1>Michael's book list</h1>
12       </div>
13       <div id="main">
14         Main content goes here
15       </div>
16       <div id="navigation">
17         This is the navigation
18       </div>
19       <div id="footer">
20         This is the footer
21       </div>
22     </div>
23   </h:body>
24 </html>
```

HTML5 knows a few more specific tags for structuring a page. We can replace some of the div elements with new semantic elements. For example, we may use <header> in favor of a div to indicate the header part of the page, as shown in Listing 11-2—but don't mix with the HTML head!

Listing 11-2. HTML Page Structured by Specific Elements

```
1    <?xml version='1.0' encoding='UTF-8' ?>
2    <!DOCTYPE html>
3    <html xmlns="http://www.w3.org/1999/xhtml"
4          xmlns:h="http://xmlns.jcp.org/jsf/html">
5      <h:head>
6        <title>Books</title>
7      </h:head>
8      <h:body>
9        <div id="wrapper">
```

```
10          <header>
11            <h1>Michael's book list</h1>
12          </header>
13          <main>
14            Main content goes here
15          </main>
16          <nav>
17            This is the navigation
18          </nav>
19          <footer>
20            This is the footer
21          </footer>
22        </div>
23      </h:body>
24    </html>
```

Only the div, which is used as a container element for the page, comes with an id. divs are broadly used and will be used in this application. A unique id helps to address the right div. As you'll see, we don't need the id right here, but for admin pages we will use such an id.

The other elements, like header, are unique within our application. By definition, these elements may occur multiple times. In such a case, an id would help again.

If we run this application, the browser would show a kind of boring page, like Figure 11-2.

Michael's book list

Main content goes here
This is the navigation
This is the footer

Figure 11-2. Structured page without layout definition

We've defined some container elements for the future content. For main, nav, and footer, the page simply contains some placeholder text.

Basic Styling with CSS

As mentioned, content and style should be separated. A web page, like a web application, is more than just content and functionality—a pleasant look and feel are also important. Cascading Style Sheets (CSS) is the technology we'll use to create that look and feel. If you're not familiar with CSS, you may want to check out Appendix B, which serves as a basic introduction.

Although it's possible to include styles in the `<style>` element of the `<html>` header of a page, it's better to put the styles into one or more separate file(s). That simplifies reuse and, due to browser caching, reduces page load time. The CSS is loaded just once instead of being loaded with every page.

Using NetBeans, right-click any folder of the project within the Projects view and choose New ➤ Other ➤ Web ➤ Cascading Style Sheet. Enter the name **books** and set the folder to `resources/css`, as shown in Figure 11-3.

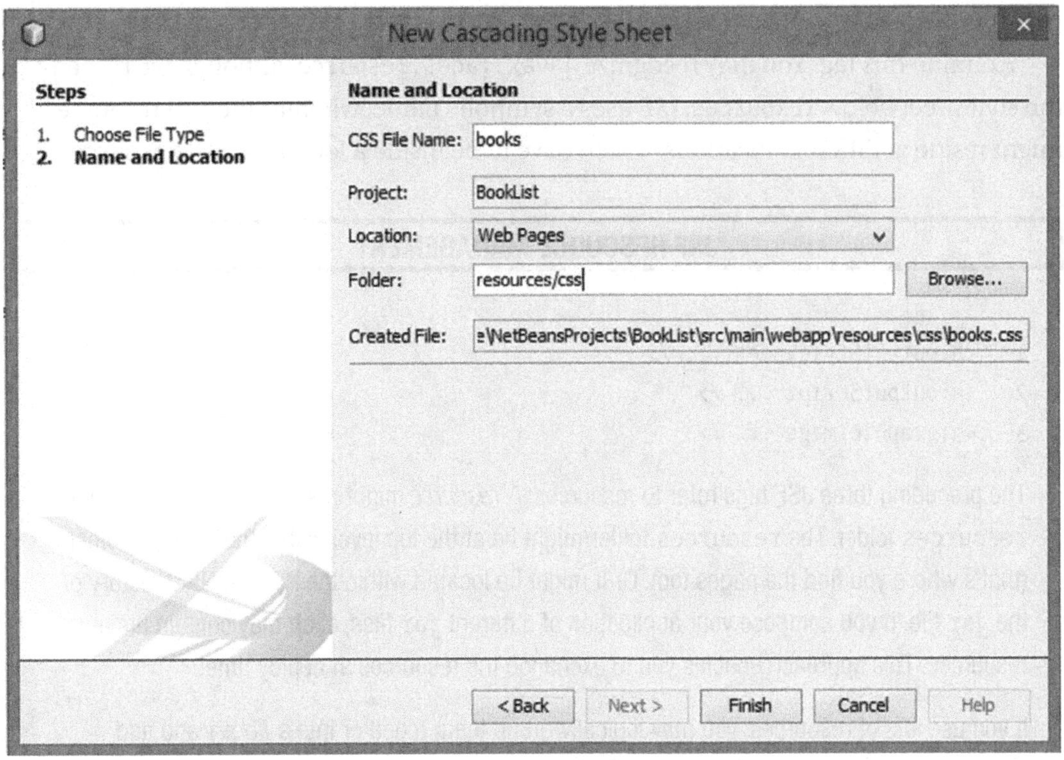

Figure 11-3. *Creating CSS with NetBeans*

You're creating a nesting subfolder structure and a file within the Web Pages folder. Alternatively, in the Web Pages folder you could create a folder called resources, then a subfolder css, and within that folder a new file, books.css.

Now we'll add a reference to that file to the JSF page, as shown in Listing 11-3.

Listing 11-3. Embedding CSS with a JSF Tag

```
1   ...
2     <h:head>
3       <title>Books</title>
4       <h:outputStylesheet name="css/books.css"/>
5     </h:head>
6   ...
```

The tag <h:outputStylesheet> will be rendered by JSF as <link type="text/css" rel="stylesheet" href="/Books/javax.faces.resource/css/books.css.xhtml"/>, which is the HTML syntax to include as CSS.

Examine this tag. You may recognize javax.faces.resource, although we placed the stylesheet below resources. JSF uses a symbolic name, whereas the real resource might reside at different locations, which have to be inside a folder named resources.

JSF RESOURCE MANAGEMENT

```
1   <h:outputStylesheet ... />
2   <h:outputScript ... />
3   <h:graphicImage ... />
```

The preceding three JSF tags refer to resources. A *resource* might reside in any folder within a resources folder. The resources folder might be at the top level within the webapp folder (that's where you find the pages too). Or it might be located within the META-INF directory of the jar file. If you compose your application of different jar files, each may contain (its own) resources. This approach enables you to exchange the resources at deploy time.

If you use lots of resources, you may logically group them together into a *library* and add an attribute library="yourLibrary". This attribute is treated as a folder—for example, <h:outputStylesheet library="muellerbruehl" name="css/books.css"/> refers to resource/muellerbruehl/css/books.css. You may ask why you can't use

`<h:outputStylesheet name="muellerbruehl/css/books.css"/>`? That does point to the same folder and will be functional, but the intent is different. By using the `library` attribute, your intent is not only to point to a specific resource file, but to a group of resources that fit together—for example, CSS, icons, and script that belong to a special theming. I cover this near the end of this book when we change an application's look and feel.

Also, using the `library` attribute, you can place an optional version folder between the `library` folder and your `resource` file path. The version folder is named according to the \ `d+(_\d+)*` pattern. By default, JSF always loads the latest version (highest number).

Without any version, `<h:outputStylesheet library="muellerbruehl"` `name=css/"books.css"/>` refers to the file `resources/muellerbruehl/css/books.css`.

Assuming a version 1_0, this file must be in `resources/muellerbruehl/1_0/css/` `books.css`. The full path to your library is composed by `resources/<library>/<versio` `n>/<name>`, where name may contain additional folders.

Let's assume we have two versions, 1_0 and 1_1, as follows:

```
resources/muellerbruehl/1_0/css/books.css
resources/muellerbruehl/1_1/css/books.css
```

Now the tag I mentioned automatically resolves to the second folder because it contains the latest version. There is no version attribute within the `h:outputStyle` tag. Thus, you may add a newer version to your folder structure, which would be resolved automatically, but you can't select a specific version.

For further info, check out the article by Bauke Scholtz at `http://stackoverflow.com/` `questions/11988415/what-is-the-jsf-resource-library-for-and-how-` `should-it-be-used`.

Listing 11-4 adds some content to the `books.css` file.

Listing 11-4. Basic CSS for Books

```
1    * {
2        margin: 0px;
3        padding: 0px;
4        border: 0px;
5        color: #000044;
6    }
7
```

```
 8    body {
 9      font-size: 12px; /* base size */
10      text-align: left;
11      font-family: Verdana, "Verdana CE",
12                   Arial, "Arial CE", "Lucida Grande CE",
13                   lucida, "Helvetica CE", sans-serif;
14      background-image: url(/Books/resources/images/books1.png);
15      background-repeat: repeat;
16      background-position: top left;
17      background-attachment: fixed;
18    }
19
20    h1, h2, h3, h4, h5, h6 {
21      color: red;
22      padding: 1.0em 0em 1.0em 0em;
23    }
24
25    h1 {
26      font-size: 2em;
27    }
28
29    h2 {
30      font-size: 1.5em;
31      font-style: italic;
32    }
33
34    h3 {
35      font-size: 1.2em;
36    }
```

With the universal selector *, some reset actions are performed. Because some default values differ from browser to browser, we set them to defined values to achieve the same (or at least similar) layout in almost every browser. This is well known as a *CSS reset* (you can read more about it at http://cssreset.com/what-is-a-css-reset/). Here, we overwrite the browser settings for padding, margin, and border. We also set the default text color to a dark blue.

Within body, we'll set the basic font size. Doing so, the font becomes independent from the browser's default font size. And we choose a font from the list of fonts. The browser tries to apply a font from this list, beginning with the first. The last one, sans-serif, is usually known by every browser and will be applied if the browser couldn't find any other font family of this list. This ensures a font without serifs. The background statements load an image as background, with a fixed (non-scrolling) positioning, which is repeated endlessly.

Next, some standard settings for the heading tags (h1 through h6) are applied. The unit *em*, a typesetting term meaning "width of the letter *M*," is a relative size. As font size, 2em doubles the size of the font. The base of this size is the size that's applied in the container element, not the size we defined in the body! The size of the body is simply the base for all other relative sizes.

For example, if we have a basic font size of 12px and define a div to which we apply a size of 2em, the resulting font size within this div would be 24px. Now, if we place a header 1 before that div, h1 would create a font of 24px (12px × 2). But if we place a header 1 within this div, then h1 would create a font size of 48px (12px × 2[by div] × 2[by h1]), because the 2em of h1 is a relative size to the font within the div, which is scaled by 2em itself.

As you can see in Figure 11-4, all content is still displayed left aligned, whatever window size you use for your browser.

Figure 11-4. Reset, background, and header styles applied

If you were to insert a long line of text for any part, such as the main content, you would see this text being extended to the right border of your browser window. Our goal is to restrict the length of our content and center it. To that end, add the content of Listing 11-5 to the books.css file.

Listing 11-5. Fix Width by CSS (Add to `books.css`)

```
1   body > div {
2       width: 80em;
3       margin: 0 auto;
4       text-align: left;
5   }
```

These styles affect the topmost `div` within our document, which is our wrapping element. Using the combined element and id selector, `div#wrapper` would have addressed the same `div`. Later on, when designing the admin pages, we'd like to reuse this style. For admin pages, the first `div` gets a different id. Thus, by using the `div#wrapper` selector, we can't reuse this style information.

`width: 80em;` limits the size of our web content by a relative size. Some years ago, it was common to set the limit to a fixed absolute size, like `width: 960px;`. This allowed creation of a fixed layout with nearly full control of the exact sizes. But we don't develop for desktop computers only. Starting with relative sizes allows for switching to a responsive layout later on. 1em is a relative unit, its width about the width of the capital *M* in whatever font and size are currently in use. Later on, we'll add so-called *media queries*, to consider smaller screen (or window) sizes.

CHECK THE WRAPPER

1. Add a long piece of text (200 characters, say) to the main content.

2. Run the application.

3. Resize the browser window from full screen width to a skinnier width.

Note that the text stays centered. That is, to the left and right of each line of text, there will be roughly equal space. When you squeeze the window size, this space is reduced. Once there's no more space, a horizontal scroll bar appears.

Our header will be as wide as the wrapper area with rounded corners, and the text displayed will be white on blue background. To get a smooth design, it will be a bit transparent and let the background shine through somewhat. The footer will look similar, but instead of a headline it will contain some text and links. Right now, it only contains pure text, so let's add some links, as shown in Listing 11-6.

Listing 11-6. Book's Footer

```
1   ...
2     <footer>
3       &copy; Michael Müller
4       |
5       <h:outputLink value="http://blog.mueller-bruehl.de">
6         Michael's Blog
7       </h:outputLink>
8       |
9       <h:link value="About" outcome="index.xhtml"/>
10    </footer>
11  ...
```

© is an HTML entity that refers to the copyright sign. Using HTML 4.x, you could use it right this way—but we declared our doctype to be HTML5, which doesn't know such entities. So, we have to declare this entity first by enhancing the doctype information at the first line of our XHTML file: `<!DOCTYPE html [<!ENTITY copy "&#169;">]>`.

The JSF tag `<h:outputLink ...>` renders an outgoing link. This kind of link leaves the application. In this page, it simply would be rendered as `<a href="http://blog.mueller-bruehl.de">Michael's Blog</a>`, which is a standard HTML link. Why should somebody use this JSF tag and not the HTML version? Because it's possible to enrich the tag with additional information. For example, you could add attributes known by JSF, such as `rendered = "#{someCondition}"`. Doing so, the link would be rendered if the condition evals to true only.

`<h:link ...>` renders to an `<a href=...>` also. It's used as an internal link (within the application) and might be enriched with JSF-specific attributes, too. Because we don't have an About page yet, it simply points to the source page. The differences of the various links are discussed later on in Chapter 18.

Having added some "real" content, we can continue to apply styles, as shown in Listing 11-7.

Listing 11-7. Basic CSS for the Page Layout and Menu (Add to `books.css`)

```
1   header, footer {
2     opacity: 0.75;
3     border-radius: 1em;
4     background-color: #000044;
```

```
 5      padding: 1em;
 6      text-align: center;
 7      box-shadow: 0 0 1em white;
 8    }
 9
10    header {
11      margin: 2em auto 1em auto;
12    }
13
14    footer {
15      margin: 0.5em auto 1em auto;
16      color: white;
17    }
18
19    header > h1{
20      color: white;
21      margin: 0;
22      padding: 0;
23    }
24
25    a {
26      text-decoration: none;
27      color: white;
28    }
29
30    a:hover{
31      color: red;
32    }
```

Although we used JSF tags, the style is always applied to the rendered HTML elements. The links are rendered as an anchor tag, (<a href=...>). Setting text-decoration: none; will omit the underlining. Rather, the link will turn red on a mouse over (by defining hover).

padding 1em; applies 1em padding to each side. Instead of one parameter, you might apply two (padding top/bottom right/left) or four (padding top right bottom left) parameters, as done for the margin. Or you may define padding-top 1em; (-right, -bottom, -left) for a given side only.

`box-shadow: 0 0 1em white;` defines a white "shadow." In fact, this seems to be a bright light. No value is added to the horizontal and vertical position. The width from opacity 100 percent to 0 is 1em.

The other elements should be fairly self-explanatory. The navigation will be placed left from the main part.

COLUMN LAYOUT

An established way to calculate layout sizes is to divide the whole content area into columns— for example, six columns with gaps in between. If we take 2 percent of the full width for such a gap, we can calculate each column width by $(100\% - 5 \times 2\%) / 6 = 15\%$ per column. Long version: in between six cols, there are five gaps. Each gap takes 2% of the width, which is a total of 10% for the gaps. We need to subtract this from the 100% width. As a result, 90% of the full width has to be devided by the six columns. In this example, we use four columns for the main part, including three gaps, and two columns for the navigation, including one gap. Last but not least, we have one remaining gap between the main part and the navigation.

I mention column layout because it's very popular and you may have heard or read about it. For Books, there's no need to arrange content in columns. The navigation will be "fixed" during scrolling; this will be realized by `position: fixed;`. See Listing 11-8.

Listing 11-8. CSS for Main Part and Navigation (Add to `books.css`)

```
1   main {
2     min-height: 40em;
3     width: 53em;
4     opacity: 0.95;
5     border-radius: 1em;
6     background-color: #eeeef3;
7     padding: 1em;
8     margin-bottom: 1em;
9     box-shadow: 0.5em 0.5em 0.5em #004
10  }
11
12  nav{
13    min-height: 40em;
```

```
14      position: fixed;
15      margin-left: 56em;
16      width: 22em;
17      padding: 1em;
18      top: 7.5em;
19      opacity: 0.85;
20      border-radius: 1em;
21      background-color: #ccccd8;
22      box-shadow: 0.5em 0.5em 0.5em #004
23    }
```

The height of an element is usually calculated by its content. The main part might get much longer than the navigation. Right now, both parts contain only a few words. To balance the height, a minimum height is defined for each of these parts. The main part's width is simply set to 53em (remember the wrapper being 80em wide). According to the box model, a padding of 2 × 1em will be added. If we assume a gap of 1em between main and nav, nav needs a left margin of 56em. And the width of nav is simply calculated by 80em – 56em – 2 × 1em (padding) = 22em.

Figure 11-5 shows the app running.

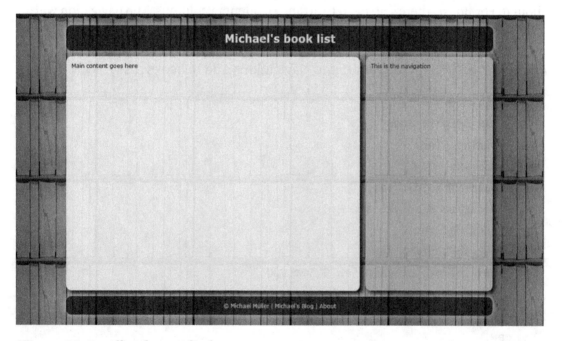

Figure 11-5. *All styles applied*

Design First Data Model

Now we can implement a first dialog. In practice, you might start implementing a big feature, like the book editor or review editor. That would make sense, because these are valuable features for the customer. But we want to assign every book to one or more categories. Thus, categories need to be available when we enter the data of a new book. In real development, we may omit this little feature to implement it later, once the customer is satisfied with the overall editor.

We haven't discussed persistence yet, and a category is one of the simplest structures within our application, so it's a good starting point to introduce data storage and access. We start to design the data model here. In Chapter 12 we will persist this data.

Ignoring the fact of different display languages, a *category* simply consists of an id and text only. So far, our data model seems to be very simple: two properties with getters and setters. See Listing 11-9.

Listing 11-9. Category

```
1   public class Category {
2     // <editor-fold defaultstate="collapsed" desc="Property Id">
3     private int _id = -1;
4
5     public int getId() {
6       return _id;
7     }
8
9     public void setId(int id) {
10       _id = id;
11     }
12    // </editor-fold>
13
14    // <editor-fold defaultstate="collapsed" desc="Property Name">
15    private String _name;
16
17    public String getName() {
18      return _name;
19    }
20
```

```
21    public void setName(String name) {
22        _name = name;
23    }
24    // </editor-fold>
25  }
```

The id is initialized with –1 to indicate there is no valid id yet.

By the way, the editor-fold comments are specific to NetBeans. They allow structuring and collapsing the code. It's a one-time presentation here.

Is that all? Nope. There's something more we need to do. As a Java developer, you might miss the hashCode and equals methods. Both are needed if objects of this class will be used in any collection. NetBeans can generate both for you. This generated code might be used as a starting point only. Using persistence, the id will be generated by the database management system.

Only this id identifies the category. There's a valid id, hashCode, and equals depend on this id only, ignoring the text. But if there's no valid id, we probably need to distinguish two different object instances. We do that by considering the text.

Usually, in our application we'll display selected properties of our entities. But if we simply put an entity onto a page, JSF would display it by its string representation. Thus, we should override the toString method to gain more informative output, as is done in Listing 11-10.

Listing 11-10. HashCode and Equals Need to Be Defined for Any Entity

```
1    @Override
2    public int hashCode() {
3      if (_id < 0) {
4        return _name.hashCode();
5      }
6      return _id;
7    }
8
9    @Override
10   public boolean equals(Object object) {
11     if (!(object instanceof Category)) {
12       return false;
13     }
```

```
14      Category other = (Category) object;
15      if (_id < 0 && other._id < 0) {
16        return _name.equals(other._name);
17      }
18      return _id == other._id;
19    }
20
21    @Override
22    public String toString() {
23      return "Category[ id=" + _id + "] " + _name;
24    }
```

Now the data model for the first dialog is ready.

First Dialog Box (Repeating Structure)

Category is the simplest data structure to be persisted and as such is a good starting point to discuss the data storage. A *category* only consists of an id and text. We could certainly design a small dialog box containing these two fields, plus two buttons, Save and Delete. Just to edit every category by its own screen. In fact, the id doesn't matter for the user; it's only used as the primary key once we move on to persistence. So, we'll put all categories into a list and edit them all at once.

We need to

- Add a category

- Modify a category's text

- Delete a category

- Save the list

To add a category or save the list, we use one button each.

It's very common to display a read-only list and add an Edit link to each row. If you click the link, the Edit dialog will be displayed. Using applications following this approach, though, I feel uncomfortable. So, we'll allow a direct and random access to each category.

Each category will be displayed as an input field. In front of this, we place a Delete icon, to delete the category of this line. Figure 11-6 gives you an impression of the completed category editor. We'll start with the core functionality on the left side in the rest of this chapter and continue with other subjects (navigation and internationalization) in subsequent chapters.

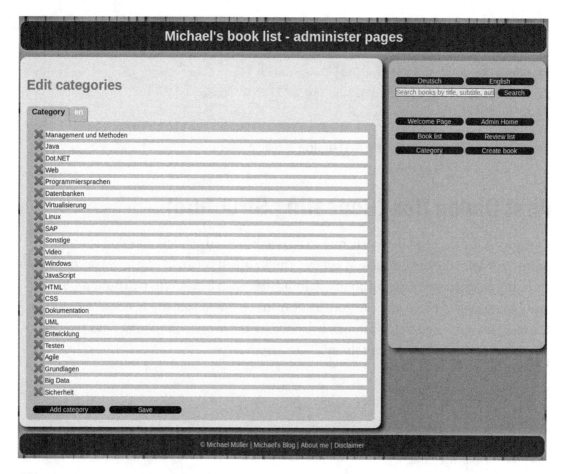

Figure 11-6. *Category editor*

We don't have a service class to retrieve categories from a database or to save them. So let's create a list with some initial categories to simulate database access. And the Save button will only perform a log, which you can observe on the NetBeans console (the Output, GlassFish Server window). See Listing 11-11.

Listing 11-11. CategoryEditor

```
1   @Named
2   @SessionScoped
3   public class CategoryEditor implements Serializable{
4     private static final long serialVersionUID = 1L;
5     private static final Logger _logger = Logger.
      getLogger("CategoryEditor");
6
7     @PostConstruct
8     private void init(){
9       _categories = new ArrayList<>();
10      _categories.add(new Category(){{setId(1); setName("Java");}});
11      _categories.add(new Category(){{setId(2); setName("Web");}});
12    }
13
14    private List<Category> _categories;
15
16    public List<Category> getCategories() {
17      return _categories;
18    }
19
20    public void setCategories(List<Category> categories) {
21      _categories = categories;
22    }
23
24    public String addCategory(){
25      _categories.add(new Category());
26      return "";
27    }
28
29    public String deleteCategory(Category category){
30      _categories.remove(category);
31      return "";
32    }
33
```

```
34      public String save(){
35         String categories = _categories
36                    .stream()
37                    .filter(cat -> !cat.getName().isEmpty())
38                    .map(cat -> cat.toString())
39                    .collect(Collectors.joining(", "));
40         _logger.log(Level.INFO, "Save categories: {0}", categories);
41         return "";
42      }
43   }
```

The code in the preceding listing uses the *lambda* and *stream* features introduced in Java 8 (my book *Java Lambdas and Parallel Streams* (Apress, 2016) is a good introduction to those, if I do say so myself). If you're not familiar with lambdas and streams, you can use a more traditional approach with a for loop. As mentioned, the save method doesn't perform a save yet, but instead does logging. See Listing 11-12.

Listing 11-12. Java 7 Version of save Method

```
1    ...
2       public String save(){
3          String categories = "";
4          for (Category category : _categories){
5             if (!category.getName().isEmpty()){
6                if (categories.length() > 0){
7                   categories += ", ";
8                }
9                categories += category;
10            }
11         }
12         _logger.log(Level.INFO, "Save categories: {0}", categories);
13         return "";
14      }
15   ...
```

The bean is simply @SessionScoped (remember to import the proper class—this is a CDI scope, not the old JSF SessionScope!). Usually, this is not the best choice. Once instantiated, such a bean will live as long as the session lasts. On a server with high traffic, this approach might result in high memory consumption.

A @SessionScoped lives for a relative long time. The server might *passivate* the bean to free resources and reload (activate) it when needed again. *Passivating* is the process of temporarily persisting the object somewhere (at the server's choice, depending on the server's implementation) by serializing the object. That's why the appropriate marker interface is needed. The serialVersionUID determines different object versions. Here, we don't use serialization besides passivation. We don't expect to load data that's activated by an object version other than passivated. So, we simply use a constant value of 1L. This prevents Java from calculating its own object version. (You can read the Java documentation for more on serialization: http://docs.oracle.com/javase/8/docs/api/java/io/Serializable.html.

Although passivating is a strategy to reduce memory consumption, it uses additional IO or other resources. Thus, a scope with a shorter lifetime is usually a better choice. The Books application is intended for only one or a few editors and lots of readers. Extending the bean's lifetime doesn't matter here. I discuss other scopes later on.

To simulate a load from a database, the category list will be created at PostConstruct time. The container will call such an annotated method just after creating an instance of the class and injecting the dependencies (if any). We could have done this initialization within the class constructor, but using the Java Persistence API (JPA—the topic of the next chapter), the appropriate service class will be injected *after* the class construction. Then we need to perform the database retrieval later, and that's why PostConstruct is ideal.

The double curly braces notation is an old Java idiom. Nevertheless, it's unknown to many developers. It's simply a shortcut to call the setters right after construction of the categories. To set properties for a newly created class, it's preferable to use a special constructor that allows attributes to pass as parameters. As you'll see in the JPA, there's no need for such a constructor, and because we're mocking database access, the data model doesn't contain it either.

The code contains three methods to add, delete, and save categories. All of them return an empty string to reload the same page. For simplicity's sake, this named bean is set into the session scope. Later on, when I introduce AJAX, we'll refine both.

Next, we need to add some content to the main part of our page, as shown in Listing 11-13.

Listing 11-13. Main Section of Category Editor

```
1   ...
2   <main>
3     <h1>Edit categories</h1>
4     <h:form>
5       <h:dataTable value="#{categoryEditor.categories}"
6                    var="cat">
7         <h:column>
8           <h:commandLink
9             action="#{categoryEditor.deleteCategory(cat)}">
10            <h:graphicImage alt="delete"
11                            name="Delete.png"
12                            library="icon/small"
13                            title="delete"/>
14          </h:commandLink>
15        </h:column>
16        <h:column>
17          <h:inputText value="#{cat.name}"/>
18        </h:column>
19      </h:dataTable>
20      <h:commandLink styleClass="button"
21                     value="Add category"
22                     action="#{categoryEditor.addCategory}"/>
23      <h:commandButton styleClass="button"
24                       value="Save"
25                       action="#{categoryEditor.save}"/>
26    </h:form>
27  </main>
28  ...
```

Besides a heading, the main part now contains a form containing three children:

- <h:dataTable...>: Renders an HTML table

- <h:commandLink...>: Renders an HTML link

- <h:commandButton...>: Renders an HTML input, type submit

The value of the <h:dataTable...> tag refers to the category list (getCategories()). Each item is bound to a variable cat. This name was freely chosen. Now, for each row, we can use this cat variable to access the current category. Within the dataTable, two columns are defined. The first displays a Delete icon, nested within commandLink. We use the current category as a parameter for the deleteCategory method. The icon is placed in the icon/small folder structure, which itself is placed in the resources folder (as we did for the CSS file). The icon itself is a 16 × 16 pixel PNG image.

The icons used for this application are the Free Application Icons, which can used in any application for free. They're distributed using the Creative Commons Attribution-Share Alike 3.0 License. The download is available from www.small-icons.com/packs/16x16-free-application-icons.htm.

Figure 11-6 showed two buttons below the table, but are those really two buttons? Frankly, no. One (h:commandLink) is rendered as a link. By defining the style class button, both—the link and the real button—will be displayed like buttons. To do that, we need to add a bit of CSS. There's one special reason to handle these buttons with different JSF tags: if one input field has the focus, and the user presses the Enter key, then the first HTML input, type submit, is invoked. This behavior is reminiscent of desktop applications, where you press Tab to move forward, but pressing Enter performs an action like saving or accepting the data. Because we've defined only one real button element, its related action, save, is invoked on Enter.

The button style is shown in Listing 11-14.

Listing 11-14. CSS to Create a Button Style

```
1   .button{
2     width: 10em;
3     border-radius: 0.5em;
4     background-color: #000044;
5     color: white;
6     display: inline-block;
7     text-align: center;
8     margin-top: 1em;
9     margin-right: 1em;
10  }
11
```

```
12   .button:hover{
13      font-weight: bold;
14      color: red;
15   }
```

In this part of the CSS file, we use a class selector, as indicated by the leading dot. Declaring the button as display: inline-block; lets us apply a defined width.

Now if you run the application, it should look like Figure 11-7.

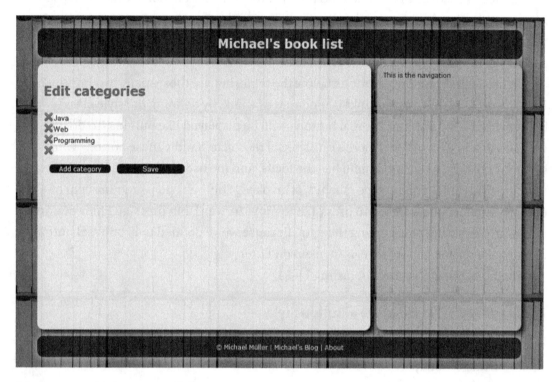

Figure 11-7. *Version 1 of the category editor*

OBSERVE THE EDITOR

As an exercise, add some categories: `edit` and `delete`.

Click the Save button and observe the GlassFish console (or log). Add three categories named x, y, and again x. Now, for the last x, click Delete. The first x category will be deleted. Do you know why?

A new category doesn't contain a valid id. According to `hashCode()` and `equals()`, categories with the same text are treated as equal. `_categories.remove(category);` removes the first occurrence. Because of the same text, removing the "wrong" entry doesn't really matter. But if we'd built the `hashCode` and `equals` method relying on the id only, then deleting any entry without a valid id would remove the first entry without a valid id, even though the text might differ.

Summary

The development of Books started with the general layout of the application. Because lots of Java developers are more familiar with desktop applications, this app starts with a "desktop first" approach rather than the currently popular "mobile first." We considered responsive design and noted that CSS is the first choice in technology to apply those styles. This chapter showed CSS's elementary usage in the application.

We developed our first dialog. Mocking away the database access, we could concentrate on the UI and introduced the first repeating structure to create an editable table.

In the next chapter, we'll persist this data.

CHAPTER 12

Java Persistence API

The data for the Books application is homogeneous, which means the overall structure is the same for every category, book, review, or piece of linking information. The classic storage method for such data (and usually the best choice) is a SQL database system.

If you're a Java SE developer and have accessed SQL DBs so far, you might have used Java Database Connectivity (JDBC). JDBC is an abstraction for SQL statements. The database is queried and returns a result set, which is transformed to lists, objects, and other things by your program. The responsibility for the transformation of persistent data to objects falls to the developer. And it's a repetitive, sometimes boring, job just to overcome the gap between relational data and objects.

If it's possible to define mapping rules, from relations to objects and vice versa, that job might be done by a piece of software. And that's exactly what an *object relational mapper* (ORM) is for. Several JPA-compatible ORMs are available. In the world of Java EE, the ORM is defined by the Java Persistence API (JPA).

Note The current version of JPA as part of Java EE 8 is 2.2. As a maintenance release of JPA 2.1, it's still defined by JSR 338 (read more about it at `https://jcp.org/en/jsr/detail?id=338`). In other words, there is no dedicated JSR for version 2.2.

Entities

If you're familiar with SQL, you probably know that a database stores entities. An *entity* is a unit of information, or simply, a thing. Mostly, an entity is represented by the columns of a table. The relations between entities are modeled by an entity–relationship model.

© Michael Müller 2018
M. Müller, *Practical JSF in Java EE 8*, https://doi.org/10.1007/978-1-4842-3030-5_12

JPA also uses the term *entity* for a unit of information—in this case, a Java object. You may annotate a class as @Entity, but a Java object might be complex. Besides simple properties, such an object may contain collections or embedded other objects. For example, if your Java object models a car, then this entity may contain a list of seat objects. As you might imagine, such complex objects can't be stored in a single table. A single Java object may be stored in a couple of different tables. A SQL entity is usually stored in a single table, whereas a JPA entity might become more complex.

Technically, a JPA entity is a *plain old Java object* (POJO) that is mapped to one or more SQL table(s). To start defining this mapping, we pick one of the simplest structures of Books: the category. At first approach, ignoring different languages, a category consists of an id and a text.

We've already created the Category class. To map this POJO to the database via JPA, it simply has to be annotated with @Entity. But here are two more important facts: an entity should implement Serializable, and declaring an id is essential. Usually this id refers to the primary key of the database table:

```
1   @Entity
2   public class Category implements Serializable{
3       @Id
4       private int id;
5       private String name;
6
7       [getters and setters omitted for brevity]
8   }
```

By default, an entity is mapped to a table with the table name equal to the uppercase class name and column names equal to the upercase attribute names. Because JPA uses *reflection* to convey database values into the objects, it can access private fields (attributes). If you let JPA create your table, you would recognize these uppercase names.

Note   The term *attribute* is used for many different things, depending on context. In the terminology of object-oriented software design, an attribute is an *instance variable*. Sometimes it's called a *field*, or, if used in conjunction with getters and setters, a *property*.

If you define the database table on your own, you might prefer so-called camelcase names over uppercase names, or you may prefer names that differ from the ones you used in your Java class. For example, many DB admins prefer column names that contain a prefix, like catId and catName (those are in camelcase, by the way). I usually prefix Java attributes with an underscore, a convention in C#. Just make sure there's a difference between the attribute name and the column name.

If for some reason the aforementioned default mapping doesn't fit, it's possible to add annotations to map table and column names.

Often, the primary key of the table is just a meaningless unique number generated by the database. JPA supports such a generation strategy. Here we need a special annotation too. Listing 12-1 shows an excerpt of the class enriched with such annotations.

Listing 12-1. Entity with Column Mapping

```
1    @Entity
2    @Table(name = "Category")
3    public class Category implements Serializable{
4        @Id
5        @GeneratedValue(strategy = GenerationType.IDENTITY)
6        @Column(name = "Id")
7        private int _id;
8
9        @Column(name = "Name")
10       private String _name;
11
12       [getters and setters omitted for brevity]
13   }
```

In the listing, all attributes are annotated with @Column. I recommended annotating all the columns or none, but this isn't crucial. You can mix annotated and non-annotated attributes within one class. In that case, all non-annotated attributes will match their uppercase names. Every attribute refers to a column within the table. If you need an attribute that shouldn't be mapped to a column, the attribute must be annotated with @ Transient.

TABLE-SPECIFIC PREFIXES

Some developers and/or DB admins prefer to add a table-specific prefix to every column name to reduce the need for aliases. Consider the following examples with and without a prefix:

```
SELECT * FROM book b JOIN category c on b.CategoryId = c.CategoryId
SELECT * FROM book JOIN category on bookCategoryId = catId
```

Using the @Column annotation, both approaches might be used.

Instead of annotating attributes, you can annotate the getter/setter pairs. You have to decide to either annotate the attributes or the getter/setter pairs. You can't mix it. Consider the example in Listing 12-2.

Listing 12-2. Mixed Field and Method-Based JPA Annotation

```
1    @Entity
2    @Table(name = "Category")
3    public class Category implements Serializable{
4      @Id
5      @GeneratedValue(strategy = GenerationType.IDENTITY)
6      @Column(name = "Id")
7      private int _id;
8
9      private String _name;
10
11     @Column(name = "Name")
12     public String getName() {
13         return _name;
14     }
15   ...
```

Here the id is mapped by a field-based annotation, whereas the name is mapped by a method-based annotation (line 11). NetBeans indicates the problem, but it compiles properly! At runtime you may recognize a misbehavior—so why doesn't it break at compile time? Because I didn't tell the whole truth. The compiler accepts this mixed annotation because it might be possible. If and only if you tell JPA by special annotations that you'll use both is it possible to mix it. So, never do it. (That's why I don't give these annotations away.)

128

In developing Books, we need more sophisticated mappings. For example, a category will display in a different language. A book is associated with different categories. These need to include collections into an entity. As a result, a single Java object might map to more than one table.

Imagine that one Java object describes a car. This object includes a few (for example, 3, 4, or 6) wheels held in a list. Now we need a table for all unique attributes of the car and a second one for the wheels. In Java, we annotate both the car class as well as the wheel class as an entity. We may store the car at once. As a rule of thumb, we need one SQL table for all non-transient attributes that are primitive types or strings, and another table for each referenced object. I talk more about this later in the book.

DECLARING A CATEGORY AS AN ENTITY

For Books, I used prefixes for the database columns. It's up to you to enrich the existing Category class with the appropriate annotations:

1. For column names, use catId and catName.

2. Don't forget to make the Category serializable.

3. If you've used NetBeans, observe the editor's output.

Have you noticed the bulb indicator on the @Entity line? You can see it in Figure 12-1.

```
     @Entity
20   @Table(name = "Category")
21   public class Category {
22
23       @Id
24       @GeneratedValue(strategy = GenerationType.IDENTITY)
25       @Column(name = "catId")
26       int _id;
27
28       @Column(name = "catName")
29       String  name;
```

Figure 12-1. *NetBeans bulb indicator before @Entity*

Hover your mouse pointer over this indicator, and NetBeans will show a popup telling you that the project has no "persistence unit" so far. In the next section, we'll talk about that.

Persistence Unit

As its name suggests, a *persistence unit* (PU) groups together artifacts for storage. These are entities that are managed by so-called *entity manager* instances. Besides that, a PU refers to information about the database connection (*data source*) and is described by an XML file. Before continuing, try creating a PU in the following exercise.

CREATE AN ENTITY WITH A PERSISTENCE UNIT

Using NetBeans, create a new project and add the JSF framework. If you haven't added anything to the freshly created project Books, you can use it here.

1. Add a package with the name `entities`.

2. In NetBeans's project tree, right-click the new package and choose New ➤ Other ➤ Persistence ➤ Entity Class.

3. NetBeans asks for the name. Choose `Category`.

4. Change the Primary Key Type to `int`.

5. Keep the Create Persistence Unit marker ticked (as shown in Figure 12-2) and follow NetBeans's steps to create the persistence unit along with the database connection.

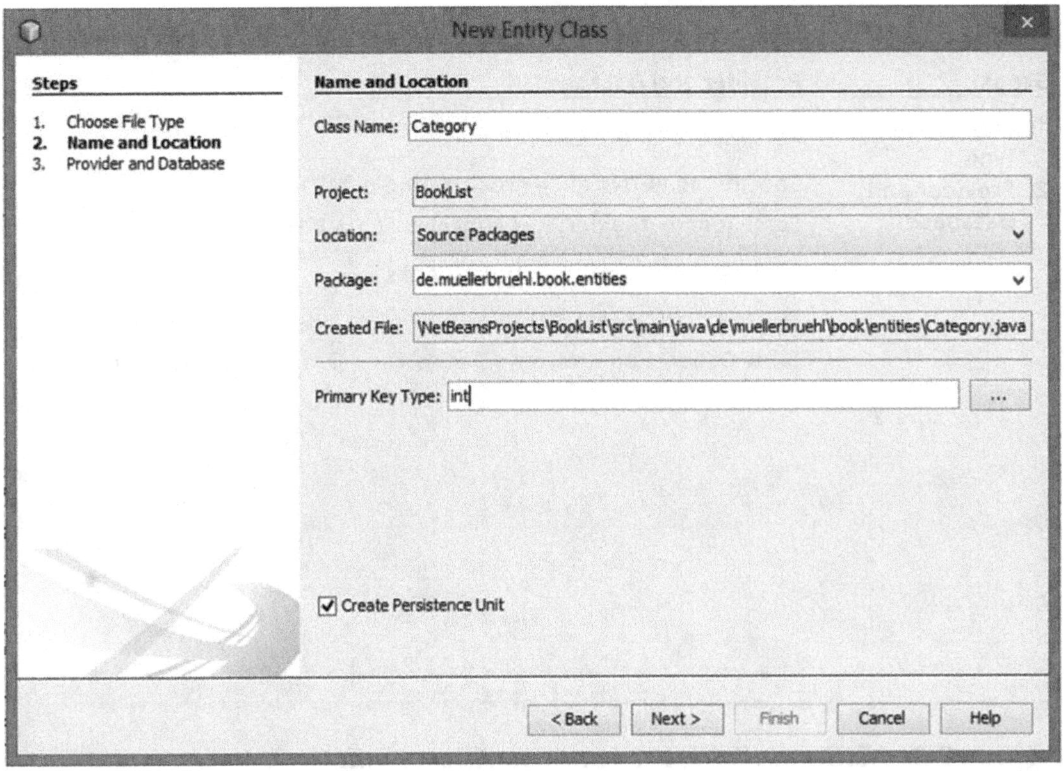

Figure 12-2. *NetBeans dialog to create an entity class*

The preceding exercise will create a persistence unit in conjunction with an entity class.

Alternatively, you can add a persistence unit only by choosing New ➤ Other ➤ Persistence ➤ Persistence Unit. NetBeans takes you directly to the New Persistence Unit wizard, shown in Figure 12-3, which is part of the whole flow initiated by the preceding exercise.

131

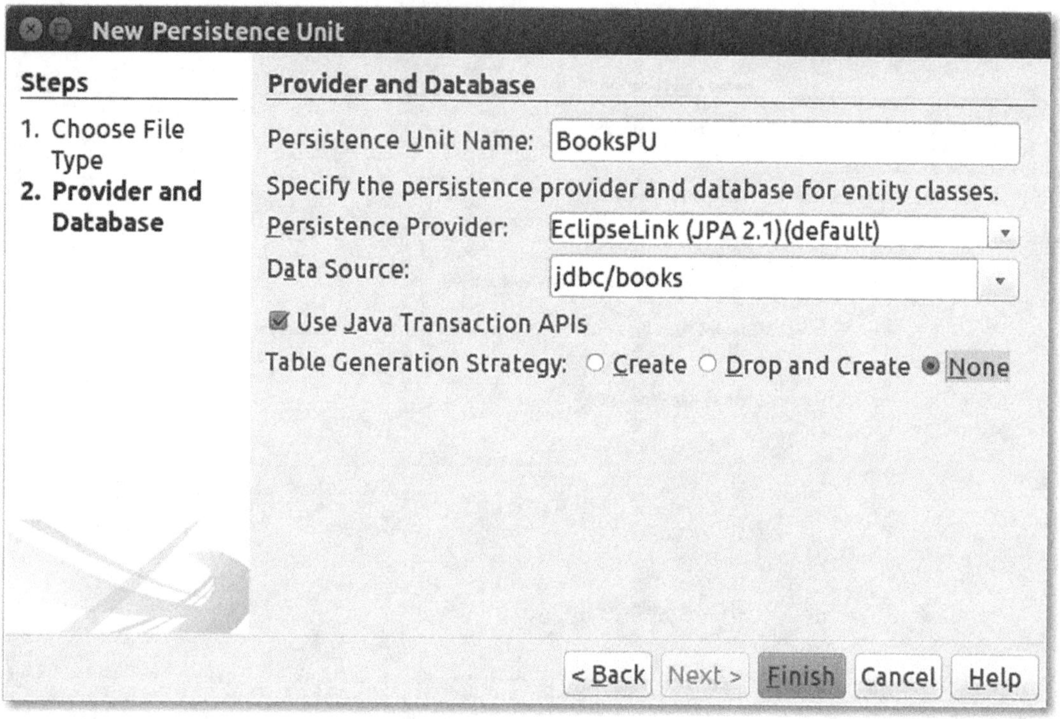

Figure 12-3. *NetBeans dialog to create a persistence unit*

In the wizard, click BooksPU for Persistence Unit Name and EclipseLink for Persistence Provider. Don't care about the current NetBeans (8.2) still offering JPA in version 2.1. You may change this later manually within the generated persistence unit. For Data Source, choose New Data Source to establish a data source pointing to your database. Enter the name **jdbc/books**. When you click Finish, NetBeans will create the persistence unit in the `src/main/resources/META-INF` folder.

If you don't use Netbeans or create the persistence unit manually, make sure to use this folder for the file `persistence.xml`. Listing 12-2 shows this file.

Listing 12-2. `persistence.xml`

```
1   <?xml version="1.0" encoding="UTF-8"?>
2   <persistence version="2.2"
3                       xmlns="http://xmlns.jcp.org/xml/ns/
                        persistence"
4                       xmlns:xsi="http://www.w3.org/2001/XMLSchema-
                        instance"
```

```
 5               xsi:schemaLocation="http://xmlns.jcp.org/xml/
                 ns/persistence
 6               http://xmlns.jcp.org/xml/ns/persistence/
                 persistence_2_2.xsd">
 7      <persistence-unit name="BooksPU" transaction-type="JTA">
 8          <jta-data-source>jdbc/books</jta-data-source>
 9          <exclude-unlisted-classes>false</exclude-unlisted-classes>
10      </persistence-unit>
11    </persistence>
```

The namespace definitions depend on the version used for this definition. In Listing 12-2 I manually updated the JPA version to 2.2 (lines 2 and 6). The interesting part starts with the tag <persistence-unit> (line 7). As you can see, in this example, there are two attributes:

- name: In the code, the PU is accessed by this name. By convention, this name often ends with *PU*.

- transaction-type: In a Java EE environment, this is "JTA". The container manages the PU, the *entity manager* (EM, explained shortly), and the transactions. The alternative value is "RESOURCE_LOCAL". If you choose this, it's the developer's responsibility to manage the EM and the transactions. This type is intended for use with Java SE.

Besides those two attributes, persistence-unit contains two elements. <jta-data-source> declares the data source (explained soon). If the tag <exclude-unlisted-classes> is set to false, no class is excluded from the PU. In other words, all classes are included by default. If set to true, a list of classes (entities) managed by this PU must be provided, as shown in the following lines:

```
<class>de.muellerbruehl.books.entities.Category</class>
<exclude-unlisted-classes>true</exclude-unlisted-classes>
```

The PU as shown here can be used if your database contains all the tables needed for the application, so the tables must be created separately. This is the preferred way, if there's a database administrator responsible for maintaining the database. And if you as a Java developer sometimes wear the DB admin cap, it might be your preferred way, too.

But if you don't like to create DB tables, JPA can perform this job for you. To configure a `create` table-generation strategy, you must add a property within the persistence-unit:

```
1   <properties>
2     <property name="javax.persistence.schema-generation.database.action"
3             value="create"/>
4   </properties>
```

Instead of `"create"`, you can use `"drop-and-create"`, which re-creates the tables.

If you don't like to remember such long properties, you can usethe NetBeans graphical editor for the PU, as shown in Figure 12-4.

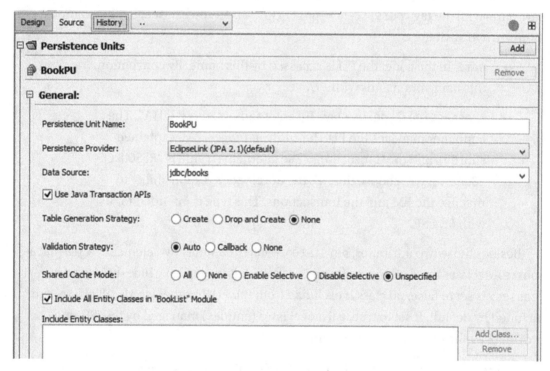

Figure 12-4. *NetBeans's graphical PU editor*

I recommend creating DB tables on their own. This separation of concerns usually increases quality. The drop-and-create strategy can be especially dangerous because it drops and re-creates your tables during app start (although it can be interesting for testing). Choosing None won't alter your table schema during the startup of your application.

Data Source

The *data source* defines the connection parameters to access the database. It's specific to the application server you use, as well to the database management system. In the case of GlassFish 4 or 5, this information is located in the file `glassfish-resources.xml` in the `src/main/setup` folder, shown in Listing 12-3. If you've chosen to create a new data source as mentioned, NetBeans would have created this file properly.

Listing 12-3. `glassfish-resources.xml`

```
1   <?xml version="1.0" encoding="UTF-8"?>
2   <!DOCTYPE resources PUBLIC
3   "-//GlassFish.org//DTD GlassFish Application Server 3.1 Resource
    Definitions\
4   //EN"
5   "http://glassfish.org/dtds/glassfish-resources_1_5.dtd">
6   <resources>
7     <jdbc-resource enabled="true"
8                    jndi-name="jdbc/books"
9                    object-type="user"
10                   pool-name="mysql_Books_booksPool"/>
11    <jdbc-connection-pool> <!-- attributes omitted for brevity -->
12        <property name="serverName" value="192.168.1.11"/>
13        <property name="portNumber" value="3306"/>
14        <property name="databaseName" value="Books"/>
15        <property name="User" value="books"/>
16        <property name="Password" value="top secret"/>
17        <property name="URL" value="jdbc:mysql://192.168.1.11:3306/Books"/>
18        <property name="driverClass" value="com.mysql.jdbc.Driver"/>
19    </jdbc-connection-pool>
20  </resources>
```

The database connection is defined in the tag `<jdbc-connection-pool>`. The content is almost self-explanatory. Remember to use your connection information. Using MySQL, you need to provide your server name or IP address in lines 12 and 17. Usually this file is generated either by creating the data source using the appropriate wizard, or by entering the information in the JDCB node on the GlassFish admin page.

`<jdbc-resource>` is a mapping between the data source name as used in the PU and the connection pool. JNDI is used for configuration in the Java EE world. Lines 7–10 define a JDBC resource that is looked up at runtime. This refers to a JDBC connection pool. Now, if we'd like to change the database connection—for example, to distinguish between development and production—we simply create a second connection pool. Switching between connections will be no more than referencing the other pool within the resource definition.

Note   The applications in this book (Books and Alumni) are designed to use the MySQL DBMS. The MySQL community server is available at `http://dev.mysql.com/downloads/`. JPA is almost independent from a special DBMS, so you might use the Derby Server that comes along with NetBeans and GlassFish. Some native queries may have to be adopted.

Usually, the user the application uses should have the minimum required rights. Thus, it's not recommended to let JPA create any database or table.

Listing 12-4 shows the SQL script to generate the `Category` table.

Listing 12-4. Create Database Table for `Category`

```
1    CREATE TABLE Books.Category (
2      catId INT NOT NULL AUTO_INCREMENT,
3      catName VARCHAR(255) NOT NULL,
4    PRIMARY KEY (catId));
```

If you let MySQL create this create script for you, it will be slightly different—MySQL surrounds each name by backticks. This is useful when you want to use names which are the same as reserved words or contain white space. You can open the MySQL Workbench and use its table editor to define a table. When you click Apply, MySQL generates and displays the script to be executed for table creation. See Listing 12-5.

Listing 12-5. Create Database Table for `Category` with Framed Names

```
1    CREATE TABLE `Books`.`Category` (
2      `catId` INT NOT NULL AUTO_INCREMENT,
3      `catName` VARCHAR(255) NOT NULL,
4    PRIMARY KEY (`catId`));
```

This kind of framing names may be vendor-specific. For example, the MS SQL Server uses square brackets instead (`create table [Category]...`). Talking in detail about SQL is beyond the scope of this book. I assume you have some knowledge of it. If not, you might read a tutorial like `www.w3schools.com/sql`.

Entity Manager

The EM handles actions like create, read, update, and delete (often abbreviated as the CRUD operations). In the web application (`transaction-type="JTA"`), an instance of the EM can be provided via injection by the container, as shown in Listing 12-6.

Listing 12-6. Inject `EntityManager`

```
1   ...
2   @PersistenceContext(unitName = "BooksPU")
3   private EntityManager _em;
4
5   protected EntityManager getEntityManager() {
6     return _em;
7   }
8
9   public void create(Category category) {
10    getEntityManager().persist(category);
11  }
12  ...
```

Besides the injection, Listing 12-5 shows how to create (*persist*) an entity. The use of the EM is explained within the service classes for the Books application.

Service Class

The entity is nothing but our data model enriched with some JPA-specific annotations. We need to add some methods to create, read, update, and delete data. Since we don't like to pollute the entity with such features, we create a service class containing the methods. Earlier you just saw an excerpt of this class.

Before we create this class, take a look at the entity lifecycle, shown in Figure 12-5.

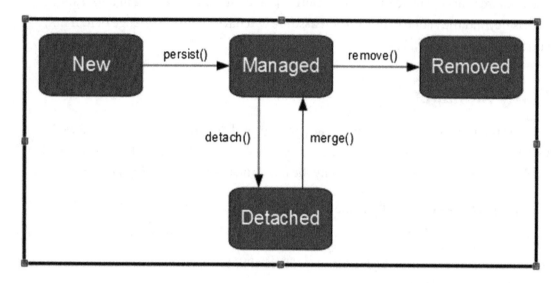

Figure 12-5. *Entity lifecycle (simplified)*

An entity that's created using the new keyword is in the state New. The same applies if the fresh entity is created by the Context and Dependency Injection (CDI) framework (using @Inject). By calling persist(entity) it's transitioned to the Managed (or attached) state. The Managed state reflects the persisted state. Thus, any change of an entity in the Managed state will be automatically stored (updated) in the database. A database retrieval might create an entity in memory that will be in the managed state. Invoking remove(entity) will delete the entity from the database.

So far, we've seen all four CRUD operations: create (persist), read (DB retrieval), update (change managed entity), and delete (remove). But Figure 12-5 shows something else—that an entity might be in detached state. Beside these operations, the figure shows a special Detached state. An entity becomes detached when it exists in memory but gets unmanaged. That may be explicitly done by calling the detach(entity) method. But there are other reasons, omitted in the simplified diagram: an entity will be detached if the EM is closed or if it's serialized and de-serialized. The latter will restore the entity in memory without being managed. For example, if the application server runs out of memory, it might passivate beans (saving somewhere, usually by serializing the values) and activate them at another time. A special method, merge(entity), will transition the entity into managed state again.

As the figure shows, a `remove()` will delete that entity. A friend of mine declined to use JPA because "a framework that needs to load an entity to perform a delete operation isn't useful, it's crazy." That's a big misunderstanding that I have seen several times. The `remove()` method is useful to delete an entity that still resides in memory. For example, the app user loads some data that's displayed on the screen—then she decides to delete that data. On the other hand, if you want to delete one entity or a batch of them that don't reside in memory, you'll use a delete operation.

The EM provides the method `contains(entity)` to check whether an entity is in the managed state or not. This method simply return true or false.

If we inject the service class into our editor bean, the Categories might become detached! Thus, to perform an update or delete, we need to merge the entity first.

Listing 12-7 shows the preliminary service class.

Listing 12-7. CategoryService

```
1    @Stateless
2    public class CategoryService {
3      @PersistenceContext(unitName = "BooksPU")
4      private EntityManager _em;
5
6
7      protected EntityManager getEntityManager() {
8        return _em;
9      }
10
11     public Category create(Category entity) {
12       getEntityManager().persist(entity);
13       return entity;
14     }
15
16     public Category read(Object id) {
17       return getEntityManager().find(Category.class, id);
18     }
19
20     public Category update(Category entity) {
21       return getEntityManager().merge(entity);
22     }
```

```
23
24     public void delete(Category entity) {
25       getEntityManager().remove(getEntityManager().merge(entity));
26     }
27
28     /**
29      * Convenience method, to create or update automatically
30      * @param entity
31      * @return managed entity
32      */
33     public Category save(Category entity) {
34       if (entity.getId() < 0){
35           return create(entity);
36       }
37       return update(entity);
38     }
39
40     public List<Category> findAll() {
41       CriteriaQuery cq = getEntityManager().getCriteriaBuilder().
         createQuery();
42       cq.select(cq.from(Category.class));
43       return getEntityManager().createQuery(cq).getResultList();
44     }
45
46   }
```

As shown before, an EntityManager will be injected using the PU as given in the annotation.

Using the annotation Stateless automatically declares the bean to be an Enterprise JavaBean (EJB). Using an EJB automatically puts the database access into a transaction scope. This simple approach assumes a fully fledged Java EE container, like GlassFish. On a servlet-only container, we have to use a different approach. Nowadays, CDI can inject an EntityManager. If you add the Weld CDI implementation to a servlet container (Listing 12-8), you need to change the class annotation (Listing 12-9).

Listing 12-8. Maven Coordinates for Weld (as Defined in Java EE)

```
1    <dependency>
2        <groupId>javax.enterprise</groupId>
3        <artifactId>cdi-api</artifactId>
4        <version>2.0</version>
5        <scope>provided</scope>
6    </dependency>
```

Listing 12-9. CategoryService

```
1    @RequestScoped
2    @Transactional
3    public class CategoryService {
```

This changes the service class from being an Enterprise JavaBean into a pure CDI bean. Because no transaction is automatically added, we need to add it with a special annotation (or manage transactions with our code). This CDI annotation also performs on a fully fledged application server.

The EntityManager has some methods for the CRUD (create, read, update, delete) operations. They are called persist, find, merge (just to reattach to managed state) and remove. The service class will expose them using the CRUD names. For brevity, the class doesn't yet contain any exception handling.

The findAll() method will retrieve all categories from the database. It's implemented by using the criteria API. Alternatively, we could have just used a JPA Query Language (JPQL) query to get the categories. I'll explain both later.

merge doesn't just reattach entities into the managed state. If an entity didn't exist before, it will be created. In Figure 12-5, persist is used to get into managed state. This is what persist is intended for. But you may use merge instead.

With this knowledge, we can simplify our service. Just omit the create and update methods and replace save with Listing 12-10.

Listing 12-10. save Method

```
1    public Category save(Category entity) {
2        return getEntityManager().merge(entity);
3    }
```

Using the CategoryService/Injection

In our category editor, we need to inject the service class we just created and adopt the init and change methods, as shown in Listing 12-11.

Listing 12-11. Controller Bean CategoryEditor

```
1    @Named
2    @SessionScoped
3    public class CategoryEditor implements Serializable{
4      private static final Logger _logger = Logger.
       getLogger("CategoryEditor");
5
6      @Inject CategoryService _categoryService;
7
8      @PostConstruct
9      private void init(){
10       _categories = _categoryService.findAll();
11       _deletedCategories = new ArrayList<>();
12     }
13
14     private List<Category> _deletedCategories;
15     private List<Category> _categories;
16
17     public List<Category> getCategories() {
18       return _categories;
19     }
20
21     public void setCategories(List<Category> categories) {
22       _categories = categories;
23     }
24
25     public String deleteCategory(Category category){
26       if (category.getId() >= 0){
27         _deletedCategories.add(category);
28       }
```

```
29        _categories.remove(category);
30        return "";
31      }
32
33      public String addCategory(){
34        _categories.add(new Category());
35        return "";
36      }
37
38      public String save(){
39        for (Category category : _categories){
40          _categoryService.save(category);
41        }
42        for (Category category : _deletedCategories){
43          _categoryService.delete(category);
44        }
45        _deletedCategories = new ArrayList<>();
46
47        return "";
48      }
49    }
```

@Inject is part of the CDI. It's up to the container to pass an object of the requested type (class) into the annotated variable. If necessary, the container will create an appropriate object and maintain its lifecycle. In the old days of JSF, you could only inject JSF managed beans with a lifetime longer than the current bean (for example, a session scoped bean into a request scoped bean, but vice versa). Rather than injecting an instance of the requested class, CDI is going to inject a proxy object. Once that proxy is injected, you use it to access the appropriate object of the requested class. The real object may change between requests.

For example, the container can inject a request scoped bean into a session scoped bean. Now, if you try to access that request scoped bean, the proxy presents a different real object for you with every request.

Only eligible beans can be injected. Otherwise, NetBeans would alert you that no bean matches the injection point. But which bean is eligible? Examples are EJBs, named beans, and more. All are identified by a special annotation or configuration file. And you might create your own annotations to "produce" eligible beans. I discuss CDI in more detail later. The problem with new technologies might be that the IDE doesn't know about them—especially for some new Java EE injectable objects NetBeans doesn't know about and alerts with such a message. Don't worry—and use it.

So far, the first version of the category editor is ready. Later, we'll refine it by using a generalized service class, by AJAXifying the JSF page, and more.

CHECK ENTITY STATE

Add a simple method to the service class to return an entity's state:

```
1    public String checkState(Category entity){
2       return entity + (_em.contains(entity) ? "attached" : "detached");
3    }
```

Call this method within findAll (CategoryService) and init (CategoryEditor), print out, and observe the states of the entities.

Summary

We covered a lot in this chapter. The Java Persistence API defines a framework for Object Relational Mapping (ORM). It's based on the core concept of entities that are managed by an entity manager (EM). An entity is a plain old Java object (POJO) with some special annotations. Only the @Entity and @Id annotations are mandatory, whereas the framework assumes default values for table and column names. Usually mappings for different table (@Table) or column (@Column) names are needed.

An entity will be in one of four different states that are managed by the EM. It's recommended to separate the data object from the data access. Thus, an entity should not contain (database-specific) logic. The data access is performed by a special service class.

The EM relies on the definition of a persistence unit, which configures the logical database access. The technical database access (driver, server properties) is configured by a data source.

This chapter also explained how to use the service class within a backing bean.

CHAPTER 13

JSF Templating

Usually an application provides a consistent look and feel. That way, the overall layout remains the same, with only content or other minor elements changing from page to page. JSF supports such an overall layout with its simple but powerful template feature.

Templating Books

A *template* is like a picture, with (mostly) rectangular holes cut into it. By placing other pictures behind these holes, you may change the picture while keeping the basic layout.

Figure 13-1 shows some different screens of the Books application.

© Michael Müller 2018
M. Müller, *Practical JSF in Java EE 8*, https://doi.org/10.1007/978-1-4842-3030-5_13

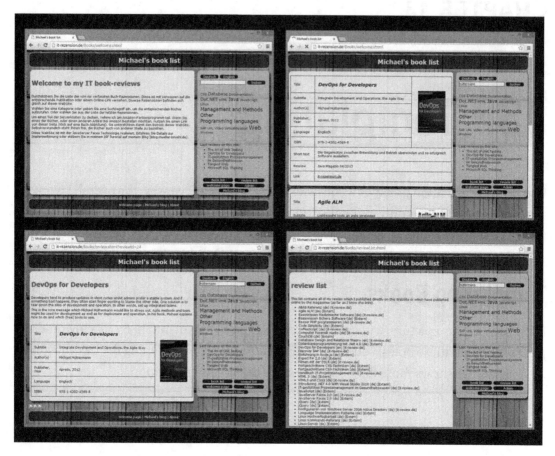

Figure 13-1. *Books in action*

As you can see, because of JSF templating (see Figure 13-2), only the main content area changes.

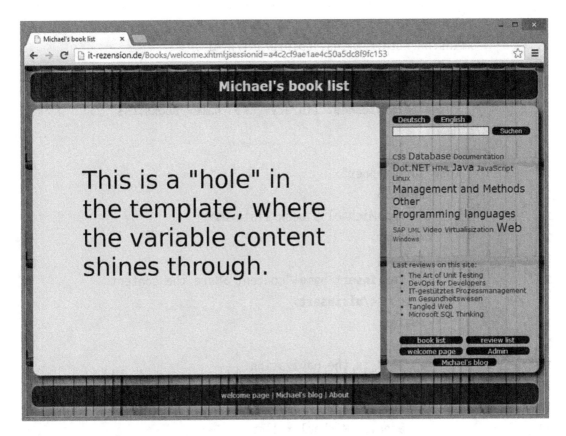

Figure 13-2. *Books in action*

For templating, at least two components are needed: the template file and the content file. Because the content file is using the template, it's called a *client*.

Let's start with the template. Remember the category editor? The first (prototype) version is still called index.xhtml. This file contains header, nav, main, and footer. The "hole" we need is exactly the main part. The simplest way to create the template is to copy this file (in the web pages branch of the projects tree, the src/webapp folder), cut the content in main, and replace it with an instruction that means "insert variable content here." That's what the <ui:insert ...> tag is for. Don't forget to insert the namespace declaration for ui:. And—voilà—the template is ready, as in Listing 13-1.

Listing 13-1. Draft of booksTemplate.xhtml

```
1    <?xml version='1.0' encoding='UTF-8' ?>
2    <!DOCTYPE html [<!ENTITY copy "&#169;">]>
3    <html xmlns="http://www.w3.org/1999/xhtml"
```

```
4              xmlns:ui="http://xmlns.jcp.org/jsf/facelets"
5              xmlns:h="http://xmlns.jcp.org/jsf/html">
6      <h:head>
7          <title>Books</title>
8          <h:outputStylesheet library="css" name="books.css" />
9      </h:head>
10     <h:body>
11         <div id="wrapper">
12             <header>
13                 <h1>Michael's book list</h1>
14             </header>
15             <main>
16                 <ui:insert name="content">Here the content
                   goes</ui:insert>
17             </main>
18             <nav>
19                 This is the navigation
20             </nav>
21             <footer>
22                 &copy;  Michael Müller
23                 |
24                 <h:outputLink value="http://blog.mueller-bruehl.de">
25                     Michael's Blog
26                 </h:outputLink>
27                 |
28                 <h:link value="About" outcome="index.xhtml"/>
29             </footer>
30         </div>
31     </h:body>
32 </html>
```

The <ui:insert ...> tag defines a placeholder with the name content, as given by the name attribute. This is the hole where the content will shine through. In a given template, more than one insert tag might be defined. The text *Here the content goes* in that tag will be replaced with the content provided by the template client.

BROWSE THE TEMPLATE

---

1. Start the application.

2. Open the template page. In the address (URL) bar of your browser, type
    http://localhost:8080/Books/booksTemplate.xhtml.

You should get the basic layout with `Here the content goes` as the main part.

Now we need to refactor `index.xhtml` to transform it into a template client. Instead of the html tag, we'll use the `<ui:composition ...>` tag. Within this tag we place `<ui:define name="content">`. The name we provide here is the same one we provided as the placeholder in our template. Whatever we want to display for the content of our template, we simply place the appropriate content in this tag.

Last but not least, we need to declare which template we want to use, as in Listing 13-2.

Listing 13-2. Template Client

```
1   <?xml version='1.0' encoding='UTF-8' ?>
2   <!DOCTYPE html>
3   <ui:composition xmlns="http://www.w3.org/1999/xhtml"
4         xmlns:h="http://xmlns.jcp.org/jsf/html"
5         xmlns:ui="http://xmlns.jcp.org/jsf/facelets"
6         template="/booksTemplate.xhtml">
7      <ui:define name="content">
8         <h1>Edit categories</h1>
9         <h:form>
10           <h:dataTable value="#{categoryEditor.categories}"
11                       var="cat">
12             <h:column>
13               <h:commandLink
14                   action="#{categoryEditor.
                         deleteCategory(cat)}">
15                 <h:graphicImage alt="delete"
16                                 name="Delete.png"
17                                 library="icon/small"
18                                 title="delete"/>
```

```
19                              </h:commandLink>
20                          </h:column>
21                          <h:column>
22                              <h:inputText value="#{cat.name}"/>
23                          </h:column>
24                      </h:dataTable>
25                      <h:commandLink styleClass="button"
26                                      value="Add category"
27                                      action="#{categoryEditor.addCategory}"/>
28                      <h:commandButton styleClass="button"
29                                        value="Save"
30                                        action="#{categoryEditor.save}"/>
31              </h:form>
32          </ui:define>>
33      </ui:composition>
```

In this example, the namespaces are defined as attributes of the <ui:composition ...> element. Sometimes you'll find JSF template clients with an html element and the namespaces declared there. Then the <ui:composition ...> is defined somewhere in this page, for example within the body. Everything outside the <ui:composition ...> will be ignored for the client. Listing 13-3 shows this approach. In my opinion, it's more concise, without such an overhead.

Listing 13-3. Template Client with Superfluous html Tag

```
1   <?xml version='1.0' encoding='UTF-8' ?>
2   <!DOCTYPE html>
3   <html xmlns="http://www.w3.org/1999/xhtml"
4        xmlns:h="http://xmlns.jcp.org/jsf/html"
5        xmlns:ui="http://xmlns.jcp.org/jsf/facelets">
6
7       This will be ignored
8
9     <ui:composition  template="/booksTemplate.xhtml">
10        <ui:define name="content">
```

```
12              Content goes here
13          </ui:define>>
14      </ui:composition>
15
16      This will be ignored
17
18  </html>
```

As we'll see later in this book, a template might be the client of another template. JSF allows you to define a cascade of nested templates.

Note   The complete source code for Books, as developed from startup to templating, is available from `http://webdevelopment-java.info`.

Summary

Creating an overall look and feel is possible through JSF's templating mechanism. It's built up by a template, which defines the overall layout. A client uses this template by replacing or adding content at predefined places. A template might be used by a couple of clients, and a template might be the client of another template, supporting cascading structures.

CHAPTER 14

Going International

An application hosted on a web server that is part of the Internet might be accessible from almost every part of the globe. Even if you don't write your application for everybody, you might address people in different countries speaking different languages. That means you need to prepare your software for an international market.

Internationalization and Localization

Books will be prepared for different languages and formats (*internationalization*) and implemented for the English (countries such as Australia, Canada, the United States, and the UK) and German (Germany) languages. Making the book available in different languages and adapting it to other surroundings is easier than it sounds.

Java does a lot of this job for us by simply letting you specify a region. We just need to provide information about the region, providing texts for all GUI elements and messages in the languages of our choice. The texts for GUI elements and messages in the chosen language will be applied, depending on the language settings of the user's system. Additionally, we may want to provide a language selector.

So far, we've developed a first version of the category editor. This editor comes with a minimal user interface. There are only a few elements to translate. But besides translating a page, we need to translate the contents (categories) as well—imagine the application displayed in a different language. So, let's first introduce and localize the welcome screen, which is a very simple page, and then come back to the category editor.

© Michael Müller 2018
M. Müller, *Practical JSF in Java EE 8*, https://doi.org/10.1007/978-1-4842-3030-5_14

INTERNATIONALIZATION AND LOCALIZATION

Internationalization (often abbreviated *i18n*) is the process of making software potentially available for other languages and regions, whereas *localization* (*L10n*) is the adaption to a special language and region.

Both involve more than simply translating GUI elements into a different language. Remember different date formats, different symbols (a German postbox looks very different from a U.S. mailbox), different wording within one language depending on the region (such as mailbox/postbox, localization/localization, cellular phone/mobile phone), and more.

Welcome Page

The welcome page (or landing page) simply informs the visitor about the intention of the application and contains some static text. With respect to international users, the text is available in different languages.

On my website (`it-rezension.de`), I offer German and English as languages, because I read books in both languages. My reviews of German books are written in German. My reviews of English books are written in German and/or English, depending on the publishing media (such as print magazine or online). Because of this, offering these two languages only is enough for my site. But the Books application is designed to be presented in other languages as needed.

On the welcome page, there is text only. We can focus internationalization on offering that text in different languages. There's no need to adapt date or number formats or icons. We'll look at such aspects later on when we work on the Alumni application.

Message Bundle

To achieve our goal, we'll use what's called a *message bundle*. This is nothing but a resource bundle made available for JSF. A *resource bundle* is a bunch of properties files that follow a special naming convention. Even if you've never developed an application for an international market, you may have used a properties file to configure your application. Each file is a kind of key-value storage. For internationalization and localization, we need such a file for each language. Each file contains the same keys but with values translated to the target locale. If the user's locale is unknown, the application must provide a default. The convention is to use the default with a simple filename and to append a language code (ISO-639 Language Code) plus optionally a region code (ISO-3166 Country Code plus a variant in rare cases). You'll find these codes on different sites on the Inernet, for example at Oracle, ISO-3166 Country Codes and ISO-639 Language Codes is available at `http://docs.oracle.com/cd/E13214_01/wli/docs92/xref/xqisocodes.html`.

Table 14-1 shows an example.

Table 14-1. *Language Codes*

Filename	Usage
messages.properties	Default
messages_de.properties	German
messages_en.properties	English
messages_en_US.properties	English, U.S.
messages_en_GB.properties	English, Great Britain

In this example, `messages` is the filename. You may choose any other name you like. Language and region (country) codes are appended after an underscore.

Now let's create a resource bundle and talk about how to use it in our web application.

Using NetBeans, choose New File ➤ Other ➤ Properties File and click Next. The New Properties File dialog appears, as shown in Figure 14-1. Provide the name **messages** and type in the folder name **src/main/resources/de/muellerbruehl/books**. You can replace `de/muellerbruehl/books` with a package name of your choice. Click Browse to browse to the existing `src/main/resources` first and then complete the name. Note that when you browse a Windows system, you'll get `src\main\resources` because Windows uses a backslash as a folder delimiter. You can enter a normal slash or a backslash—both will be recognized by the dialog. Click Finish to create the properties file.

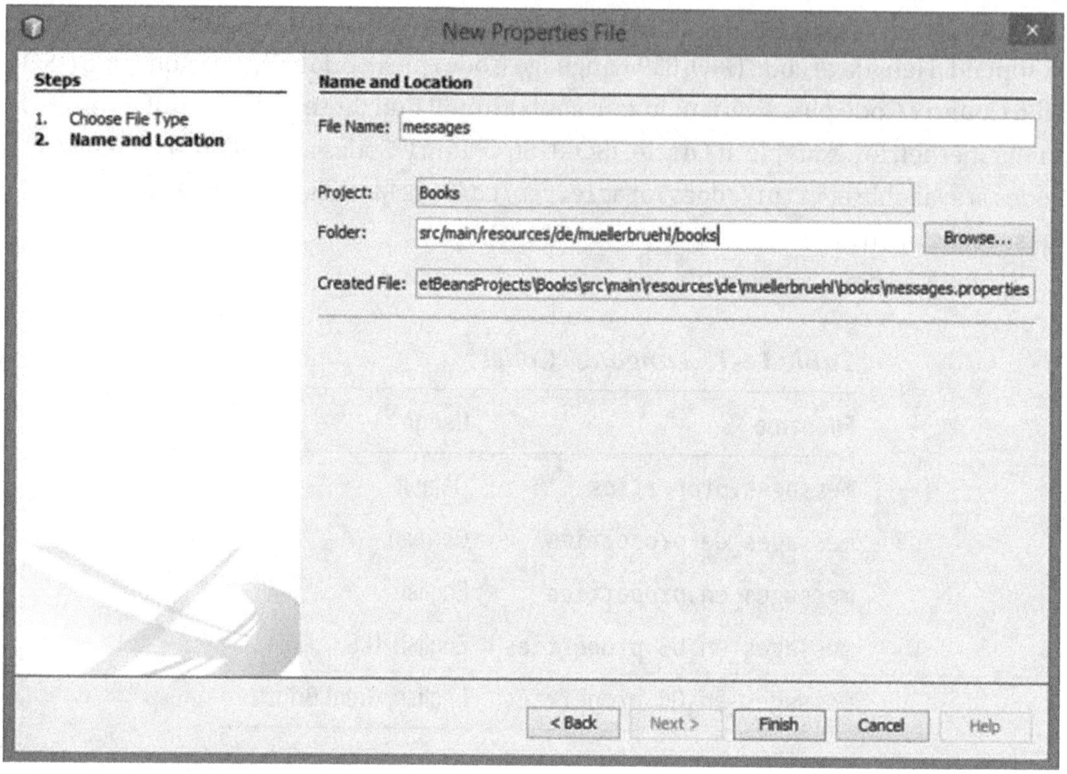

Figure 14-1. *New Properties File dialog*

NetBeans creates a new file and opens it in its editor. If NetBeans has placed any content into this files, delete it, save the file, and close it in the editor.

On the Projects tree, right-click the `messages.properties` file (Figure 14-2) and choose Add ➤ Locale.

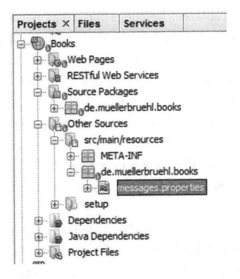

Figure 14-2. *Projects tree*

NetBeans displays the New Locale wizard, shown in Figure 14-3.

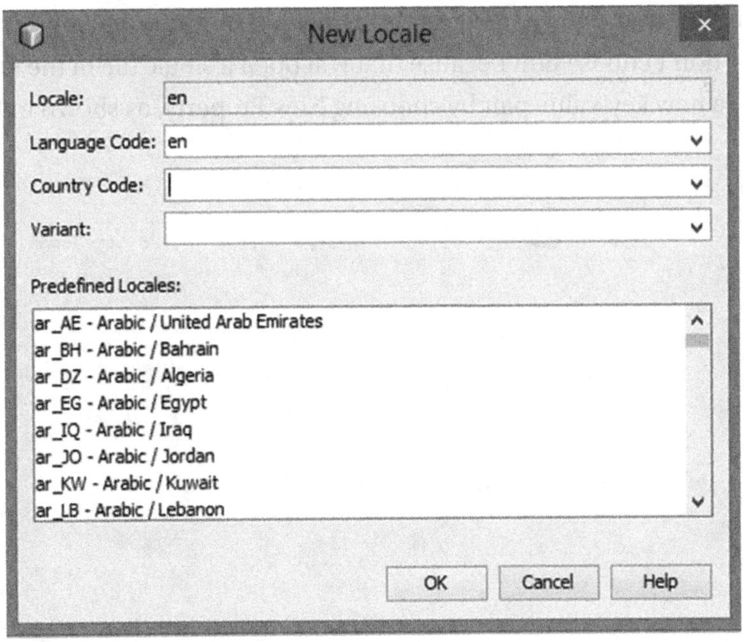

Figure 14-3. *New Locale wizard*

As you can see, you can choose a language and a region (country and variant). For Books, enter **en** and click OK or press Enter. NetBeans creates the appropriate properties files for you (messages.properties and messages_en.properties). Add a second file for **de** (for German), creating a messages_de.properties file). If you know about the language codes, you don't need the New Locale wizard; you can just create the files with respect to the correct names, which involves nothing more than appending the correct language code to the properties filename. You can also do this if your favorite IDE doesn't offer such a wizard. To offer different versions of a language, you need to append the correct variant, such as messages_en_US.properties U.S. English) or messages_en_GB.properties (British English).

We want to offer two languages, but we've created three properties files in total. Of course, we could have used the default for German and the other for English, but I recommend using a specific file for each language and the default as a fallback.

The text for our page's headline is in the key headWelcome. You can edit the properties file, as in Figure 14-4, but you'd have to enter the key into every file to keep the files synchronized, which might be an annoying job. For easy editing, NetBeans offers a special properties editor, shown in Figure 14-4. Right-click any of the properties files and choose Open—don't choose Edit because that will open a single file in the text editor. You can create a new key-value pair by choosing New Property, as shown in Figure 14-5.

Figure 14-4. *Properties files editor*

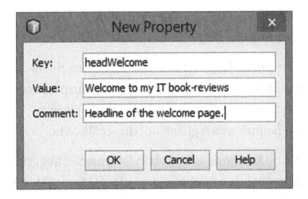

Figure 14-5. *New Property dialog*

For Key enter **headWelcome**, and for Value enter **Welcome to my IT book-reviews**. Optionally provide a comment. Click OK or press Enter.

NetBeans inserts the new property into every properties file—not into every properties file of the project, but the resource bundle `messages`. An entry looks like this: `headWelcome=Welcome to my IT book-reviews`. Now only one file, for German, has to be adapted, which might be done directly in the properties files editor: `Willkommen zu meinen IT-Rezensionen`.

Next, create a property with the key `textWelcome`. Its value will become a multi-line text with some line breaks. For example:

Discover the books I've reviewed. Get references to the printed publication or links to online reviews.

Please choose from the categories or enter a term for searching. Or you might choose from the list of reviews published on this site.

To help offset parts of the server fees, I participate the Amazon partner program. If you follow a link from a cover image to buy something from Amazon, you will help to finance this site. Of course, you may buy the books wherever you like.

This site is powered by JavaServer Faces technology. Read about the implementation in my book <a href="http://leanpub.com/jsf"> Web Development with Java and JSF</a> and in my blog <a href="http://blog.mueller-bruehl.de/en/">[blog.mueller-bruehl.de]</a>.

Click the appropriate field of the *de – German* column and enter a German version of the welcome text, something like this:

> Durchstöbern Sie die Liste der von mir verfassten Buch-Rezensionen. Diese ist mit Verweisen auf die entsprechende Publikation oder einem Online-Link versehen. Diverse Rezensionen befinden sich gleich auf dieser WebSite.
>
> Wählen Sie eine Kategorie oder geben Sie eine Suchbegriff ein, um die entsprechenden Bücher aufzurufen. Oder wählen Sie aus der Liste der letzten Rezensionen.
>
> Um einen Teil der Serverkosten zu decken, nehme ich am Amazon-Partnerprogramm teil. Wenn Sie eines der Bücher, oder einen anderen Artikel bei Amazon bestellen möchten, nutzen Sie einen Link von dieser Seite (Klick auf eine Buch-Abbildung). Sie unterstützen damit den Betrieb dieser WebSite. Selbstverständlich steht Ihnen frei, die Bücher auch von anderer Stelle zu beziehen.
>
> Diese WebSite ist mit der JavaServer Faces Technologie realisiert. Erfahren Sie Details zur Implementierung in meinem Buch <a href="`http://leanpub.com/jsf`"> "Web Development with Java and JSF"</a> oder stöbern Sie in meinem JSF Turorial auf meinem Blog <a href="`http://blog.mueller-bruehl.de/en/`"> [blog.mueller-bruehl.de]</a>.

Once you've created the properties files, how do you use it with JSF?

You need to create a `faces-config.xml` file (see "Configuration files" in Part I) in the `WEB-INF` folder, shown in Listing 14-1. If you create this file with NetBeans, it will be generated with the appropriate namespaces.

Listing 14-1. `faces-config.xml`

```
1  <?xml version='1.0' encoding='UTF-8'?>
2  <faces-config version="2.3"
3              xmlns="http://xmlns.jcp.org/xml/ns/javaee"
4              xmlns:xsi="http://www.w3.org/2001/XMLSchema-instance"
5              xsi:schemaLocation="http://xmlns.jcp.org/xml/ns/javaee
```

```
6              http://xmlns.jcp.org/xml/ns/javaee/web-faces
               config_2_2.xsd">

7
8      <application>

9        <locale-config>
10         <default-locale>en</default-locale>
11         <supported-locale>de</supported-locale>
12         <supported-locale>en</supported-locale>
13       </locale-config>
14       <resource-bundle>
15         <base-name>de.muellerbruehl.books.messages</base-name>
16         <var>msg</var>
17       </resource-bundle>
18       <message-bundle>de.muellerbruehl.books.messages</message-bundle>
19      </application>

20
21    </faces-config>
```

Within the `<application>` tag, we define the different locales we want to use (lines 9-14). Within `<locale-config>`, we can define our default language as well as other languages. Because Books supports (at least) two languages, we need to declare English and German here. English (en) is used as the default locale (line 10), and German (de) is defined as supported locale (line 11). English is defined as supported locale, too (line 12). Although you could use English without re-declaring it as supported locale, this declaration is useful to query all the supported languages. Any locale that should be supported by the application needs to be declared here.

Next, we define a resource bundle (`<resource-bundle>`, lines 14 to 17). This defines the resources we want to access in our pages. It's defined by the full package and filename, without the `properties` extension. `<var>` defines the variable name we can use within a JSF page to address this bundle.

Sometimes it's very useful to overwrite a couple of JSF's standard messages. We'll do this by providing a localized text stored together with the same key JSF uses. `<message-bundle>` (line 18) declares the properties files (without locale and extension). Within Books we use one file group for all of our texts. Thus, the message bundle points to the same files. It could have been a different group of properties files.

In web.xml (located in the same folder), we change the welcome file entry to
<welcome-file>welcome.xhtml</welcome-file>.

Naive Welcome Page Implementation

The welcome page should simply display the heading and the text. Like the category
editor, it uses the existing template. Thus, we have to define a <ui:composition>. This
is a first naive implementation, as shown in Listing 14-2, with the output shown in
Figure 14-6.

Listing 14-2. First Draft of welcome.xhtml

```
1    <?xml version='1.0' encoding='UTF-8' ?>
2    <!DOCTYPE html>
3    <ui:composition xmlns="http://www.w3.org/1999/xhtml"
4                    xmlns:h="http://xmlns.jcp.org/jsf/html"
5                    xmlns:ui="http://xmlns.jcp.org/jsf/facelets"
6                    template="/booksTemplate.xhtml">
7
8      <ui:define name="content">
9        <h1>#{msg.headWelcome}</h1>
10       <p>
11         #{msg.textWelcome}
12       </p>
13     </ui:define>
14
15   </ui:composition>
```

If you're familiar with HTML, you might be able to guess what the problem will be:
HTML ignores line breaks made by CR or CRLF. And the embedded HTML elements
(links) wouldn't be interpreted. As a result, the welcome text wouldn't be properly
formatted. Anyway, you can use this page to check the localization. Using a browser with
German as default locale, the page would be displayed in German, otherwise it would be
shown in English.

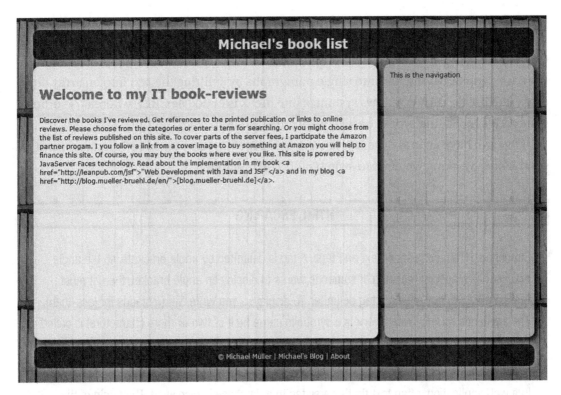

Figure 14-6. *Welcome page with innocent implementation (English version)*

CHECK ANOTHER LOCALE

Try changing the language setting of your browser. For example, in Firefox choose Options
➤ Content ➤ Languages. Add the desired language if not present and move it to the top.
Using Chrome, you have to expand the settings to the extended view first. Declare German as
the default (or if your default had been German, set it to English). Reload the application. The
language should change.

Then set the default to any other (non-English, non-German) language and reload the app. It
should display the English version.

Use Paragraphs and <ui:repeat>

Once the message bundle is set up properly, we can tackle the formatting problem. First, we chop down the text into single paragraphs by splitting the text into an array on every line break. On a Windows system, a line break is coded as CRLF, whereas on other systems it's LF. So, the breaks have to be normalized first.

Once we have an array, we can use the `<ui:repeat>` tag to iterate all elements, and to get the links working we need to switch off HTML escaping.

HTML ESCAPING

Simplified, HTML consists of text and tags. A tag is delimited by angle brackets, so the angle bracket has a special meaning. If someone wants to display an angle bracket, then, it must first be *escaped* from being a tag delimiter. To display <, you write < (*lt* stands for less-than). The sequence &xxx; (where xxx is a symbolic name built of two or more characters) is called an HTML entity and is used to escape special characters. A character might be escaped by its code too. < is also the less-than sign.

In a web application, often text that's persisted to a database is displayed. The origin of this text might be a user input. Now, if that text is treated as HTML, a vicious person could insert code pointing to a malicious website or containing a malicious script. To prevent such injection attacks, JSF commonly escapes the output by default.

The text for our welcome page doesn't depend on any user input. It's stored in a resource file. We'll trust our own content (someone could hack the application server, but for our purposes here we'll assume they don't) and switch off HTML escaping, as shown in Listing 14-3.

Listing 14-3. Refined Welcome Page

```
1   <?xml version='1.0' encoding='UTF-8' ?>
2   <!DOCTYPE html>
3   <ui:composition xmlns="http://www.w3.org/1999/xhtml"
4                   xmlns:h="http://xmlns.jcp.org/jsf/html"
5                   xmlns:ui="http://xmlns.jcp.org/jsf/facelets"
6                   template="/booksTemplate.xhtml">
7
```

```
 8     <ui:define name="content">
 9       <h1>#{msg.headWelcome}</h1>
10       <ui:repeat value="#{msg.textWelcome.replace('\\r', '').
         split('\\n')}"
11                     var="text">
12         <p>
13           <h:outputText value="#{text}" escape="false"/>
14         </p>
15       </ui:repeat>
16     </ui:define>
17
18   </ui:composition>
```

The trick is to split the output text into an array that's traversed by the <ui:repeat...> element. <ui:repeat...> might be used to traverse arrays, collections, or maps.

Each element will be available in a variable named text. Each paragraph is surrounded by a paragraph tag (<p>).

So far, we've used <h:dataTable...> and <ui:repeat...> as repeating elements. Later in the book, we'll look at more repeating structures and discuss the advantages and pitfalls of each.

All we need now for a pretty format is some CSS code to introduce padding above and below a paragraph. Because we defined links to be displayed with white color, and the content background is a bright one, we have to choose a dark color, as is done in Listing 14-4.

Listing 14-4. Additional Formating Statements of books.css

```
1   p {
2     margin: 5px  0 5px  0;
3   }
4
5   p > a {
6     color: blue;
7   }
```

Note   Run the application and check the formatting behavior. You should get a couple of paragraphs with a short gap in between and real links.

Language Switcher

Usually it's adequate to choose the display language, depending on the user's environment. I use a language switcher on my web site, http://it-rezension.de. Switching the language seems to be straightforward:

```
1   FacesContext.getCurrentInstance().getViewRoot()
2               .setLocale(new Locale(getLanguageCode()));
```

Get the view root of the current FacesContext instance and set the locale to a new locale. Seems easy! But if you switch the language that way, you'll find that the old language is soon restored. What happened?

The JSF specification states that the locale has to be set with every request to the user's setting. This will overwrite the language switcher. So, #{msg.headWelcome} will display the language according to the user's setting, and not according to the result of the switcher. The trick I originally used for Books was to remember the language selection in a session scoped bean and retrieve all values with a utility class.

Listing 4-5 shows the excerpt of the page.

Listing 14-5. Insert Localized String into Web Page

```
1   ...
2   <h1>#{sessionTools.getMessage('headWelcome')}</h1>
3   ...
```

And Listing 14-6 shows the relevant Java code.

Listing 14-6. Refer a Locale Specific String by Its Key

```
1   public String getMessage(String key) {
2     ResourceBundle messageBundle;
3     Locale locale = new Locale(getLanguageCode());
4     messageBundle = ResourceBundle
5                     .getBundle("de.muellerbruehl.books.messages",
                        locale);
6     return messageBundle.getString(key);
7   }
```

For brevity, only the principle is shown here.

Since JSF 2.0, it's been possible to register listeners to System Events. I'll discuss these events in detail further on. Here I'll just how to use it for a better version of the language switcher. The trick still is to remember the selected language in a @SessionScoped bean, because once the user changes the language, we want to remember that setting. But just before rendering the page, we switch to the selected language. JSF will then use the strings from the appropriate resource bundle. So, we simply can access the message bundle within the page definition via #{msg.XXX}.

To do that, we need to register a listener to the preRenderView event, as in Listing 14-7. This event occurs whenever the page should be rendered. A companion preRenderComponent event will be fired before rendering a single component.

Listing 14-7. Embed Listener for the Language Switcher

```
1   ...
2   <f:metadata>
3     <f:event type="preRenderView"
4       listener="#{sessionTools.preRenderView}"/>
5   </f:metadata>
6   ...
7   <h1>#{msg.headWelcome}</h1>
8   ...
```

A listener for a system event is a method of type void with a parameter of type ComponentSystemEvent, as in Listing 14-8.

Listing 14-8. SystemEvent Listener to Set the Locale Before Rendering

```
1   public void preRenderView(ComponentSystemEvent event) {
2     Locale locale = new Locale(getLanguageCode());
3     FacesContext.getCurrentInstance().getViewRoot().setLocale(locale);
4   }
```

Last but not least, you might use the <f:view> tag to define the locale. This defines the ViewRoot, the root of the component tree. So, all other JSF components must be included within a <f:view>. Using Facelets as VDL, the view root is defined implicitly. Usually the explicit definition would only be used in conjunction with JSP as VDL.

Nevertheless you can use a view root definition with Facelets. A page definition would be similar to Listing 14-9.

Listing 14-9. Skeleton of a Page Definition with Explicit Definition of the View Root

```
1    <html xmlns="http://www.w3.org/1999/xhtml"
2         xmlns:ui="http://xmlns.jcp.org/jsf/facelets"
3         xmlns:h="http://xmlns.jcp.org/jsf/html"
4         xmlns:f="http://xmlns.jcp.org/jsf/core">
5
6      <f:view locale="#{sessionTools.language}">
7        <h:head>
8          ...
9        </h:head>
10       <h:body>
11         ...
12       </h:body>
13     </f:view>
14   </html>
```

<f:view> may take an optional attribute locale to define a special locale for this view. As before, we'll get the value stored for the current session.

I assume it would be no problem to fit all those pieces together. Or try the language switcher, which is included in the source of the complete application.

Localized Content

Now we're going to translate our content using an enhanced version of the category editor. For Books we have to distinguish two kind of users:

- The administrator, the editor who edits and maintains the data

- Visitors to the website who want to gather some information

The administer area should be indicated by an optical effect.

Preparing the Administer Area

There are different solutions for the administer pages. All of them need the same look and feel, consistent with the overall feel of the application. So, a different background color is chosen while keeping the rest. But there is one part that differs from the reader's point of view: the navigation.

One approach is to exchange the navigation part. We may include a *visitor navigation* or a *administer navigation,* depending on the pages we display. Another approach is to use a different template, and that's the approach Books takes.

To preparing the pages, follow these steps:

1. In your Web Pages (webapp) folder, create a subfolder and give it the name admin.

2. Copy booksTemplate.xhtml into the admin folder and rename the target to adminTemplate.xhtml.

3. Move the index.xhtml file into the admin folder and rename it to categoryEditor.xhtml.

4. In the header of this page, change booksTemplate to adminTemplate.

5. In the admin folder create a welcome.xhtml page. As in the existing welcome page, put some welcome text for the administrator in there.

Include into Page

By copying the template, we've doubled the markup for the footer. In this case, it's only a small part, but it's good practice to reuse code. Just to remind you, the footer is shown in Listing 14-10.

Listing 14-10. Footer

```
1   ...
2     <footer>
3       &copy; Michael Müller
4       |
5       <h:outputLink value="http://blog.mueller-bruehl.de">
6         Michael's Blog
7       </h:outputLink>
```

```
8        |
9        <h:link value="About" outcome="/welcome.xhtml"/>
10   </footer>
11   ...
```

JSF offers the `<ui:include src="..."/>` tag to include (what else?) a portion of one page into another.

We'll put the common parts into their own directory. Thus, we create a folder in our Web Pages folder and name it common.

Next, let's create a new file footer.xhtml in that folder. This file contains a `<ui:composition>`, as seen before, and contains our footer, as shown in Listing 14-11.

Listing 14-11. Footer Refactored as HTML Fragment

```
1    <?xml version='1.0' encoding='UTF-8' ?>
2    <!DOCTYPE html [<!ENTITY copy "&#169;">]>
3    <ui:composition xmlns="http://www.w3.org/1999/xhtml"
4                    xmlns:h="http://xmlns.jcp.org/jsf/html"
5                    xmlns:ui="http://xmlns.jcp.org/jsf/facelets">
6
7      &copy; Michael Müller
8        |
9      <h:outputLink value="http://blog.mueller-bruehl.de">
10        Michael's Blog
11     </h:outputLink>
12       |
13     <h:link value="About" outcome="/welcome.xhtml"/>
14   </ui:composition>
```

The footer part in both templates (booksTemplate as well as adminTemplate) can now be rewritten to reference the new file, as shown in Listing 14-12.

Listing 14-12. Include HTML File

```
1    ...
2      <footer>
3        <ui:include src="/common/footer.xhtml"/>
4      </footer>
5    ...
```

That will insert the part within the `<ui:composition>` tag into the template. Pretty easy and straightforward, isn't it?

Besides a static `include`, it's possible to get the file to be included from an EL expression:

```
1    <ui:include src="#{someBean.someProperty}"/>
```

Now if you calculate the property, you might dynamically determine which source to include. For example, you can mimic a tab control and insert the content of a tab depending on the current selection.

Back to the category editor. Figure 14-7 shows two different tabs, one for Category, the other for a translation. Clicking one of the tab's captions will trigger a reload and include a different part of the view description.

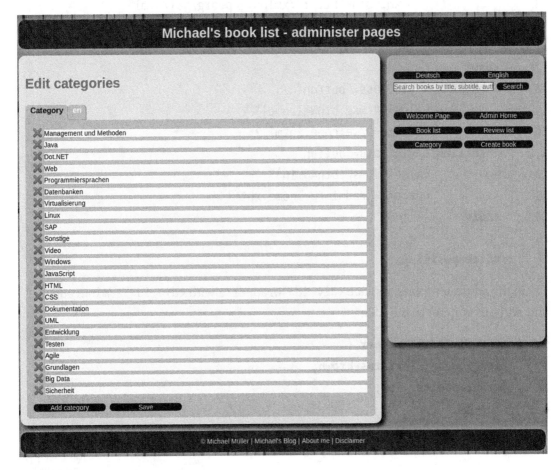

Figure 14-7. *Category editor*

Common Navigation

Create a file include\commonNavigation.xhtml and insert it into the <nav> areas of both templates. In the admin template, add two buttons within one div above the common navigation, to navigate to \admin\categoryEditor.xhtml and \admin\bookEditor. xhtml. Create a new file \admin\bookEditor.xhtml (which will be used in Chapter 15). See Listing 14-13.

Listing 14-13. Simple Navigation

```
1    <?xml version='1.0' encoding='UTF-8' ?>
2    <!DOCTYPE html [<!ENTITY copy "&#169;">]>
3    <ui:composition xmlns="http://www.w3.org/1999/xhtml"
4                    xmlns:h="http://xmlns.jcp.org/jsf/html"
5                    xmlns:ui="http://xmlns.jcp.org/jsf/facelets">
6
7      <div>
8        <h:link styleClass="button"
9                value="#{msg.btnWelcome}"
10               outcome="/welcome.xhtml"/>
11       <h:link styleClass="button"
12               value="#{msg.btnAdmin}"
13               outcome="/admin/welcome.xhtml"/>
14     </div>
15
16   </ui:composition>
```

In the admin template, replace <div id="wrapper"> with <div id="adminWrapper"> and add this snippet to the CSS:

```
1    body > div#adminWrapper {
2      background-color: rosybrown;
3      border-radius: 1em;
4    }
```

Topics

Although the original version of Books was created to support two languages only, we want to design the category editor to support any language in principle. For the translation, we need the category in the original (default) language and one additional column for each additional language we want to support. Every category will be displayed on its own row. It might become quite a wide table, so let's implement another solution: with a couple of pages we'll build up a look and feel of a tab control, one register tab for every language (as shown in Figures 14-7 and 14-8).

The first page is similar to our existing editor. It's used to add (edit, delete) categories in default language. All other tabs will display two columns for each category. The first one is read only and displays the existing categories in default language. The second column is editable to enter the translation in one of the target languages. Because most of my reviews are written in German, I defined de as the default language. Figure 14-8 shows the editor for the English translation.

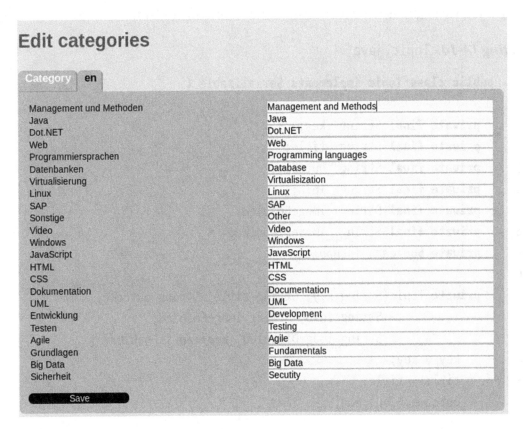

Figure 14-8. *Category editor, translation*

Each register tab has a short headline—for example, Category, en, es, fr, and so on depending on the language count we want to support. Or, instead of displaying the language abbreviation, we might prefer to display a flag to indicate the language. (We'll ignore for now potential issues like different flags representing the same language. Should the Union Jack or Stars and Stripes stand for English? Can one flag represent different languages, such as Switzerland's standing for German, French, or Italian, or Canada's standing for English or French?)

Okay, for each register tab we need some information like heading or flag, URL, and more. We'll place that information into a container called Topic. The topics of the editor will be maintained in a collection structure we'll call Topics. A topic might be used not for the category editor only, so it contains some more elements than needed for this editor. Depending on the editor, a topic needs to contain a heading only or key, heading and URL, or another combination of elements. There are different solutions for such a container class—for example, one parameterless constructor and getters/setters for each field, or different constructors taking different arguments. Or—and this is how it's built for Books—we might use a builder class, as shown in Listing 14-14.

Listing 14-14. Topic.java

```java
1    public class Topic implements Serializable {
2
3        private final String _key;
4        private final String _title;
5        private final String _outcome;
6        private final String _info;
7        private final String _imageEnabled;
8        private final String _imageDisabled;
9        private boolean _isEnabled;
10
11       private Topic(String key, String title, String outcome,
12                     String info, String imageEnabled,
13                     String imageDisabled, boolean isEnabled) {
14           _key = key;
15           _title = title;
16           _outcome = outcome;
```

```
17        _info = info;
18        _imageEnabled = imageEnabled;
19        _imageDisabled = imageDisabled;
20        _isEnabled = isEnabled;
21      }
22
23
24      public String getKey() {
25        return _key;
26      }
27
28      public String getTitle() {
29        return _title;
30      }
31
32      ... other getters omitted ...
33
34      public String getImageDisabled() {
35        return _imageDisabled;
36      }
37
38      public String getImage() {
39        return _isEnabled ? _imageEnabled : _imageDisabled;
40      }
41
42      public boolean isIsEnabled() {
43        return _isEnabled;
44      }
45
46      public void setIsEnabled(boolean isEnabled) {
47        _isEnabled = isEnabled;
48      }
49
50      ... hashCode and equals omitted ...
51
```

```
52
53     public static class TopicBuilder {
54
55       private final String _key;
56       private String _title = "";
57       private String _outcome = "";
58       private String _info = "";
59       private String _imageEnabled = "";
60       private String _imageDisabled = "";
61       private boolean _isEnabled = true;
62
63       static public TopicBuilder createBuilder(String key) {
64         return new TopicBuilder(key);
65       }
66
67       private TopicBuilder(String key) {
68         _key = key;
69         _title = key;   // defaults to key
70       }
71
72       public TopicBuilder setTitle(String title) {
73         _title = title;
74         return this;
75       }
76
77       ... other chain elements omitted ...
78
79       public Topic build() {
80         return new Topic(_key, _title, _outcome, _info,
81                          _imageEnabled, _imageDisabled, _isEnabled);
82       }
83     }
84   }
```

Listing 14-15 shows the list of Topics:

Listing 14-15. Topics.java

```java
public class Topics implements Serializable {

  private Optional<Topic> _activeTopic = Optional.empty();
  private final Set<Topic> _topics = new LinkedHashSet<>();

  public Set<Topic> getTopics() {
    return _topics;
  }

  public void clear() {
    _topics.clear();
  }

  public void addTopic(String title) {
    addTopic(Topic.TopicBuilder.createBuilder(title).build());
  }

  public void addTopic(Topic topic) {
    _topics.add(topic);
  }

  public void remove(String key) {
    Optional<Topic> topic = findTopic(key);
    topic.ifPresent(t -> _topics.remove(t));
  }

  public void remove(Topic topic) {
    _topics.remove(topic);
  }

  public Optional<Topic> findTopic(String key) {
    return _topics.stream()
```

```
33              .filter(topic -> topic.getKey().equals(key))
34              .findAny();
35      }
36
37      /* pre-Java 8 code example
38      public Topic findTopic(String key) {
39      for (Topic topic : _topics) {
40      if (topic.getKey().equals(key)) {
41      return topic;
42      }
43      }
44      return Topic.TopicBuilder.createBuilder("").build();
45      }
46      */
47      public Optional<Topic> getActiveTopic() {
48        return _activeTopic;
49      }
50
51      public void setActive(String key) {
52        _activeTopic = findTopic(key);
53      }
54
55  }
```

Each topic is intended to hold the information of a specific tab page. The first will be our existing category editor page, which has to be only slightly adapted. And for every supported locale, we'll add another tab page. To perform this task, we need information about the supported languages, so we'll create a small method to collect this info. And because we might reuse this, we'll put it into a Utilities class, as in Listing 14-16.

Listing 14-16. Utilities.java

```
1   public class Utilities {
2     public static Set<String> getSupportedLocales(HandleDefault
      defHandler) {
3       Application app = FacesContext.getCurrentInstance().
        getApplication();
```

```
4      Set<String> languageCodes = new HashSet<>();
5      for (Iterator<Locale> itr = app.getSupportedLocales(); itr.
       hasNext();) {
6        Locale locale = itr.next();
7        languageCodes.add(locale.getLanguage());
8      }
9
10     String defaultLang = app.getDefaultLocale().getLanguage();
11     if (defHandler == HandleDefault.Exclude) {
12       languageCodes.remove(defaultLang);
13     } else {
14       languageCodes.add(defaultLang);
15     }
16     return languageCodes;
17   }
18
19   public enum HandleDefault {
20
21     Include, Exclude
22   }
23 }
```

The locales are defined in the faces-config.xml file, which is valid for the whole
application. Hence, it's the application object we have to query. getSupportedLocales()
is an iterator, not an iterable, so we can't use a for each loop. Depending on the
configuration file, the default language might be included within the supported locales
or not. We'll tackle this problem by explicitly excluding or including the default locale,
depending on the parameter defHandler.

Because the application should potentially support many languages, and we need
to save space, the topics will just contain the locale code as is. But the first tab will be
named Category, or in German *Kategorie*. It needs to be translated, so we have to get the
message bundle and the appropriate translation out of it. To do that, we'll add another
method to our Utilities class, as in Listing 14-17.

Listing 14-17. Retrieve Localized Message with Key

```
1   public static String getMessage(String key) {
2     ResourceBundle messageBundle = ResourceBundle
3             .getBundle("de.muellerbruehl.books.messages");
4     try {
5       return messageBundle.getString(key);
6     } catch (MissingResourceException e) {
7       return "<unknown resource: " + key + ">";
8     }
9   }
```

Now we can initialize and use the topics within the CategoryEditor class.
initTopics() will be called from the existing init() method, as shown in Listing 14-18.

Listing 14-18. Topic Handling in CategoryEditor.java

```
1    ...
2      private static final String CATEGORY = "category";
3      private Topics _topics;
4
5      private void initTopics() {
6        _topics = new Topics();
7        Topic topic = Topic.TopicBuilder
8                .createBuilder(CATEGORY)
9                .setTitle(Utilities.getMessage("lblCategory"))
10               .setOutcome("categoryEditor.xhtml")
11               .build();
12       _topics.addTopic(topic);
13       for (String lang : Utilities.getSupportedLocales(HandleDefault.
         Exclude))
14       {
15         topic = Topic.TopicBuilder
16                 .createBuilder(lang)
17                 .setOutcome("categoryTranslator.xhtml")
18                 .build();
19         _topics.addTopic(topic);
```

```
20        }
21        _topics.setActive(CATEGORY);
22    }
23
24    public String changeTab(String newTopicKey) {
25      if (_topics.getActiveTopic().get().getKey().equals(newTopicKey)) {
26        return "";
27      }
28      _topics.setActive(newTopicKey);
29      return _topics.getActiveTopic().get().getOutcome();
30    }
31
32    public Set<Topic> getTopics() {
33      return _topics.getTopics();
34    }
35
36    public boolean isActive(Topic topic) {
37      Optional<Topic> activeTopic = _topics.getActiveTopic();
38      if (activeTopic.isPresent()) {
39        return activeTopic.get().equals(topic);
40      }
41      return false;
42    }
```

If the user clicks a topic, it performs a call to changeTab that returns the page to navigate to. The topics will be displayed, and to grant access to them we have to expose them by getTopics. The last method shown is a convenience method to check whether the parameter is currently the active topic.

Once we prepare the topics, we can use them within our page layout. The existing CategoryEditor now becomes one of diverse tab pages. To do that, we introduce a new template categoryTemplate.xhtml and make categoryEditor.xhtml become a client of this. And we move the heading from the existing editor into the new template. See Listing 14-19.

Listing 14-19. categoryTemplate.xhtml

```
1   <?xml version='1.0' encoding='UTF-8' ?>
2   <!DOCTYPE composition PUBLIC "-//W3C//DTD XHTML 1.0 Transitional//EN"
3     "http://www.w3.org/TR/xhtml1/DTD/xhtml1-transitional.dtd">
4   <ui:composition xmlns:ui="http://xmlns.jcp.org/jsf/facelets"
5                   template="adminTemplate.xhtml"
6                   xmlns:h="http://xmlns.jcp.org/jsf/html"
7                   xmlns:c="http://java.sun.com/jsp/jstl/core"
8                   xmlns:f="http://xmlns.jcp.org/jsf/core">
9
10    <ui:define name="content">
11
12      <h1>Edit categories</h1>
13
14      <h:form id="form">
15        <div class="tab">
16          <ul class="tab">
17            <c:forEach items="#{categoryEditor.topics}" var="topic">
18              <li class="#{categoryEditor.isActive(topic)
                  ?'activetab':'tab'}">
19                <h:commandLink value="#{topic.title}"
20                               action="#{categoryEditor.changeTab
                                 (topic.key)}">
21                  <f:param name="langCode" value="#{topic.key}"/>
22                </h:commandLink>
23              </li>
24            </c:forEach>
25          </ul>
26        </div>
27      </h:form>
28      <div class="editor">
29        <ui:insert name="editContent">Content</ui:insert>
30      </div>
```

```
31      </ui:define>

32

33    </ui:composition>
```

Each topic is wrapped into a list item `<li>` of an unordered list `<ul>`. `<c:forEach>` is used to iterate through all topics. Why not `<ui:repeat value="#{categoryEditor.topics}" var="topic">` like we used before? If you try that, you'll get an error. Technically, `<c:forEach>` is a tag handler. As such, it doesn't become part of the component tree. It's evaluated, and the result of the repetition will be used to build up the component tree. On the other hand, `<ui:repeat>` is a component that will be part of the component tree. Its child components will be inserted only once into the component tree, independent of the repetition. And it will be evaluated at a time when the topics map doesn't exist. Scary? Nope. But you have to consider a couple of differences between repeating structures. I'll discuss the details and differences in Chapter 23.

For now, let's talk about the other noteworthy elements here. For each list item, we choose the style class depending on whether it's the active topic or not. In conjunction with CSS, this will mimic the tabs. All translations will be handled by the same page (`categoryTranslator.xhtml`). To determine the right language, we pass this as a parameter into this page using the `<f:param>` tag, which defines a parameter by its name and its value, which in fact become a key-value pair, accessible by the called page.

To prepare the next steps and test the application so far, create an empty `categoryTranslator.xhtml` page (more precisely, `ui:composition`). Use your existing category editor as your boilerplate. If you don't have the code at your disposal, take a look at Listing 14-20. To get our tabs up and running, we finally need to add some CSS voodoo.

Listing 14-20. Tab Lookalike Formatting (`book.css`)

```css
1    main div.tab {
2      display: block;
3    }

4

5    main ul.tab {
6      list-style-type: none;
7      display: inline;
8    }

9

10   main li.tab,
```

```
11   main li.activetab {
12     list-style-type: none;
13     display: inline;
14     border-style: solid;
15     border-width: 2px 2px 1px 2px;
16     border-top-left-radius: 0.5em;
17     border-top-right-radius: 0.5em;
18     background-color: #ccccd8;
19   }
20
21   main li.tab {
22     border-color:  #cccccc #aaaaaa #aaaaaa #cccccc;
23   }
24
25   main li.activetab {
26     border-color:  #cccccc #aaaaaa #ccccd8 #cccccc;
27   }
28
29   main li.tab a,
30   main li.activetab a {
31     padding: 0 0.5em 0 0.5em;
32     font-size: 1.2em;
33     text-decoration: none;
34     font-weight: bold;
35   }
36
37   main li.activetab a {
38     color: #000044;
39   }
40
41   .editor {
42     background-color: #ccccd8;
43     border-radius: 0.5em;
44     border-top-left-radius: 0;
45     padding: 1em;
46   }
```

Figure 14-9 shows the result of our efforts.

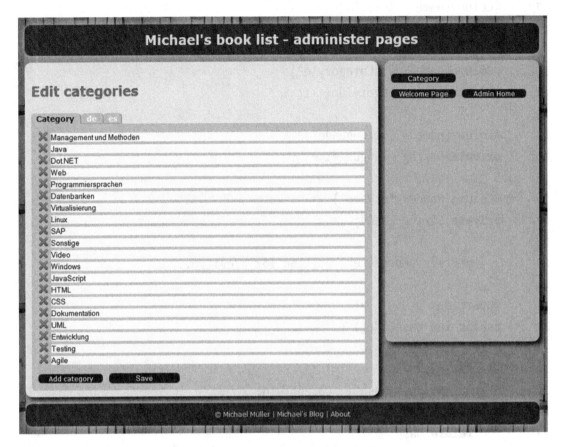

Figure 14-9. *Category editor using a tab control lookalike*

Enhancing the Category Entity

Before we can realize the category translator, we need to prepare an appropriate translation entity and enhance the category entity. The translation entity refers to the category id and provides the translated name for one language. See Listing 14-21.

Listing 14-21. Important Parts of `CategoryTranslation.java`

```
1   @Entity
2   @Table(name = "CategoryTranslation")
3   public class CategoryTranslation implements Serializable {
4
5       @Id
```

```
6    @GeneratedValue(strategy = GenerationType.IDENTITY)
7    @Column(name = "ctId")
8    private int _id = -1;
9
10   @Column(name = "ctCategoryId")
11   private int _categoryId = -1;
12
13   @Column(name = "ctLanguage")
14   private String _language;
15
16   @Column(name = "ctName")
17   private String _name;
18
19   ... getters and setters omitted for brevity ...
20
21   @Override
22   public int hashCode() {
23     if (_id < 0) {
24       int hash = 3;
25       hash = 89 * hash + _categoryId;
26       hash = 89 * hash + Objects.hashCode(_language);
27       return hash;
28     }
29     return _id;
30   }
31
32   @Override
33   public boolean equals(Object object) {
34     if (!(object instanceof CategoryTranslation)) {
35       return false;
36     }
37     CategoryTranslation other = (CategoryTranslation) object;
38     if (_id < 0 && other._id < 0) {
39       return _categoryId == other._categoryId
40               && _language.equals(other._language);
```

```
41        }
42        return _id == other._id;
43     }
44  }
```

Again, we need hashCode and equals to be the same for two objects with the same valid id. Otherwise, both are determined by _categoryId and _language. See Listing 14-22.

Listing 14-22. Create Statement for CategoryTranslation (MySQL)

```
1   CREATE TABLE `CategoryTranslation` (
2     `ctId` int(11) NOT NULL AUTO_INCREMENT,
3     `ctCategoryId` int(11) NOT NULL,
4     `ctLanguage` varchar(10) NOT NULL,
5     `ctName` varchar(45) NOT NULL,
6     PRIMARY KEY (`ctId`),
7     KEY `FK_CategoryTranslation_Category2` (`ctCategoryId`),
8     CONSTRAINT `FK_CategoryTranslation_Category2`
9       FOREIGN KEY (`ctCategoryId`)
10      REFERENCES `Category` (`catId`)
11  );
```

The preceding statement creates the table for a MySQL database—if you use another DBMS, you may need to adapt it. See Listings 14-23 and 14-24.

Listing 14-23. Create Statement for CategoryTranslation (MS SQL Server Version)

```
1   CREATE TABLE CategoryTranslation(
2         ctId int IDENTITY(1,1) NOT NULL,
3         ctCategoryId int NOT NULL
4           CONSTRAINT FK_CategoryTranslation_Category2
5           FOREIGN KEY(ctCategoryId) REFERENCES Category (catId),
6         ctLanguage varchar(10) NOT NULL,
7         ctName varchar(45) NOT NULL,
8     PRIMARY KEY (ctId)
9   )
```

Listing 14-24. Create Statement for `CategoryTranslation` (MySQL Version)

```
 1 CREATE TABLE Books.CategoryTranslation (
 2    ctId INT NOT NULL AUTO_INCREMENT,
 3   ctCategoryId INT NOT NULL,
 4   ctLanguage VARCHAR(10) NOT NULL,
 5   ctName VARCHAR(45) NOT NULL,
 6   PRIMARY KEY (ctId),
 7   INDEX fk_CategoryTranslation_1_idx (ctCategoryId ASC),
 8   CONSTRAINT fk_CategoryTranslation_1
 9     FOREIGN KEY (ctCategoryId)
10     REFERENCES Books.Category (catId)
11     ON DELETE NO ACTION
12     ON UPDATE NO ACTION);
```

As you can see, a foreign key is defined to add referential integrity to the existing Category table. We may translate it into "this translation belongs to a category." In fact, to one category no, one, or many translations may belong. Each category contains a collection of translations, which might be empty.

Listing 14-25 enhances the category entity to model this one-to-many relationship.

Listing 14-25. One-To-Many Relationship with List

```
1   ...
2     @OneToMany
3     @JoinColumn(name = "ctCategoryId", referencedColumnName = "catId")
4     private List<CategoryTranslation> _catTranslations;
5   ...
```

This relationship is defined by the @OneToMany annotation. We use a second table with a foreign key. This is modeled by the @JoinColumn annotation with the two columns that are used to join these tables. This should be pretty self-explanatory. All translations will be held by a list.

With JPA, you might model other kinds of one-to-many relationships, such as using a dedicated join table. Usually such a dedicated join table is superfluous for a one-to-many relationship. You'll need it for a many-to-many relationship.

Thinking about the category translations, it would be useful to access a translation directly by its language code. Thus a Map<String, CategoryTranslation> would fit better than a list. No problem—we only have to define which field of the translation would become the map's key.

We also need accessors to this map, and for future use some convenience methods to access a single translation. See Listing 14-26.

Listing 14-26. Translation Enhancement of Category.java

```
1    ...
2    @OneToMany(fetch = FetchType.LAZY,
3               cascade = CascadeType.ALL,
4               orphanRemoval = true)
5    @JoinColumn(name = "ctCategoryId", referencedColumnName = "catId")
6    @MapKey(name = "_language")
7    private Map<String, CategoryTranslation> _catTranslations =
8                       new HashMap<>();
9
10   public Map<String, CategoryTranslation> getCategoryTranslations() {
11     return _catTranslations;
12   }
13
14   public void setCategoryTranslations(
15         Map<String, CategoryTranslation> catTranslations) {
16     _catTranslations = catTranslations;
17 }
18
19   public String getTranslatedName(String langCode) {
20     if (_catTranslations.containsKey(langCode)) {
21       return _catTranslations.get(langCode).getName();
22     }
23     return "";
24   }
25
26   public void setTranslatedName(String langCode, String name) {
27     if (_catTranslations.containsKey(langCode)) {
28       _catTranslations.get(langCode).setName(name);
29     } else {
```

```
30          CategoryTranslation translation = new CategoryTranslation();
31          translation.setLanguage(langCode);
32          translation.setCategoryId(_id);
33          translation.setName(name);
34          _catTranslations.put(langCode,  translation);
35        }
36      }
37
38      public String getTranslatedNameOrDefault(String langCode) {
39        if (_catTranslations.containsKey(langCode)) {
40          String name = _catTranslations.get(langCode).getName();
41          if (name.isEmpty()) {
42            return _name;
43          }
44          return name;
45        }
46        return _name;
47      }
48    ...
```

Although the convenience methods should need no further explanation, some information for the @OneToMany annotation is noteworthy. fetch = FetchType.LAZY will load the translation only when first accessed. EAGER will load it together with the category itself. Which one performs best depends on the data structure and usage. Imagine a big object graph, with many parts of it rarely used. In such a case, lazy loading would often be the better choice. In case of our categories, the translations are small and often used, so I prefer an eager loading (and introduced lazy first for didactic reasons).

Depending on cascade, operations might be cascaded or not—for example, persisting a category will persist its translations or not. Here, we use CascadeType.ALL to cascade all operations. Other values are DETACH, MERGE, PERSIST, REFRESH, and REMOVE.

In line 6 of Listing 14-26 we use @MapKey(name = "_language"). This line tells JPA to use the field _language of the CategoryTranslation class. And to use its column name @Column(name = "ctLanguage"). If we omit the @MapKey annotation, JPA tries to guess the column name by adding _KEY to the uppercase field name. It would use _CATTRANSLATIONS_KEY, which slightly differs from the column name we use.

All our translations are held within a Map<LanguageCode = Translation>. This map will be automatically saved when we save the category. Suppose we remove an entry of that map and save the category again. What will happen to the removed translation entry? Because we cascaded all operations, saving the category will affect the CategoryTranslation too. Without further definition, JPA will set the category id of the translation to NULL and update the appropriate database table. And if we delete the category, all translations will be kept in the database with a category id set to NULL. This behavior works well for aggregations. Imagine a shelf object containing a list of books. If the shelf were deleted, you'd still keep the books and put them on another shelf. Unlike category and its translation, this is a typical composition. Without its category, the translation becomes a useless orphan. orphanRemoval = true will ensure the deletion of such orphans.

The Category Translation Page

Now we've prepared all the pieces of the puzzle. It's time to put them all together and create the category translator. In fact, most of the job is already done. We need a page definition and some additional methods for the bean.

The page shown in Listing 14-27 is quite simple. Most of it is already known.

Listing 14-27. categoryTranslator.xhtml

```
1   <?xml version='1.0' encoding='UTF-8' ?>
2   <!DOCTYPE html>
3   <ui:composition xmlns="http://www.w3.org/1999/xhtml"
4                   xmlns:h="http://xmlns.jcp.org/jsf/html"
5                   xmlns:ui="http://xmlns.jcp.org/jsf/facelets"
6                   template="categoryTemplate.xhtml"
7                   xmlns:f="http://xmlns.jcp.org/jsf/core"
8                   xmlns:c="http://xmlns.jcp.org/jsp/jstl/core">
9
10    <ui:define name="editContent">
11     <h:form>
12       <h:dataTable value="#{categoryEditor.categories}"
13                    var="cat"
14                    styleClass="wide">
```

```
15            <h:column>
16              <h:outputText styleClass="wide" value="#{cat.name}"/>
17            </h:column>
18            <h:column>
19              <h:inputText styleClass="wide"
20                   value="#{cat.categoryTranslations[param.langCode].
                     name}"/>
21            </h:column>
22          </h:dataTable>
23
24          <h:commandButton styleClass="button"
25                           value="Save"
26                           action="#{categoryEditor.save}">
27            <f:param name="langCode" value="#{param.langCode}"/>
28          </h:commandButton>
29        </h:form>
30      </ui:define>
31    </ui:composition>
```

The #{cat.categoryTranslations[param.langCode].name} grants access to the translation map of the category. Within the brackets we provide the key, which is the language code. Remember, we passed this code with a <f:param> tag into this page. Now we can access it from the parameter map, which holds the request parameters. The param.langCode refers to the parameter langCode using a common dot notation. The Save button will trigger a page navigation that reloads the same page. To access the language after this reload, we need to pass it again by a param tag.

All we have to do in our bean is initialize the translation, which means add those translations that haven't been retrieved from the database. See Listing 14-28.

Listing 14-28. CategoryEditor.java

```
1   public String changeTab(String newTopicKey) {
2     if (_topics.getActiveTopic().get().getKey().equals(newTopicKey)) {
3       return "";
4     }
5     _topics.setActive(newTopicKey);
6     if (!newTopicKey.equals(CATEGORY)) {
```

```
 7        initTranslation(newTopicKey);
 8      }
 9      return _topics.getActiveTopic().get().getOutcome();
10    }
11
12    private void initTranslation(String langCode) {
13      // ensure there is an element in the map for this language
14      _categories.stream().forEach(c -> {
15        if (c.getTranslatedName(langCode).isEmpty()) {
16          c.setTranslatedName(langCode, "");
17        }
18      });
19    }
```

Last but not least, Figure 14-10 shows a quick look at the translation editor.

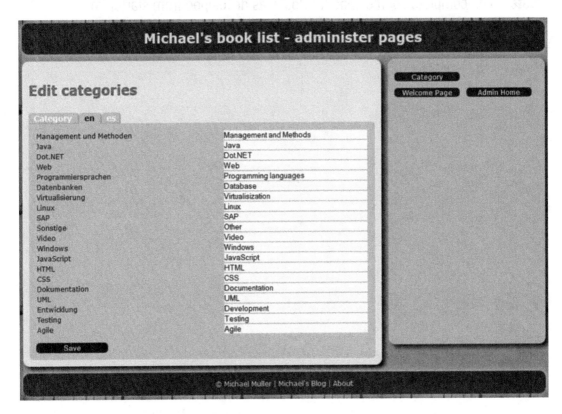

Figure 14-10. *Category translator*

Summary

The process of internationalization covers the preparation of software to be potentially usable in other countries and languages. Localization is the adaptation to a specific language or country (or region). Localization doesn't just mean translation, but also adapting date and number formats, character sets, writing direction, images, and more.

Java supports translation of literal text with message bundles. Sometimes content has to be translated too. The chapter demonstrated a possible solution by adding translation to objects and the database.

This chapter also discussed a language switcher, HTML escaping, joining tables by JPA, and passing parameters between pages. It introduced some repeating structures of JSF (some based on the JSP tag library). Some differences were addressed, but a detailed discussion of repeating structures comes later in the book.

Note   The complete source code for Books as developed from startup to internationalization is available from `webdevelopment-java.info`.

CHAPTER 15

Bean Validation

As I've pointed out, Books is an application that's maintained by just one author, who should know about the expected data. So there's no user interface that gives an immediate response after each input or that offers lots of hints. Of course, those features are essential for an application intended for potentially unknown users. Later on, when developing a second application called Alumni, I'll cover those features in detail. Right now, validation will be useful in preventing a user from entering data that might not fit the database.

Remember the JSF lifecycle: during phase 3, the input values will be converted and validated. In the HTML page, every input is treated as simple text. With help from the EL, these inputs are bound by value expressions to the data model. Usually this is done by using the properties of a Java bean. In Java, all properties are strongly typed. That means conversions are needed, from text (string) to the target type and vice versa. This job is done by converters. JSF offers standard converters for a wide range of built-in Java types. Later on, we'll discuss custom converters. If a conversion fails, JSF throws an exception. Accordingly, converters perform raw validation.

JSF also includes a couple of standard validators that you can use to define a validation at a finer level. For example, you can allow positive numbers only, or force a string to a maximum length, and so on. I cover this kind of validator later on.

A JSF validator will validate the input on the server side just after the user entered it and before applying values to the model. Sometimes only validating the input isn't enough. Data might be changed at the business layer. When you want to persist that altered data to a database, the program might crash because the data doesn't fit the database schema. In such a case, validating the data again just before storing would be very helpful. The same applies for validating at any other place within the application.

Luckily, Java EE offers exactly this kind of validation: it's known as *bean validation*. JSF takes advantage of it and uses this validation too, if defined in the model the data is applied to. In our application, we'll edit and store information about books. We're going to add bean validation by simply applying special annotations to the book entity. Now this validation will be used both by JSF and JPA. And if needed, you may additionally call the validation programmatically.

© Michael Müller 2018
M. Müller, *Practical JSF in Java EE 8*, https://doi.org/10.1007/978-1-4842-3030-5_15

Book Entity

Every book is described by its title, subtitle, author, and by certain other information, including a short description. The description might be presented to the user in different languages. So, we'll need a second table containing the translations, like we did for the categories. For brevity's sake, I'm only going to talk about essential parts of the entities. You can download the complete files.

Tables 15-1 and 15-2 show the two tables we'll use for the book and the translation.

Table 15-1. *Book*

Column Name	Data Type
bookId	int
bookTitle	varchar(200)
bookSubtitle	varchar(200)
bookAuthor	varchar(255)
bookPublisher	varchar(45)
bookYear	int
bookLanguage	varchar(10)
bookISBN	varchar(45)
bookShorttext	varchar(500)
bookReference	varchar(500)
bookAdReference	varchar(50)

Table 15-2. *Book Translation*

Column Name	Data Type
btId	int
btBookId	int
btLanguage	varchar(10)
btShorttext	varchar(500)
btReference	varchar(50)

Next we'll define the book entity and implement a property (field plus getter and setter) for every column as we did before in Chapter 12. Listing 15-1 shows just one property.

Listing 15-1. Entity Class Book

```
1   [...]
2
3   @Entity
4   @Table(name = "Book")
5   public class Book implements Serializable {
6
7   [...]
8
9     // <editor-fold defaultstate="collapsed" desc="Property Title">
10    @Size(max = 200)
11    @Column(name = "bookTitle")
12    public String getTitle() {
13      return _title;
14    }
15
16    public void setTitle(String title) {
17      _title = title;
18    }
19
20    private String _title;
21    // </editor-fold>
22
23  [...]
24  }
```

The <editor fold> tags are specific to NetBeans and are used to collapse the code. They'll be ignored by most other IDEs.

Let's focus on the @Size(max = 200) annotation (line 10). It checks the size of the property, which is limited to a maximum of 200 characters. That's exactly what we defined in the table. If the property title contains more characters, the validation will throw an exception. This validation takes place just before storing the data. Without bean validation, we would get an exception while inserting/updating the database with a string that exceeds that size.

At first glance, it may seem not that valuable to replace an IO exception with a validation exception (we may save the database access). But as mentioned, bean validation will be invoked by JSF also. And bean validation isn't restricted to entities. You can annotate your data access object (DAO) class or any other kind of data model you've chosen. The annotation might be placed to a field or a property (getter method).

During lifecycle phase 3, conversion and validation, JSF will invoke the JSF validators as well as bean validation. If a value expression like #{book.name} points to a property or field that's annotated for bean validation, this check will be invoked. Instead of simply (re-)throwing an exception, JSF recognizes possible violations. If a message tag is defined within the page, as shown in the next section, then this exception triggers the output of an appropriate message. And as a real benefit of bean validation in combination with JSF, the user gets an immediate response.

There are a couple of annotations defined by bean validation—for example, @Min and @Max to define integer limitations, or @Future and @Past to define date constraints. As you can see, these constraints seem simple. Indeed they are, so I won't explain them in detail. One of the most sophisticated constraints is @Pattern, which compares the value of a property or field with pattern matching. For a list of possible constraints (as of Java EE 8), take a look at the Java EE 8 tutorial at https://javaee.github.io/tutorial/bean-validation002.html. Another useful source is http://beanvalidation.org.

Bean validation is included with Java EE application server. It's not part of a pure servlet container or Java SE. Adding bean validation just means adding an appropriate library to your classpath. At http://beanvalidation.org you'll find a list of certified implementations.

Book Editor

If a validation failure occurs, it should be reported to the user. To do that, we need a placeholder for the message in our editor page. Listing 15-2 shows this page.

Listing 15-2. Extract of bookEditor.xhtml

```
1    <div class="inputGroup">
2      <h:outputLabel styleClass="label" for="title" value="#{msg.
       lblTitle}"/>
```

```
3      <h:inputText id="title" styleClass="inputFull"
4                      value="#{bookEditor.book.title}"/>
5      <h:message id="msgTtitle" for="title" styleClass="warning"/>
6   </div>
```

In this extract, we have a label, an input field, and a message. This message will contain the validation message—if, and only if, there is one. There's no need to place the message nearby the input field (somebody may group all messages together somewhere at the page). Both components (inputText and message) are bound together by for="title". Here "title" is the id of the input field.

The validation will be invoked in phase 3 of the JSF lifecycle. All possible exceptions will be collected under the hood, including the dedicated messages. If at least one exception occurs, the lifecycle will branch after phase 3 directly to phase 6, *render response*. The previous page will be rerendered, including all messages.

Sometimes the standard messages won't fit, so you'll need to customize them. One approach is to add a ValidationMessages.properties file to the default package in the src/main/resources folder. Now, with the right properties within that file, you can customize the messages. The property names follow the structure javax.validation. constraints.XXX, where *xxx* represents the constraint name, such as javax.validation. constraints.Size.message. You'll find a list for example at http://grepcode.com/file/ repo1.maven.org/maven2/org.hibernate/hibernate-validator/4.0.0.CR1/org/ hibernate/validator/ValidationMessages.properties. If you need to translate the messages, just add resource files with the proper locale code, as we did before.

Especially in the case of the pattern matcher, a single message like must match "{regexp}" isn't very useful to the user. Who outside the IT world would understand such a message? Depending on the pattern, we need different messages. For example, if we use a regular expression to define a valid email, then the message should reflect that bean validation offers a simple solution: the message can be defined within the annotation:

```
@Pattern(regexp = ".*@.*", message = "Please enter a valid email address.")
```

This simple regular expression isn't a very sophisticated email checker, mind you— it's just to show the principle. As you can see, it's possible to define a different message for each constraint. Here, the message is just a literal. If we need to display the message in different languages, then we need to transform the message into a key that refers to the properties file. If we surround the message with curly braces, then the content within these curly braces is treated as a key:

```
@Pattern(regexp = ".*@.*", message = "{validation.constraints.email.
message}")
```

Now we can add this key to the properties files. In `ValidationMessages_en.properties`, we add the following:

```
validation.constraints.email.message=Please enter a valid email address
```

And within `ValidationMessages_de.properties`, we add this line:

```
validation.constraints.email.message=Bitte geben Sie eine gültige E-Mail-
Adresse an
```

Don't forget about the `ValidationMessages.properties` file to place the text for your default language. Using NetBeans's properties editor, you'll see the default as well as the different languages at one glance.

In the preceding example, we used the `message` attribute for just one key. Usually that's what you want to do. In fact, you might mix literal text and keys. Every occurrence of a pair of curly braces is treated as a key. So, we may combine multiple keys and literal text. The following alerts the localized text about a wrong format, followed by the three hash signs and our message for the email:

```
{validation.constraints.wrong.format.message} ### {validation.constraints.
email.message}
```

Summary

During its validation phase, JSF doesn't just perform a JSF-specific validation, it also invokes standard bean validation if defined within the data model. Thus, validation constraints might not only ensure that fields will fit the database during storage, but can also provide qualified feedback to the user.

This chapter explained how to use bean validation on a fundamental level. We'll dig into it a bit deeper later in the book.

CHAPTER 16

Contexts and Dependency Injection

Sometimes you need an instance of an object with a type that might be changed or determined at runtime, and you need a reliable mechanism to perform that task. Luckily, Java EE 8 comes with Contexts and Dependency Injection (CDI), which can solve the problem.

From new() to CDI

If you write a class that needs access to an underlying object-oriented service, you need to obtain an instance of this service and call its methods. One simple approach is to create a new object of the service class:

```
DataService dataService = new DataService();
```

That approach has a couple of disadvantages. What would happen if you could choose between different compatible services? Let's declare DataService as an abstract class or an interface and implement a concrete service. You could use

```
DataService dataService = new MySQLDataService();
```

or

```
DataService dataService = new PostgreSQLDataService();
```

Now your application still needs to know one of the concrete services. If you need the flexibility to choose the service at runtime, one solution would be to use an if-cascade or switch to select the concrete class depending on a configuration string. Your class still needs to know the concrete implementations. And if you want to add another implementation, your class needs to know that too. This is a dependency you usually don't want to have.

201

© Michael Müller 2018
M. Müller, *Practical JSF in Java EE 8*, https://doi.org/10.1007/978-1-4842-3030-5_16

The trick is to move the decision into a static factory method of the service. This is one of the patterns Erich Gamma and coauthors discussed in their book *Design Patterns: Elements of Reusable Object-Oriented Software* (Addison-Wesley, 1994).

Now our class becomes independent from the concrete implementations:

```
DataService dataService = DataService.createService("MySQL")
```

But besides that interface (or abstract class), our class still has to know the service and is responsible for creating the object, even though we delegate the creation to the service. In traditional programming, our code is responsible for the flow of control.

Now, imagine our class is an extension of a framework[1] that includes the desired service. Then the framework might be responsible for the flow of control. So, our class is an extension point that's called by the framework. And the framework might create the service and inject it into our class. The flow of control is inverted compared to traditional programming. This approach, called inversion of control (IoC), was described by Martin Fowler back in 2005 (you can read more about it at `http://martinfowler.com/bliki/InversionOfControl.html`).

CDI is an IoC provided by Java EE. Injection became quite easy by simply annotating the wanted object with `@Inject`. We've used it in our projects before.

With CDI the container will create all desired objects and inject it into our classes. But it doesn't only inject objects that belong to the framework into our class. CDI also injects particular objects of our application (or another one) into our class.

But how does CDI know which object to inject? How does it figure out whether an object is to be created or if an existing instance might be used?

You can annotate your classes with special keywords that will be recognized and interpreted by CDI. We've used such an annotation before: `@Named` of the `javax.inject` package, which declares a bean as a CDI bean. Such a named bean can be injected by Java EE into the consuming class. Besides CDI beans, CDI can also inject Enterprise Java Beans (EJBs).

---

[1]Of course, that's the intention of a framework: although we control the flow of our application when we use the methods of a library, a framework dictates its flow to us. It offers extension points, where the developer may add or change behavior.

Note   Without discussing EJBs, we've used them before in our service classes by using the @Stateless annotation, which declares a class as a stateless EJB. Using this kind of bean, we benefit from the container's automatic transaction management. On the other hand, using a CDI bean for such a service class used to force the developer to add the transaction handling manually. One general solution is to create an interceptor to add a transaction to every JPA access. Nowadays this is included in CDI with the @Transactional annotation.

Besides such a static declaration of named beans, a developer may declare any method that returns an object as a producer method. This is the CDI equivalent of a factory method.

Once CDI knows what to inject, it needs to know about the object's lifecycle to determine whether an existing one can be used or a new object needs to be injected. CDI offers a couple of annotations for this purpose too. Building Books, we still used some of them. Remember the xxxScoped ones? Table 16-1 lists a short overview of common annotations of this group.

Table 16-1. Predifined CDI Scopes

Annotation	Description
@ApplicationScoped	A bean is bound to the application lifecycle: it's created when the application starts (at least on the first usage of the bean) and destroyed when the application shuts down.
@SessionScoped	A bean annotated with that marker is bound to the lifecycle of the current session.
@RequestScoped	A bean annotated with @RequestScoped is bound to a single HTTP request.
@ConversationScoped	This binds the lifecycle to the period of a so-called *conversation*. By default, a conversation is in *transient* mode, which means it's bound to a single request. But by invoking its start method, a conversation is set into *long-running* mode and will live until the end method is called. This allows the developer to control the lifecycle.
@Dependent	This is a pseudo scope: the bean's lifecycle depends on its owner's lifecycle. This means its lifecycle depends on the bean it's injected into. This is the default if no scope is defined.

You can also define your own scopes. JSF has defined two other scopes based on the CDI scopes: @ViewScoped and @FlowScoped. The first is bound to one page, regardless of how many subsequent requests are made to this. The latter can be used for a series of pages (called a *flow*).

Don't mix this up with the older JSF scopes, which became deprecated with Java EE 8 and which won't be covered in this book. Using these JSF scopes, there had been one rule: only beans with a wider lifecycle context could be used in another bean. With CDI, it's possible to inject beans with a short lifecycle into one with a longer lifecycle.

At a first glance, it's hard to imagine how that would work. The bean with the shorter lifecycle might have been destroyed by the time I want to use it in a bean. CDI uses a simple trick: except in dependent mode, CDI doesn't inject a direct reference to an object. Rather, a proxy object is created and a reference to the proxy gets injected. As a result, when accessing the object with the shorter lifecycle, it might be replaced under the hood by a new one.

Remember FacesContext.getCurrentInstance(), which we used for printing the component tree? Although the FacesContext hadn't been injectable up to JSF 2.2 (yeah, it's possible in JSF 2.3), we have similar behavior: every time you access the getExternalContext() of the FacesContext, you get information about the current request, even though you may have gotten your reference some requests ago.

Discussing all aspects of CDI is far beyond the scope of this book. But we'll use (and discuss) some aspects of CDI in some upcoming chapters. Developing the book editor, we're going to use @ConversationScoped.

Summary

CDI is an implementation of the Inversion of Control pattern. It enables the framework to create an appropriate instance of a class or interface and provide (inject) it for our application. Java classes annotated with @Named automatically become eligible for injection and will be injected at appropriate places by the @Inject annotation.

CDI itself offers much more. For example, you might define your own annotations by defining interfaces for producers. That's beyond this book's scope. In this book, we'll commonly use the predefined injections.

CHAPTER 17

Conversation Scope

Contexts and Dependency Injection (CDI) offers a couple of different scopes that you may use to define the lifetime of an object. Most scopes (such as request scope) are bound to predefined cycles like a single request, a session, or the application lifetime. The lifetime of one predefined scope, the *conversation scope*, can be controlled programmatically, so this scope becomes interesting for a couple of features.

Multi-page Editor

Our next task is to create a new book entry or edit an existing one. The book editor will consist of a tab panel offering one page for the book's metadata, including title, author, publisher, and one page for each language, where you can edit a review. It must be possible to switch between these pages without losing data, so it's not very hard to imagine that we need a backing bean living longer than just one request.

During one session, the user may edit more than one book. Unlike the categories (where all of them were edited together), we have to offer a function to edit one book after the other. That means a session scope won't fit here. We need a scope longer than just one request but shorter than a session. According to the table in Chapter 16, using the built-in CDI scope @ConversationScoped would be the choice.

The book editor will be invoked with a parameter representing the book id. The bookId is extracted from the request map (line 22), which we can access via the external context (lines19f). For the sake of simplicity, if the bookId is unknown or not an integer, we'll always create a new book (lines 24 and 28). In a mission-critical application, we would choose a different strategy, but for Books this is sufficient. Once the book is loaded or created, we turn the conversation into a long-running one, as seen in Listing 17-1.

© Michael Müller 2018
M. Müller, *Practical JSF in Java EE 8*, https://doi.org/10.1007/978-1-4842-3030-5_17

Listing 17-1. Excerpt of BookEditor.java

```java
1   [...]
2   @Named
3   @ConversationScoped
4   public class BookEditor implements Serializable {
5     [...]
6     @Inject Conversation _conversation;
7
8     @PostConstruct
9     private void init() {
10      [...]
11      loadOrCreateBook();
12      if (_conversation.isTransient()) {
13        _conversation.begin();
14      }
15
16
17    private void loadOrCreateBook() {
18      FacesContext fc = FacesContext.getCurrentInstance();
19      Map<String, String> paramMap = fc.getExternalContext()
20              .getRequestParameterMap();
21      try {
22        int bookId = Integer.parseInt(paramMap.get("bookId"));
23        _book = _bookService.find(bookId);
24        if (_book == null) {
25          _book = new Book();
26        }
27      } catch (NumberFormatException e) {
28        _book = new  Book();
29      }
30    }
31
32  [...]
33  }
```

Helped by CDI, we get an instance of `Conversation` injected into our `BookEditor` (line 6). For simplicity, we assume this is a fresh instance. Such a fresh instance acts in the so-called *transient* mode and will terminate with the current request. Until now, the `BookEditor` behaves like a request scoped bean. But a `Conversation` might become long running, as requested by our application. We'll prolong the conversation within the `init()` method. Due to the `@PostConstruct` annotation, this method is automatically called when the construction of the `BookEditor` finishes.

Anyway, it's important to first check whether the conversation is transient (not long running). Only in this state is it allowed to start the long run. In line 12 of Listing 17-1, we perform the check of whether the conversion isn't yet long-running as indicated by `isTransient()`. If this isn't the case, we start the long-running part by calling `begin()`.

Starting the long run is quite easy, but ending it can become complicated. Of course, it's nothing but calling `end()` on our conversation object. The only question is: when do we terminate the long-running mode? If the editor had a Save and Close button, this would be a wonderful candidate to store the data and quit the long-running mode of the conversation—after saving a book, the editor would be closed. But using Books, the user may save and stay in the open dialog. He may continue to edit, and so we can't end the conversation. Or the user may hit any navigation button to move to a different location—to create a new book, say, or edit another one. Having no single point for leaving the editor requires some more effort.

Let's examine when JSF will reuse an existing conversation or inject a new one. A book bean will be created every time it's used in a new request and either the conversation is transient, or, in the case of a long-running conversation, a new conversation is used. In such a case, the `init()` method is invoked. So we can track new conversations by tracking calls to this method, as seen in Listing 17-2.

Listing 17-2. `BookEditor.java: log init`

```
1   [...]
2   @Named
3   @ConversationScoped
4   public class BookEditor implements Serializable {
5       [...]
6       private static final Logger LOGGER = Logger.getLogger("BookEditor");
7
8       @PostConstruct
9       private void init() {
```

```
10        LOGGER.log(Level.INFO, "init in BookEditor");
11        [...]
12      }
13
14    [...]
15    }
```

Once the bean is prepared as such, it will log every creation (more precisely, it will log every time it's created by CDI—if created by a new, init wouldn't be called). Now we can invoke our book editor in different ways to observe the behavior.

For testing purposes, in Listing 17-3 we'll add two links to the book editor to the navigation section of adminTemplate.xhtml.

Listing 17-3. Test Links: Navigation to bookEditor.xhtml

```
1   <h:form>
2     <h:commandLink styleClass="button"
3                     value="#{msg.btnNewBook} commandLink"
4                     action="/admin/bookEditor.xhtml"/>
5   </h:form>
6   <h:link styleClass="button"
7           value="#{msg.btnNewBook} link"
8           outcome="/admin/bookEditor.xhtml"/>
```

DIFFERENCES BETWEEN THE LINK TAGS: TRY AND OBSERVE

1. Start Books and navigate to the book editor via the commandLink button.

2. When the book editor opens, click the commandLink button again.

3. Observe the log output live in NetBeans output, the GlassFish window.

4. Restart the application and repeat your observations using the link button.

commandLink and link provide different navigation models. commandLink implements a more traditional JSF navigation using a post back, but link, introduced with JSF 2.0, realizes a navigation via get. In the next section, we'll discuss the differences and the impact on conversation handling.

POST and GET Navigation

In HTML, you can use a form to gather data. As part of the form you can place a button below the input fields to submit the data to the server. In traditional HTML this data is transferred via an HTTP POST request to the server. This is a request to the same URL, which is why it's called a *postback*. And as a result, the server often sends back a confirmation that's displayed on a different page. This kind of navigation is called *postback navigation*. Before JSF 2.0, this was the common navigation model of JSF.

If you read articles about REST, you may know that an HTTP GET is used to retrieve a resource, whereas a POST is used to create one. And you may have read about JSF not implementing the original design goals of HTTP because of this postback navigation. As mentioned, postback navigation was the common navigation type before REST, so it's not against the principles of HTTP. If some evangelists want to tell you something else, don't believe them.

Although postback navigation feels like a natural navigation, there is one drawback: data is posted to the original URL while the response might display a fresh page. Thus, the URL shown in the browser is often one step behind. Because of this, some purists argue, JSF isn't bookmarkable. JSF often is used for applications, so what do you think: should an application be bookmarkable in every state? Or just for well-defined pages (entry points)?

To update the current URL in the browser's display, one strategy offered by JSF is a redirect: just after the postback, a GET to the target page is invoked. Or you can use a GET navigation with link.

Have you observed the browser's URL and the server's log from the previous exercise? Invoking the commandLink button for the first time doesn't update the URL to the book editor. This is a typical postback navigation. When the book editor is displayed for the first time, a new conversation is started (as indicated by the log). Subsequent clicks to this button will refresh (reload) the page, but won't start a conversation.

But if you use the link button, the URL directly points to the book editor. This is navigation by GET request. A new conversation is started with every click, and thus a new instance of the book editor is created with every click. Behind the scenes, CDI holds the former instances because the conversations are still running. We need to handle this.

Note   Using the postback navigation, JSF reuses an existing conversation. Using the GET navigation, JSF will create a new conversation.

As we will discuss later, it's possible to keep an existing conversation during a GET navigation.

Begin and End the Conversation

As shown in this chapter, we started the conversation within the init() method during the @PostConstruct. If the user saves the book information, she may stay on the editor page to continue editing, which means we have to keep the conversation. And there's no single exit point from the editor—the user may use any navigation offered by the navigation panel. To solve this issue, *every* navigation triggered by a navigation button will end the conversation.

In such a navigation case, we call a method to finish the current conversation, as shown in Listing 17-4.

Listing 17-4. Method to Stop a Long-Running Conversation

```
1    public void endConversation(Conversation conversation) {
2        if (!conversation.isTransient()) {
3            LOGGER.log(Level.INFO,
4            "Conversation stopping: {0}", conversation.getId());
5            conversation.end();
6        }
7    }
```

Summary

Most of CDI's predefined scopes have well-defined lifetimes that depend on the context of the request, session, or application. There is one scope (@ConversationScoped) that might be set into a programmatically controlled long-running mode. This allows the programmer to use a scope with a lifetime longer than a request, but different from a session or application.

A conversation might be transitioned into the long-running mode by begin() and put back to its shorter lifetime by end().

CHAPTER 18

Links

Books isn't just a list of reviewed books. You can also use it to create and display reviews. Aside from these *internal* reviews, most reviews are published somewhere else, in printed media and/or online. The goal of this chapter is to create a list of reviews that contains links to both internal and *external* reviews.

Internal Reviews

Links to internal reviews will be created from the review entities. Such an entity contains these properties:

- `Id`
- `BookId`
- `Date`
- `Language`
- `Text`
- `Book`

The last property isn't stored in the appropriate SQL table. The only reference to a book stored in the database is the `BookId`. But using the `Book` as additional property will enable us to display some information about the book itself without the need to code an additional database call. In SQL terms, we do a kind of select `...from Review join Book....` We simply need to define a relation, as shown in Listing 18-1. JPA will perform the SQL stuff. Listing 18-1 shows an excerpt of the `Review` class.

© Michael Müller 2018
M. Müller, *Practical JSF in Java EE 8*, https://doi.org/10.1007/978-1-4842-3030-5_18

Listing 18-1. Entity for Internal Reviews

```
 1 @Entity
 2 @Table(name = "Review")
 3 public class Review implements Serializable {
 4
 5   private static final long serialVersionUID = 1L;
 6
 7   // <editor-fold defaultstate="collapsed" desc="Property Id">
 8   @Id
 9   @GeneratedValue(strategy = GenerationType.IDENTITY)
10   @Column(name = "rvId")
11   private Integer _id;
12
13   public Integer getId() {
14     return _id;
15   }
16
17   public void setId(Integer id) {
18     _id = id;
19   }
20     // </editor-fold>
21
22   // <editor-fold defaultstate="collapsed" desc="Property BookId">
23   @Column(name = "rvBookId")
24   private Integer _bookId;
25
26   public Integer getBookId() {
27     return _bookId;
28   }
29
30   public void setBookId(Integer bookId) {
31     _bookId = bookId;
32   }
33     // </editor-fold>
34
```

```
35  // <editor-fold defaultstate="collapsed" desc="Property Book">
36  @ManyToOne
37  @JoinColumn(name = "rvBookId", insertable = false, updatable = false)
38  private Book _book;
39
40  public Book getBook() {
41    return _book;
42  }
43  // </editor-fold>
44
45  [... other fields, hashCode etc. omitted for brevity...]
46
47 }
```

The book is referenced in lines 36–42. You can write a couple reviews (for example, using different languages) for the same book. That's why we use a many-to-one relationship here. We assume that the book we write a review for exists in the database. When we store the review, we need to include a reference to the book. In the database table, we only need a column for the BookId (lines 23–32). The property book I mentioned before is retrieved from the database by exactly this id.

So far, we have two properties that depend on that one property. JPA doesn't allow two properties writing the same column. We need to declare one of them as not writeable. Because we only want to save the bookId and not the entire book, we advise JPA to ignore the bookId of the book property for inserts and updates (line 37).

External Reviews

The external links are stored in their own table. As for reviews, we create a convenient property of type Book. Listing 18-2 shows how.

Listing 18-2. Entity to Manage Links to External Reviews

```
1  @Entity
2  @Table(name = "ReviewLink")
3  public class ReviewLink implements Serializable {
4
```

```
 5     private static final long serialVersionUID = 1L;
 6
 7     @Id
 8     @GeneratedValue(strategy = GenerationType.IDENTITY)
 9     @Column(name = "Id")
10     private Integer _id;
11
12     @Column(name = "BookId")
13     private Integer _bookId;
14
15     @Column(name = "LanguageCode")
16     private String _language;
17
18     @Column(name = "URI")
19     private String _URI;
20
21     [getter/setter omitted]
22
23     @ManyToOne
24     @JoinColumn(name = "BookId", insertable = false, updatable = false)
25     private Book _book;
26
27     public Book getBook() {
28       return _book;
29     }
30
31     [HashCode and more omitted]
32   }
```

Listing 18-2 shows an excerpt of the ReviewLink class. Accessing the book (lines 23ff) is quite similar that described for the Review class.

JSF Links

JSF offers three different tags to create a link. How do they differ, and which one would be appropriate to perform this goal? Table 18-1 lists these tags.

Table 18-1. *JSF Tags for Creating a Link*

Tag Name	Description
commandLink	Renders an HTML link <a href=...> that also performs a submit.
link	Renders an HTML link <a href=...> that can be used for bookmarkable JSF navigation.
outputLink	Renders an HTML link <a href=...> that's mostly used to navigate outside the app.

commandLink

commandLink is the classic JSF link. Indeed, it renders an HTML link element but acts more like a submit element. While rendering the commandLink, JSF assigns a function call to the element's onClick event. This function, located in the JSF JavaScript library, dynamically adds a hidden input element and performs a submit. This approach is transparent to the developer.

A Submit element would perform a POST request. This is HTML standard for submitting forms. Thus, the commandLink needs to be nested into an <h:form> element. A POST request sends data for the current URI. If a commandLink is used to navigate to another page, the browser still displays the former URI while displaying the new page. With this kind of navigation, the URI displayed in the browser's headline is one page behind.

link

The link tag was introduced in JSF 2.0 to enable JSF navigation using GET requests. A GET request is the same one you use when you enter a URI directly into your browser. The server sends the content of the requested page, and using the GET navigation, the browser displays the URI of the current page. Because of that, the URI becomes bookmarkable.

outputLink

The outputLink tag is the classic tag to create an HTML link element for a GET request. As its name suggests, it's used to navigate outside your application. Using this tag, you simply create links, not JSF navigation, but you can use it to navigate within your application.

Choosing the Right Link

The postback navigation is no problem if the user starts our application with a defined entry point—for example, a login page. Maybe you offer your user some additional starting points for the application. Once the application is started, it follows its workflow. The user acts within the application without caring about the URI. In such a case, it doesn't matter—the URI is one step behind.

In case of Books, the review list should link to reviews. These reviews will be direct addressable. They should also be searchable by a search engine, so we need to access them via GET request. commandLink won't fit these requirements.

But which of the other two link elements is best? Or do we need both? Before I discuss them, I invite you to figure out the behavior by yourself in the next exercise.

 Investigating Links

Create a new web application called testLinks and add the JSF framework. As JSF servlet URL pattern, use *.xhtml. You may want to revisit TinyCalculator and read up on how to create such an app using NetBeans.

NetBeans will automatically create the page index.xhtml during application setup. If you're using a different IDE, you may need to create such a page by yourself. Add a second page, page2.xhtml.

To the index.xhtml page, add <h:link...> (outcome="link") as well as <h:outputLink...> (value="link") with the following targets:

- /page2
- /page2.xhtml

- /testLink/page2

- /testLink/page2.xhtml

- http://it-rezension.de

Run the project and try and observe the links.

Listing 18-3 shows a simple version of the index.xhtml page. It's not very sophisticated—just for demonstration.

Listing 18-3. Link Demo (testLink) index.xhtml

```
1    <?xml version='1.0' encoding='UTF-8' ?>
2    <!DOCTYPE html">
3    <html xmlns="http://www.w3.org/1999/xhtml"
4          xmlns:h="http://xmlns.jcp.org/jsf/html">
5      <h:head>
6        <title>Facelet Title</title>
7      </h:head>
8      <h:body>
9        Hello from Facelets
10
11       <div>
12         <h:link value="/page2" outcome="/page2"/>
13       </div>
14       <div>
15         <h:link value="/page2.xhtml" outcome="/page2.xhtml"/>
16       </div>
17       <div>
18         <h:link value="/testLink/page2" outcome="/testLink/page2"/>
19       </div>
20       <div>
21         <h:link value="/testLink/page2.xhtml" outcome="/testLink/page2.
             xhtml"/>
22       </div>
23       <div>
```

217

```
24          <h:link value="http://it-rezension.de" outcome="http://it-
            rezension.de"/>
25
26      </div>
27      <hr/>
28      <div>
29        <h:outputLink value="/page2">
30          /page2
31        </h:outputLink>
32      </div>
33      <div>
34        <h:outputLink value="/page2.xhtml">
35          /page2.xhtml
36        </h:outputLink>
37      </div>
38      <div>
39        <h:outputLink value="/testLinks/page2">
40          /testLinks/page2
41        </h:outputLink>
42      </div>
43      <div>
44        <h:outputLink value="/testLinks/page2.xhtml">
45          /testLinks/page2.xhtml
46        </h:outputLink>
47      </div>
48      <div>
49        <h:outputLink value="http://it-rezension.de">
50          http://it-rezension.de
51        </h:outputLink>
52      </div>
53
54    </h:body>
55  </html>
```

Figure 18-1 shows the output.

```
Hello from Facelets
/page2
/page2.xhtml
/testLink/page2: This link is disabled because a navigation case could not be matched.
/testLink/page2.xhtml: This link is disabled because a navigation case could not be matched.
http://it-rezension.de: This link is disabled because a navigation case could not be matched.

/page2
/page2.xhtml
/testLinks/page2
/testLinks/page2.xhtml
http://it-rezension.de

   • Unable to find matching navigation case from view ID '/index.xhtml' for outcome '/testLink/page2'
   • Unable to find matching navigation case from view ID '/index.xhtml' for outcome '/testLink/page2.xhtml'
   • Unable to find matching navigation case from view ID '/index.xhtml' for outcome 'http://it-rezension.de'
```

Figure 18-1. *Output of* testLink

link creates links both for /page2 and /page2.xhtml, but no other. If you omit the file extension, JSF automatically adds the .xhtml. The slash / determines the root within our application—*not* an absolute path.

/testLink is the context path of the application, a kind of "outside the application." And the link to my review page points to a different website. link is used for a JSF navigation and as such, for any other link, it can't find a navigation.

On the other hand, outputLink simply creates every link we provide, as specified. If not provided, JSF automatically precedes the current host to complete the link. Thus /page2 becomes http://localhost:8080/page2. Such a link would point to a nonexisting page. Only /testLinks/page2.xhtml and http://itrezension.de point to existing pages.

Draw the Conclusion

link can only be used for internal navigation. outputLink might be used for external as well for internal links. For an internal link, the context path needs to be added.

For the review list, (at least) two alternative solutions might be used:

- Use both link and outputLink together with a condition that selects the appropriate element depending on the kind of link. Listing 18-4 shows the principle of this approach.

- Or always use an outputLink for both internal and external links. For internal links, you need to add the context path to the page's address, making the URI fully qualified.

Books uses the second approach.

Listing 18-4. Principle of Determining Internal versus External Link

```
1   <h:link rendered="#{review.intern}" .../>
2   <h:outputLink rendered="#{not review.intern}" .../>
```

Listing 18-5. Excerpt of reviewList.xhtml

```
1   <h:outputLink value="#{review.url}"
2                 target="#{review.intern ? '_self' : '_blank'}">
3     #{review.title}
4   </h:outputLink>
```

External links are stored in the ReviewLink table. They define a complete URI and are used as stored in the database. Internal links are created dynamically by appending the bookId and language to the page and prefixing it with the context path. The context path is available from the external context of the Faces context, as shown in Listing 18-6.

Listing 18-6. Creation of Internal Links

```
1   private String buildUrl(int bookId, String language) {
2     String path = FacesContext.getCurrentInstance()
3             .getExternalContext().getRequestContextPath();
4     return path + Page.UserReview.getUrl() +
5             "?bookId=" + bookId + "&language=" + language;
6   }
```

buildUrl is part of the ReviewInfo.class.

Summary

JSF offers three different type of links. commandLink renders an HTML link (href element). While rendering this link, JSF adds an onClick handler redirecting this link to an input submit element. As a result, such a link initiates a postback navigation.

`link` renders a real link that's used for a JSF navigation case (internal navigation), whereas the intention `outputLink` creates a link element that's not used for regular JSF navigation but for navigating to an external page. Anyway, we can use it for a navigation within our application.

CHAPTER 19

Responsive Design

Some years ago, it was common to develop web applications with a fixed-width page size of 960 pixels. This size was a good choice for the popular 17-inch desktop monitor displays.

Times have changed. Desktops and modern laptops have high-resolution screens, and many people are using quite large screens. Full HD for example is 1920 pixels wide. Even if this allows more information on the screen, you won't use more than about 1200 pixels per line to keep the text readable. The rise of mobile devices like tablets and smartphones dominates the marketplace with applications running on smaller displays, starting with less than 400 pixels. Although the physical resolution of a modern smartphone sometimes is better than full HD, they often use *logical* pixels, which are built up by a group of physical pixels. The challenge is to create web pages and applications that automatically adapt to the resolutions of large, medium, *and* small screens. This is achieved with *responsive design*. You may read about *adaptive design*, which also adapts to the screen resolution. The two techniques are a little different, but we'll ignore these small differences in this book.

This chapter introduces some techniques to make the application responsive to various screen sizes.

Making Books Responsive

The application Books uses an easy form of such a responsive design. On a PC, this can be simulated by resizing the browser window. Figures 19-1 through 19-4 show how the Books application automatically changes its layout in response to the changing window size.

© Michael Müller 2018
M. Müller, *Practical JSF in Java EE 8*, https://doi.org/10.1007/978-1-4842-3030-5_19

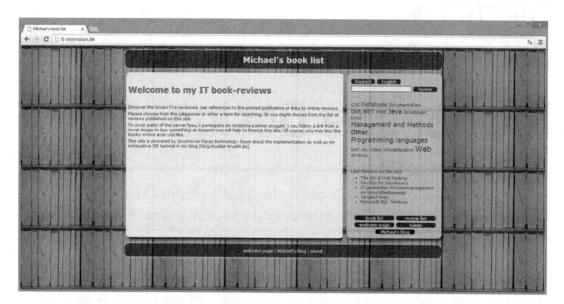

Figure 19-1. *Books on wide display*

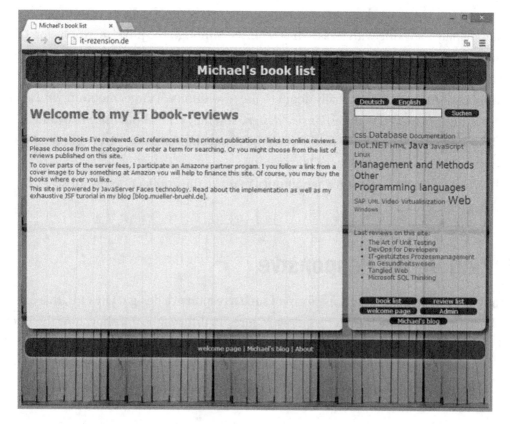

Figure 19-2. *Books on mid-sized display*

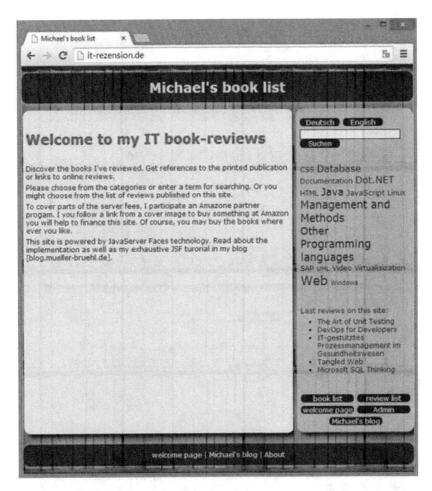

Figure 19-3. *Books on tablet-sized display*

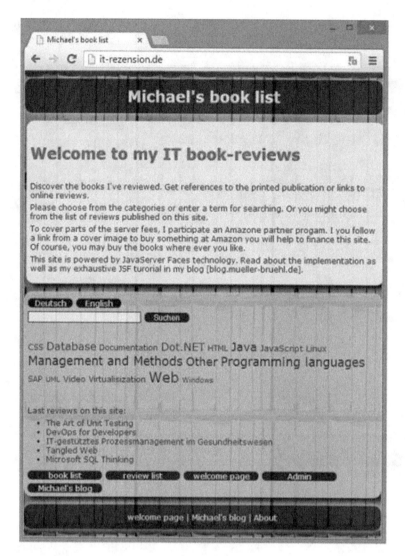

Figure 19-4. *Books on smartphone-sized display*

To make the application responsive, there's no need to change the code or content of the application. The application is made responsive by modifying its CSS layout.

As the previous figures show, there are different display strategies depending on the screen size used. As a software developer, I assume you personally use a high-resolution screen. You can simulate different device sizes by resizing your browser window. Let's start with a full screen and the reduce the window size.

For a wide display, the content and navigation size are limited by a maximum size. We use this maximum size to keep the content readable. If the browser window width is more than that, we add a margin to center the content. If you reduce the window size, the margins left and right will be reduced, keeping the size of content and navigation. Then, at a certain width, the strategy changes: the width of content and navigation will be reduced according to the window size. At another particular width, the strategy changes again: the navigation is displayed below the content. These special widths, where the display strategy is changed, are called *breakpoints*.

The trick is to apply different styles depending on the size of the screen. Especially for mobile devices, some manufacturers apply a kind of logical pixel size to their *viewport* (the visible area of the browser window), which may differ from the real pixel size. So, we need to prepare this scaling with a simple entry in the `<h:head>` section of our JSF template, as shown in Listing 19-1.

Listing 19-1. Scaling of the Viewport in `booksTemplate.xhtml`

```
1    <meta name="viewport" content="width=device-width, initial-scale=1.0"/>
```

Next, we define the breakpoints using media queries. *Media queries* start with `@media`, followed by the media's name, such as `@media screen` or `@media print`. There are also two more options: `speech` (for speech synthesizers) and `all` (used for all devices). Although first recommended in 1994, media queries were widely introduced with HTML 4 and CSS 2 for tailoring styles to different media. Driving responsive design became possible when other attributes like `width` were added. This scheme became a W3C recommended standard in 2012.

For implementing a responsive design, we'll use media queries for the screen in conjunction with the viewport size to decide which styles we want to apply. We'll define the breakpoints, the discrete sizes at which the styles will change.

But first, let's take a look into the relevant excerpt of the CSS file, shown in Listing 19-2.

Listing 19-2. Excerpt from `books.css` Before Becoming Responsive

```
1    body > div {
2      width: 80em;
3      margin: 0 auto;
4      text-align: left;
5    }
6
7    main {
```

```
8        min-height: 40em;
9        width: 53em;
10       opacity: 0.95;
11       border-radius: 1em;
12       background-color: #eeeef3;
13       padding: 1em;
14       margin-bottom: 1em;
15       box-shadow: 0.5em 0.5em 0.5em #004
16     }
17
18   nav{
19       min-height: 40em;
20       position: fixed;
21       margin-left: 56em;
22       width: 22em;
23       padding: 1em;
24       top: 7.5em;
25       opacity: 0.85;
26       border-radius: 1em;
27       background-color: #ccccd8;
28       box-shadow: 0.5em 0.5em 0.5em #004
29     }
```

Remember, body > div declares some attributes of the application's space. Using a relative unit (em) for the width allows for growing or shrinking the space as the user changes the browser's font size. But we have to choose our breakpoints according to the screen size, which is given in pixels.

The content of our application on a wide viewport uses 80em. If the viewport's width is more than that, the browser adds some empty space on the right or left. Shrinking the window will reduce this space. If the viewport's size becomes smaller than our maximum content size, we need to shrink the content width. Thus, the first breakpoint seems to be reached when the viewport width is equal or less than the width of the body div element.

Caution   Although it's possible to use em for the media width, that results in some funny behavior. Suppose we define a breakpoint at 60em. Below that size, we'll reduce the font size in pixels, and that will change the width of 1em. In other words, we'll change our scale base. Shrinking the viewport to less than these 60em will suddenly result in a viewport with of more than 60em. Can you imagine what would happen? It's really unexpected. A rule of thumb: don't alter the scale base of your breakpoints.

It's best to define exact pixels for the screen width. So, we need to calculate pixels from our width:

$$\textit{Width in pixels} = \textit{Width in em} \times \textit{Font size in pixels}$$

Because we defined a default font size of 12 pixels, the width is 80em × 12px = 960px.

If the screen size is smaller than that, the application size must be reduced. If no size is defined, the size is determined by the browser's display width. Thus, it's possible to omit the width. We only need to define a maximum width for large browser windows. To do that, we'll replace line 2's `width: 80em` with `max-width: 80em`. No special breakpoint is needed.

The main part is 53em plus padding left and right, which is 1em each. Thus, we get a total width of 55em. This is 55/80 × 100% = 68.75% of our 80em width. If we shrink the window, we'd first like to shrink the main part too by keeping this relative size. In our application, 1em equates to 1/80 × 100% = 1.25%. Using this information, we can refine all widths by replacing the em sizes with percent sizes.

Caution   Sizes in percent are relative sizes. Beware: these aren't relative to the screen but to the surrounding container.

If we shrink the width, fewer characters of text may be displayed in each line. But we don't change the line's height, so in many cases it's best to keep vertical sizes in em.

For the responsive design, we divide our main and nav classes into two parts. One of them contains all styles that are independent from the viewport width (see Listing 19-3, lines 7–20), whereas the other parts contain viewport-dependent styles. These parts will be different for each breakpoint. Lines 23–37 use the original values as seen in the previous listing.

Listing 19-3. Excerpt from books.css, First Responsive Approach

```
1   body > div {
2     max-width: 80em;
3     margin: 0 auto;
4     text-align: left;
5   }
6
7   main {
8     opacity: 0.95;
9     border-radius: 1em;
10    background-color: #eeeef3;
11    margin-bottom: 1em;
12    box-shadow: 0.5em 0.5em 0.5em #004;
13  }
14
15  nav{
16    opacity: 0.85;
17    border-radius: 1em;
18    background-color: #ccccd8;
19    box-shadow: 0.5em 0.5em 0.5em #004;
20  }
21
22  @media screen and (min-width: 960px){
23    main {
24      min-height: 40em;
25      width: 53em;
26      padding: 1em;
27    }
28
29    nav{
30      min-height: 40em;
31      position: fixed;
32      margin-left: 56em;
33      width: 22em;
34      top: 7.5em;
```

```
35      padding: 1em;
36    }
37  }
38
39  @media screen and (min-width: 600px) and (max-width: 960px){
40    main {
41      min-height: 45em;
42      width: 66.25%;
43      padding: 1.25%;
44    }
45
46    nav{
47      min-height: 45em;
48      position: fixed;
49      margin-left: 70%;
50      width: 27.5%;
51      padding: 1.25%;
52      top: 7.5em;
53    }
54  }
55
56  @media screen and (max-width: 600px){
57    main {
58      width: 97.5%;
59      padding: 1.25%;
60    }
61
62    nav{
63      width: 97.5%;
64      padding: 1.25%;
65      bottom: 1em;
66    }
67  }
```

In line 22 you'll find the first media query. It applies to a viewport size on the screen with a minimum width of 960px. Every style declaration between the opening curly brace on that line and the corresponding closing one on line 37 will be applied to the HTML page if, and only if, that minimum width condition is true. The next breakpoint is reached with a size of 960px. Within the condition of the corresponding media query, we define the width as mentioned before in percent, not in em (lines 39–54). If the size is less than 600px, we rearrange the navigation now being displayed below the main content. As you can see, media queries are enhanced by one or more width conditions. I assume these are mostly self-explanatory.

There's one important detail to talk about. Look at Listing 19-4.

Listing 19-4. Cascaded Media Queries

```
1   @media screen and (min-width: 960px){...}
2   @media screen and (min-width: 600px) and (max-width: 960px){...}
3   @media screen and (max-width: 600px){...}
```

In this definition, `max-width` of the smaller screen (or window) equals the `min-width` of the bigger screen. Are these overlappings okay? Listing 19-5 seems to show a better way.

Listing 19-5. Cascaded Media Queries, Nonoverlapping

```
1   @media screen and (min-width: 960px){...}
2   @media screen and (min-width: 600px) and (max-width: 959px){...}
3   @media screen and (max-width: 599px){...}
```

Now the sizes don't overlap, and this is what you'll find in some books or blogs talking about responsive design. At a first glance, such a nonoverlapping definition seems to be correct. But it really isn't: we now have *two* gaps, one between 959 and 960px, and the other between 599 and 600px. Eh?

Try an experiment: replace the media queries with the nonoverlapping version. Start with a wide browser window and reduce its width. When you reach a breakpoint, slowly increase and reduce the window size and observe what happens. Depending on your system or browser settings (you may have fonts enlarged, or the browser window zoomed), most browsers will display the navigation below the main content when you reach the breakpoint. That's because there's a 1-pixel gap and a calculated size just between both definitions. None of the definitions will be used, so the navigation won't be displayed as expected.

Take a look at Figure 19-5. Here the browser calculates a width of 959.167px, which falls into this 1-pixel gap.

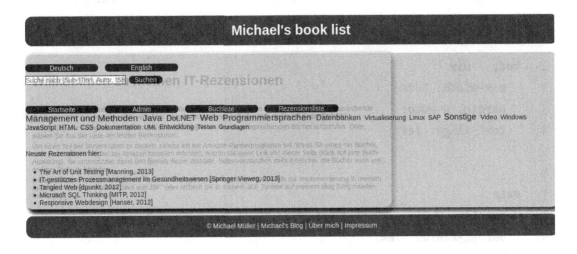

Figure 19-5. *Width = 959.167px*

Due to this problem, Books uses the overlapping approach. To avoid ambiguity, CSS uses the last definition found in the CSS file.

In our first responsive approach, we still use em for the wide viewport size. But because the container is restricted to 80em, even if the viewport is wider, relative sizes in percent in the main part can't grow. So we can use the same sizes as used for the smaller window in percent.

The navigation floats out of the body > div container. Its container is the display area of your browser, and it will grow as the window grows. To keep the navigation size, it still has to be defined using em. This said, we can refactor the style sheet. See Listing 19-6.

Listing 19-6. Excerpt from books.css, Refined Responsive Definition

```
1   body > div {
2       max-width: 80em;
3       margin: 0 auto;
4       text-align: left;
5   }
6
7   main {
8       opacity: 0.95;
9       border-radius: 1em;
10      background-color: #eeeef3;
11      margin-bottom: 1em;
12      box-shadow: 0.5em 0.5em 0.5em #004;
13  }
14
15  nav{
16      opacity: 0.85;
17      border-radius: 1em;
18      background-color: #ccccd8;
19      box-shadow: 0.5em 0.5em 0.5em #004;
20  }
21
22  @media screen and (min-width: 600px){
23      main {
24          width: 66.25%;
25          padding: 1.25%;
26      }
27
```

```
28    nav{
29      position: fixed;
30      top: 7.5em;
31    }
32  }
33
34  @media screen and (min-width: 960px){
35    main, nav {
36      min-height: 40em;
37    }
38
39    nav{
40      margin-left: 56em;
41      width: 22em;
42      padding: 1em;
43    }
44  }
45
46  @media screen and (min-width: 600px) and (max-width: 960px){
47    main, nav {
48      min-height: 45em;
49    }
50
51    nav{
52      margin-left: 70%;
53      width: 27.5%;
54      padding: 1.25%;
55    }
56  }
57
58  @media screen and (max-width: 600px){
59    main {
60      width: 97.5%;
61      padding: 1.25%;
62    }
```

```
63
64    nav{
65      width: 97.5%;
66      padding: 1.25%;
67      bottom: 1em;
68    }
69  }
```

In line 22 you'll find a common definition for all sizes greater than or equal to 600px.

Responsive Pixel Layouts

As we've seen, making a layout that's responsive isn't too hard. Luckily, we created our first (nonresponsive) version of the layout sizes relative not to the screen, but to the font size. However, many pages are designed with pixel dimensions. Here the transition needs a little more effort, as Listing 19-7 shows.

Let's assume the original layout had been designed to be accurate using pixels.

Listing 19-7. Excerpt of a Pixel-Dimensioned Layout

```
1   main {
2     min-height: 500px;
3     width: 640px;
4     opacity: 0.95;
5     border-radius: 10px;
6     background-color: #eeeef3;
7     padding: 10px;
8     margin-bottom: 10px;
9     box-shadow: 5px 5px 5px #004
10  }
11
12  nav{
13    min-height: 500px;
14    position: fixed;
15    margin-left: 670px;
16    width: 270px;
```

```
17      padding: 10px;
18      top: 90px;
19      opacity: 0.85;
20      border-radius: 10px;
21      background-color: #ccccd8;
22      box-shadow: 5px 5px 5px #004
23    }
```

Beware, it's not the same! For example, nav's left margin is 670px, whereas the original layout used 56em = 672px. Here, the designer preferred sizes that can be divided by 10, or at least by 5. In my experience, this is typical for a layout that's been designed on fixed pixel counts.

Most books on responsive design start with an example of how to make a pixel layout responsive. The common method suggested is to calculate the relative width of one pixel and multiply every pixel width by that accurate factor. Let's do that:

Total width = 960 pixels, thus one pixel is $1/960 \times 100\%$ = 0.1041666666666667%.

640px = $640 \times 0.1041666666666667\%$ = 66.66666666666667%.

670px = $670 \times 0.1041666666666667\%$ = 69.79166666666667%.

And so on.

Now the CSS looks ugly. In most instances, such accuracy isn't needed. Get up the nerve to round these values to, at most, two-fraction digits. Trust me when I say users won't notice any difference.

Calculating Sizes

Listing 19-8 calculates some sizes.

Listing 19-8. Excerpt of Navigation Layout

```
1    @media screen and (min-width: 960px){
2      nav{
3        margin-left: 56em;
4        width: 22em;
5        padding: 1em;
```

```
 6      }
 7    }
 8
 9    @media screen and (min-width: 600px) and (max-width: 960px){
10      nav{
11        margin-left: 70%;
12        width: 27.5%;
13        padding: 1.25%;
14      }
15    }
```

By shrinking the screen size, we switched from a padding, which is relative to the current font size, to the percent dimension, which is relative to the surrounding container. That means the padding itself will be diminished. Sometimes it's useful to keep the padding relative to the font size. Using CSS 3, it's no problem to mix different dimensions and keep accuracy.

In our example, the element width plus its padding will result into a total width of 1.25% + 27.5% + 1.25% = 30%. Let's assume we have a requirement to keep the padding of 1em. Then the element width has to be 30 percent minus 2em. And that's exactly what you can do:

```
width: calc(30% - 2em);
```

I assumed the padding will be added to the box width. That's what most browsers do. (Old versions of Internet Explorer declare width including the padding and border.) Using CSS 3, you can change the behavior of box sizing in such a way that the width includes the padding and the borders (by `box-sizing: border-box;`).

Tip   You can read about the CSS box model at W3Schools. Check out `www.w3schools.com/css/css_boxmodel.asp` and `www.w3schools.com/cssref/css3_pr_box-sizing.asp`.

Mobile-First and Desktop-First

At first Books was developed for desktop computers only. Then with the rise of mobile devices came a need to adapt it to smaller screen sizes. This procedure is what today is called a *desktop-first* approach.

Books simply places the navigation at the bottom when the screen size shrinks. Usually, for a small-sized screen, the height is very limited. It may be a good idea to replace the navigation by a folding menu to save some space. This can be solved by CSS also. Mobile devices sometimes only have smaller bandwidth (cellular network speed) available. So, often I advise reducing the user interface. For example, you may omit the background image. Or you may have to reduce content.

The latter might become a hard job. Which parts are less important and can be eliminated? With that question in mind, lots of people prefer a *mobile-first* approach: develop an application with a minimal interface, and then adapt it to larger screens, adding some decorative padding.

Don't worry about people saying one or the other approach is best. Just do it your way.

Summary

Some years ago an application could be designed for a certain screen resolution, but today we need to consider different kinds of screens and sizes. Users may not use a desktop PC only. We have to consider laptop sizes, tablets, and other mobile devices. Because we can't expect the user to scroll long content on small screens, we need to adapt the content of our application pages to different screen sizes.

One key technique to make a web application *responsive* is to define different breakpoints within CSS's media queries. This chapter showed a pure CSS approach. That might be complemented by the aid of JavaScript, which we'll use for the Alumni application.

To create a responsive application, you can start with a mobile layout first (mobile-first) or a desktop layout (desktop-first).

CHAPTER 20

Summary and Perspective

Books is an application intended to be managed by mainly one author, publishing for many readers. We expect the author of the reviews (that's me) to know how to interact with the application. That means we can have a reduced set of requirements regarding the user interface, especial with regard to validating input. Nevertheless, Books is a fully fledged interactive web application.

After going over basic JSF tags for forms and text (in our discussions of TinyCalculator), we discussed more JSF features like loops, conditions, tables, and the different kinds of links, as well as more advanced features like templating. We outlined how JSF integrates with other Java EE technologies. Books takes advantage of the Java Persistence API (JPA), Context and Dependency Injection (CDI), and bean validation. We discussed some aspects of internationalization and how to make the application responsive to different screen sizes using CSS.

The source code for the Books application is available as a zip file for download from `http://webdevelopment-java.info/webdevelopment/resources/download/BooksComplete.zip`. To open the compressed archive, use the password `MdkJ47(kq!`. If you check the code, you'll find some techniques not discussed so far. For example, there's a rare usage of `<f:ajax>`. These techniques will be described in the next part.

Speaking of the next part, the next application, Alumni, is designed to be a social platform. All users need to be registered and will enter data. We'll need to discuss security and increase our requirements for the user interface. All user input has to be validated, and the user should obtain immediate responses. Validators, AJAX, authentication, custom components, and more will all be introduced in the context of working with Alumni.

© Michael Müller 2018
M. Müller, *Practical JSF in Java EE 8*, https://doi.org/10.1007/978-1-4842-3030-5_20

PART III

Intermezzo

CHAPTER 21

Intermezzo

So far, we've talked about two web applications, TinyCalculator and Books. In this part, we will discuss some aspects of web development with JSF detached from developing concrete applications.

© Michael Müller 2018
M. Müller, *Practical JSF in Java EE 8*, https://doi.org/10.1007/978-1-4842-3030-5_21

Intermezzo

CHAPTER 22

JSF Lifecycle Revisited

Let's recall JSF's lifecycle. There are six phases, starting with the restore view phase. Or, in the case of a new page, the view has to be created. Figure 22-1 should refresh your memory of the JSF lifecycle.

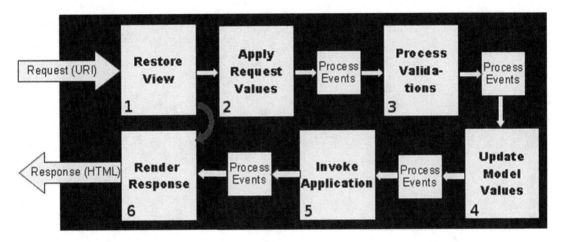

Figure 22-1. *JSF lifecycle*

As a main part of the view, the component tree has to be (re-)created during phase 1. This tree is a logical representation of the UI components. HTML components will be derived from the component tree during the render phase (phase 6). But there may not be a one-to-one relationship between UI components and HTML components.

Among other things, a JSF tag is interpreted as *tag handler* or as *UI component*. A tag handler is processed while creating the component tree, but it wouldn't be included itself within the tree. On the other hand, UI components *will* become part of the component tree. And during the render phase, one component might be used to create a couple HTML elements.

247

M. Müller, *Practical JSF in Java EE 8*, https://doi.org/10.1007/978-1-4842-3030-5_22

You may imagine tag handlers as processing instructions to build the tree, and UI components as processing instructions to create the output. The next chapter will discuss such matters using the example of repetitive structures.

CHAPTER 23

Repetitive Structures

So far, we've used three different tags for repetitive structures:

- c:forEach
- ui:repeat
- h:dataTable

In this chapter we'll discuss the differences and coverage among these.

The first two elements are used to repeat everything between the opening and closing tags. As a developer, it's up to you to choose the right structure within the HTML. Without a special structure, you may simply concatenate strings to a paragraph. Or you may nest it within a table tag and repeat the rows to render a table. Or you might create a list using the HTML <ul> or <ol> elements with nested items (<li>). Whatever you choose to do, you have full control.

As its name suggests, the third element, h:dataTable, repeats its content within the predefined structure of an HTML table. This offers fewer options but a simpler way to create tables.

Tag Handler vs. Component

forEach is a tag handler, whereas the other two elements are components. Remember, a tag handler comes to life during the compilation of the component tree. When the component tree is built, JSF adds the enclosed components for each cycle of the loop.

Consider the forEach tag handler: it's simply an instruction for a repetitive processing of its child elements, as shown in Listing 23-1.

© Michael Müller 2018
M. Müller, *Practical JSF in Java EE 8*, https://doi.org/10.1007/978-1-4842-3030-5_23

Listing 23-1. `c:forEach` Example, Facelets Source

```
1   <c:forEach items="#{controller.friends}" var="friend">
2     <div>
3       <h:outputText value="#{friend.name}"/>
4     </div>
5   </c:forEach>
```

Let's assume the friend list contains three friends: three names are displayed. If you examine the rendered HTML page (in Firefox, for example, you can press Ctrl+U to display the HTML source), you'll see three divs with the names, as you might have expected, as shown in Listing 23-2.

Listing 23-2. `c:forEach` Example, Rendered HTML

```
1   <div>Sally
2   </div>
3   <div>Bob
4   </div>
5   <div>John
6   </div>
```

In Listing 23-3 you can take a look at similar logic, except using repeat instead of forEach.

Listing 23-3. `ui:repeat` Example

```
1   <ui:repeat value="#{controller.friends}" var="friend">
2     <div>
3       <h:outputText value="#{friend.name}"/>
4     </div>
5   </ui:repeat>
```

If you run this example (as part of a complete page), you'll get the same output, visually and as HTML code. Where is the difference?

Well, one observable difference is the component tree. Figure 23-1 shows the component tree for both structures. As a result of the forEach (tag handler), three outputTexts will be inserted into the component tree. The tag handler itself won't be inserted. On the other hand, repeat (a component) itself is inserted into the component tree and just one nested outputText. That's two components as defined in the source page, and no repetition.

Figure 23-1. *Component tree*

The repetition takes place as recently as the render output phase is invoked. If we want to display three friends, the body of forEach will be repeated three times and will insert three names belonging to three diffs. As a result, the HTML source of both structures will be the same.

If you use a tag handler for your loop, the loop is iterated while building the component tree. If you use a component, it will show up only once within the component tree. Iteration takes place while interpreting the tree (rendering the page).

Other than the component tree, there's no observable difference in this short example. But it wouldn't be hard to imagine that the different timing and different component tree might result in distinctly different behavior, depending on the complexity of the application.

Let's examine a slightly modified example of the forEach loop, as shown in Listing 23-4.

Listing 23-4. c:forEach Example with Condition

```
1   <c:forEach items="#{controller.friends}" var="friend">
2     <c:if test="#{friend.name.length() > 0}">
3       <div>
4         <h:outputText value="#{friend.name}"/>
5       </div>
6     </c:if>
7   </c:forEach>
```

The only difference is an additional test for non-empty names. Because all friends have names, the output is still the same.

Next, in Listing 23-5, we'll modify the repeat in the same manner.

Listing 23-5. ui:repeat Example with Condition

```
1   <ui:repeat value="#{controller.friends}" var="friend">
2     <c:if test="#{friend.name.length() > 0}">
3       <div>
4         <h:outputText value="#{friend.name}"/>
5       </div>
6     </c:if>
7   </ui:repeat>
```

If you run the preceding example, no name will be displayed.

TAG HANDLER VS. COMPONENT PUZZLER

Run the preceding examples and think about what happened. Try to figure it out on your own before you continue reading. How could you modify the display condition to get it right?

Because a tag handler is interpreted during the compile time (of the component tree), all information must be available at that time too. At compile time, a component is simply inserted into the tree. It's processed during the render phase.

Although that's a simplified view, it's sufficient to describe what happened: forEach and if are both tag handlers. While compiling the tree, the loop is performed and the condition is checked. So far, everything is okay. But repeat is a component, which means the loop isn't performed until the render phase. At compile time, no loop is performed, no variable friend is known, and thus, no test becomes true.

One possible solution is to use the component panelGroup. Using layout="block" in conjunction with any style class, this will render a div, if and only if the rendered condition becomes true. Within a component, the condition is evaluated during the same phase as the loop is performed. If you omit either the layout or styleClass, then JSF won't insert a div and your browser will display all names on a single line. See Listing 23-6.

Listing 23-6. ui:repeat Example Using Rendered

```
1   <ui:repeat value="#{controller.friends}" var="friend">
2     <h:panelGroup rendered="#{friend.name.length() > 0}"
3                   layout="block"  styleClass="dummy">
4       <h:outputText value="#{friend.name}"/>
5     </h:panelGroup>
6   </ui:repeat>
```

Using a predefined JSF tag (panelGroup) requires some useless effort. An HTML-friendly approach seems much clearer, as you can see in Listing 23-7.

Listing 23-7. ui:repeat Example Using an HTML-Friendly Approach

```
1   <ui:repeat value="#{controller.friends}" var="friend">
2     <div jsf:rendered="#{friend.name.length() > 0}">
3       <h:outputText value="#{friend.name}"/>
4     </div>
5   </ui:repeat>
```

Performance Issues

Take a look at the source code of loopDemo in Listing 23-8 and recap your knowledge of the forEach loop. Within the method getNames() we'll print a short message. What do you think: how many times will a single call to loopDemo invoke that method? Not even once, once, or three times?

Listing 23-8. Loop Puzzler

```
 1   private static void loopDemo(){
 2     for (String name : getNames()){
 3       System.out.println("Name is " + name);
 4     }
 5   }
 6
 7   private static List<String> getNames() {
 8     System.out.println("withing  getNames");
 9     List<String> names = new  ArrayList<>();
10     names.add("Bob");
11     names.add("Anne");
12     names.add("Eve");
13     return names;
14   }
```

That shouldn't have been really that hard: the list is built exactly once.

You might expect something similar when retrieving the values for the loop variable. To verify the behavior of these different tags, let's perform some tests.

We'll create three simple classes, a (non-persistent) Friend entity, a named bean "controller" to handle the JSF part, and a data provider that mimics the relatively slow access to persistent data (for example, a database).

Listing 23-9. Friend

```
 1   public class Friend {
 2       private final String _name;
 3       private final List<Book> _books = new ArrayList<>();
 4
```

```
5        public Friend( String name){
6            _name = name;
7        }
8
9        public String getName() {
10           return _name;
11       }
12
13       public List<Book> getBooks() {
14           return _books;
15       }
16
17   }
```

A Friend has a name and holds books. To keep everything as simple as possible, we grant direct access to the book list by returning the complete list. This simple approach lets us add a book directly to the list. In a real application, you may hide the list and implement an addBook() method. Although a *book* contains other info than its title, we'll use a very simple Book class for this demonstration. Create a new class Book with just a field plus getter and setter for Title. Let NetBeans create the hashCode and equals methods.

Next, we create a named bean, which is simply request scoped. All it does is offer the friend list to our page. To do that, the data has to be obtained from some data provider. In a real app, this might be a JPA service. See Listing 23-10.

Listing 23-10. Controller

```
1    @Named
2    @RequestScoped
3    public class Controller {
4
5      private int _counter;
6
7      public int getCounter() {
8        return _counter;
9      }
10
11     public List<Friend> getFriends() {
```

```
12        _counter++;
13        return DataProvider.instance.getFriends();
14     }
15   }
```

Besides the getter for the friends, this controller contains a field to count the accesses to the list. And it provides a getter to access this counter.

Next, you see the simple data provider, as shown in Listing 23-11. It creates a fixed list of five friends and assigns a random number of books to each. When somebody tries to access the friend list, we call the retrieveDatafromDB() method. Because this should mimic a longer-running method, the thread sleeps for 100 ms. In a real Java EE app, we don't use sleep() because the server will control the threads for us. But for this little test, it's quite okay.

Listing 23-11. DataProvider

```
1   public class DataProvider {
2
3     private final List<Friend> _friends = new ArrayList<>();
4
5     public static DataProvider instance = new DataProvider();
6
7     private DataProvider() {
8       createData();
9     }
10
11    /**
12     * retrieves a list of friends
13     * @return friends
14     */
15    public List<Friend> getFriends() {
16      retrieveDatafromDB();
17      return _friends;
18    }
19
20    private void retrieveDatafromDB() {
21      // here might be an access to a DB
```

```
22      // simulate it by a sleep (yea, shouldn't use sleep in an EE
        environment)
23      try {
24          Thread.sleep(100);   // slow db access
25      } catch (InterruptedException ex) {
26          // ignore
27      }
28   }
29   private void createData() {
30      _friends.clear();
31      String[] names = {"Sally", "Bob", "John", "Mary", "Jim"};
32      for (int i = 0; i < 5; i++){
33          addFriend(names[i]);
34      }
35   }
36
37   private void addFriend(String name) {
38      Friend friend = new Friend(name);
39      Random random = new Random();
40      int count = random.nextInt(5);
41      for (int i = 0; i < count; i++) {
42          String title = "Book." + name.substring(0, 1) + i;
43          Book book = new Book(title);
44          friend.getBooks().add(book);
45      }
46      _friends.add(friend);
47   }
48 }
```

Now we need a page to display the friend list. We'll create this page in three different flavors to examine the different repetitive structures. The intention is to display a list of friends, and for each friend we'll display a table with its books. See Listing 23-12.

Listing 23-12. Display Friends by Repeat (repeat.xhtml)

```
1    <?xml  version='1.0'  encoding='UTF-8'  ?>
2    <!DOCTYPE html>
3    <html xmlns="http://www.w3.org/1999/xhtml"
4          xmlns:h="http://xmlns.jcp.org/jsf/html"
5          xmlns:f="http://xmlns.jcp.org/jsf/core"
6          xmlns:ui="http://xmlns.jcp.org/jsf/facelets"
7          xmlns:c="http://xmlns.jcp.org/jsp/jstl/core">
8      <h:head>
9        <title>LoopCompare</title>
10     </h:head>
11
12     <h:body>
13       <h1>Test loop ui:repeat</h1>
14
15       AccessCount:  #{controller.counter}
16
17       <ui:repeat value="#{controller.friends}" var="friend">
18         <div>
19           #{friend.name} (Access no #{controller.counter})
20             <h:dataTable value="#{friend.books}" var="book">
21               <h:column>
22                 - #{book.title} (Access no #{controller.counter})
23               </h:column>
24             </h:dataTable>
25         </div>
26       </ui:repeat>
27
28       AccessCount:  #{controller.counter}
29
30       <div>
31         <h:button value="forEach" outcome="forEach"/>
32         <h:button value="repeat" outcome="repeat"/>
33         <h:button value="table" outcome="table"/>
```

```
34        </div>
35       </h:body>
36    </html>
```

In line 15 we simply display the counter before invoking the loop, and in line 28 after that. Lines 17–26 show the loop, constructed by the repeat component. This is the part we'll adopt in each file. Lines 31–33 create three buttons to switch between the three test pages.

For the other two pages, only the part that differs is shown in Listings 23-13 and 23-14.

Listing 23-13. Display Friends by forEach (forEach.xhtml)

```
1    [...]
2        <h1>Test loop c:forEach</h1>
3
4        AccessCount: #{controller.counter}
5
6        <c:forEach  items="#{controller.friends}" var="friend">
7          <div>
8            #{friend.name}  (Access no #{controller.counter})
9            <h:dataTable value="#{friend.books}" var="book">
10             <h:column>
11               - #{book.title} (Access no #{controller.counter})
12             </h:column>
13           </h:dataTable>
14         </div>
15       </c:forEach>
16
17       AccessCount:  #{controller.counter}
18   [...]
```

Listing 23-14. Display Friends by dataTable (table.xhtml)

```
1    [...]
2        <h1>Test loop h:dataTable</h1>
3
4        AccessCount: #{controller.counter}
5
```

```
6      <h:dataTable value="#{controller.friends}" var="friend">
7        <h:column>
8          #{friend.name} (Access no #{controller.counter})
9          <h:dataTable value="#{friend.books}" var="book">
10           <h:column>
11             - #{book.title} (Access no #{controller.counter})
12           </h:column>
13         </h:dataTable>
14       </h:column>
15     </h:dataTable>
16
17     AccessCount: #{controller.counter}
18   [...]
```

Each of these pages contains a loop that retrieves the friend list from the controller. Within this list, another loop is used to display the book list of each friend. At various places, we print out the current counter. Because the controller is request scoped, it will be re-created for every page, and thus the counter starts at 0.

RUN AND OBSERVE

Start the project, click another page, click the same page, and observe the results. Compare your observations to your expectations.

Figure 23-2 takes a look at a sample output (using JSF 2.3 with GlassFish 5.0).

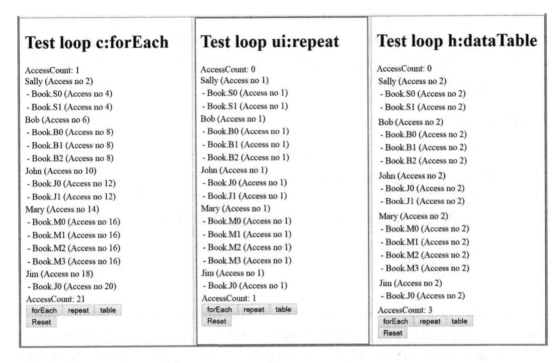

Figure 23-2. *Loop problem*

Without digging into implementation details, some results are obvious: repeat accesses the list only once, as you might have expected, according to the access to a loop variable, whereas forEach performs massive calls to the getFriends method. In fact, the number of calls depends on the number of friends and on the nested table. If you omit the book list, forEach calls getFriends $1 + n$ times. Including the book list, it needs $1 + 4 \times n$ accesses. dataTable calls the method three times, regardless of how many friends and independently of whether we use it with or without the inner table.

If you're wondering why forEach's counter starts with 1, it's a tag handler. Its loop is resolved while building the component tree. Thus there's a first access before the page is rendered.

The massive access count may cause problems in your application. From this point of view, repeat might be the best choice. But for specific applications, you might need to access individual components within the loop. As a component, repeat doesn't repeat its children. It simply repeats the generated output. So, sometimes there's a need for a tag handler performing the loop.

The massive method calls depend on the implementation of the ForEachHandler. Ed Burns (JSF spec lead) is going to investigate this problem. I created a slightly bigger demo to show the problem, which you can download from webdevelopment-java.info.

To mitigate this problem, you might use a local caching, as seen in Listing 23-15.

Listing 23-15. Local Cache

```
1   private List<Friend> _friends;
2   public List<Friend> getFriends() {
3     if (_friends == null) {
4       _friends = DataProvider.instance.getFriends();
5     }
6     return _friends;
5   }
```

Listing 23-15 shows how we might modify the Controller class. If, and only if, the friend list is empty, we'll perform the slow database access. This is a really short-term cache because the Controller object is destroyed once the request is finished. But if we use the forEach tag handler, that might boost performance significantly.

Summary

JSF offers a couple of different repetitive structures, and we need to distinguish between components and tag handlers. Whereas tag handlers are resolved during compile time, components are included into the component tree. This difference has a great impact on how and when the repetition is performed and may lead to performance problems. Caching might be a good practice to mitigate such problems.

PART IV

Alumni

CHAPTER 24

Alumni

Alumni is a social network application. People may register for one or more classes at their old school, university, or similar institution. They may use bulletin boards, organize events, share photos, or engage in peer communication.

Every user may enter and edit information. Because we can't expect them to be experts, all dialogs need to be fault-tolerant and provide quick response. In addition to the techniques discussed so far, we'll be using the following (as well as others):

- Converters and validators

- AJAX

- Authentication and authorization

- Container-based security

- Composing components

- WebSockets

- Changing look and feel

There's not enough room in this book to discuss the entire application in every detail. Rather, I'll explain a few techniques in depth, sometimes describing them in broader terms than we'll need for Alumni. I'll start with basic implementations to guide you from a simple to a customized solution.

Preparing the Application

Every time we've created a new application so far, we've used a NetBeans wizard to create a skeleton for us. We may do that for Alumni too, but because NetBeans doesn't support Java EE 8 out of the box at the time of writing, we'll need to modify the Project Object Model (POM) for using Java EE 8 (as described in Chapter 9).

265

© Michael Müller 2018
M. Müller, *Practical JSF in Java EE 8*, https://doi.org/10.1007/978-1-4842-3030-5_24

Even more, Alumni isn't built as a single module application but is divided into smaller parts for GUI, business layer, storage, and other services. Maven supports such a split by a multi-modules project. We need to tweak the POM and create sub POMs for each different module. The following excerpts of selected POMs focus on the aspects of Java EE 8 as well as the modularization, omitting other stuff like testing. Listing 24-1 starts with the main POM.

Listing 24-1. Main POM of Alumni (Excerpt)

```
01 <?xml version="1.0" encoding="UTF-8"?>
02 <project xmlns="http://maven.apache.org/POM/4.0.0"
03          xmlns:xsi="http://www.w3.org/2001/XMLSchema-instance"
04          xsi:schemaLocation="http://maven.apache.org/POM/4.0.0
05          http://maven.apache.org/xsd/maven-4.0.0.xsd">
06
07    <modelVersion>4.0.0</modelVersion>
08
09    <properties>
10      <java.version>1.8</java.version>
11      <project.build.sourceEncoding>UTF-8</project.build.sourceEncoding>
12    </properties>
13
14    <groupId>de.mueller-bruehl</groupId>
15    <artifactId>Alumni</artifactId>
16    <version>2017.0.0-SNAPSHOT</version>
17    <packaging>pom</packaging>
18
19    <modules>
20      <module>AlumniGui</module>
21      <module>AlumniBusiness</module>

22      <module>AlumniData</module>
23      <module>AlumniAccount</module>
24    </modules>
25
26    <build>
27      <plugins>
```

```
28        <plugin>
29          <groupId>org.apache.maven.plugins</groupId>
30          <artifactId>maven-compiler-plugin</artifactId>
31          <version>3.7.0</version>
32          <configuration>
33            <source>${java.version}</source>
34            <target>${java.version}</target>
35          </configuration>
36        </plugin>
37        <plugin>
38          <groupId>org.apache.maven.plugins</groupId>
39          <artifactId>maven-war-plugin</artifactId>
40          <version>3.1.0</version>
41        </plugin>
42      </plugins>
43    </build>
44
45  <dependencyManagement>
46    <dependencies>
47      <dependency>
48        <groupId>javax</groupId>
49        <artifactId>javaee-api</artifactId>
50        <version>8.0</version>
51        <scope>provided</scope>
52      </dependency>
53
54      ... other dependencies go here ...
55
56    </dependencies>
57  </dependencyManagement>
58
59 </project>
```

Beginning with line 19, we define the modules of our application. We'll create three modules that will compose the Alumni application:

- AlumniGui (GUI layer)

- AlumniBusiness (business layer)

- AlumniData (database access)

A fourth module, AlumniAccount, will be an independent service used by Alumni (covered in detail in Chapter 33). Within the dependency management, we predefine dependencies for our modules. Here we refer to the Java EE 8 API (lines 47-52). Besides that parent POM, we need to define a POM for each module. Listing 24-2 shows the POM of AlumniGui. (The other POMs are quite similar—it should be no problem to derive them too. I'll explain some relevant details later on when explaining selected aspects.)

Listing 24-2. POM of Module AlumniGui (Excerpt)

```
01 <?xml version="1.0" encoding="UTF-8"?>
02 <project xmlns="http://maven.apache.org/POM/4.0.0"
03          xmlns:xsi="http://www.w3.org/2001/XMLSchema-instance"
04          xsi:schemaLocation="http://maven.apache.org/POM/4.0.0
05            http://maven.apache.org/xsd/maven-4.0.0.xsd">
06   <modelVersion>4.0.0</modelVersion>
07
08   <name>AlumniGui</name>
09
10   <parent>
11     <groupId>de.mueller-bruehl</groupId>
12     <artifactId>Alumni</artifactId>
13     <version>2017.0.0-SNAPSHOT</version>
14     <relativePath>../pom.xml</relativePath>
15   </parent>
16
17   <artifactId>AlumniGui</artifactId>
18   <packaging>war</packaging>
19
20   <dependencies>
21     <dependency>
```

```
22        <groupId>javax</groupId>
23        <artifactId>javaee-api</artifactId>
24        <scope>provided</scope>
25      </dependency>
26
27      <dependency>
28        <groupId>${project.groupId}</groupId>
29        <artifactId>AlumniBusiness</artifactId>
30        <version>${project.version}</version>
31      </dependency>
32
33      <dependency>
34       <groupId>${project.groupId}</groupId>
35        <artifactId>AlumniData</artifactId>
36        <version>${project.version}</version>
37      </dependency>
38
39      <dependency>
40       <groupId>${project.groupId}</groupId>
41        <artifactId>AlumniService</artifactId>
42        <version>${project.version}</version>
43      </dependency>
44
45      ... other dependencies omitted for brevity ...
46
47    <build>
48      <finalName>${project.artifactId}</finalName>
49      <resources>
50        <resource>
51          <directory>src/main/resources</directory>
52          <filtering>true</filtering>
53        </resource>
54      </resources>
55    </build>
56
57 </project>
```

The GUI module depends on Java EE 8 as well as on the other layers of the application.

For simple access to entities, the business layer won't add any value. We either use the business layer to delegate all data access to the data layer or we allow the GUI to bypass the business layer and directly access the data layer. Because we're using JPA, the application only deals with Java objects. So, the GUI never needs to know about the database, even if we bypass the business layer. For simplicity's sake, I've chosen the later approach. Because of that, AlumniGui needs to depend on both AlumniBusiness as well as AlumniData.

The other modules, as I've mentioned, are defined by similar POMs. To avoid circular dependencies, no other module will depend on AlumniGui.

Registration Form

Alumni can be used by members only. That means a user must register first. Once registered, the user may log in at any time. We only collect a small amount of mandatory personal data during this registration.

The welcome page of Alumni offers a login form and a link to the registration dialog for new users. Although the registration isn't the first dialog of the application, it represents the first action every user needs to perform before using Alumni. And it's a good starting point to introduce the next JSF and Java EE features.

Like all other dialogs, this form will validate user input and report potential problems by displaying messages. That prevents the user from entering invalid data. It also protects the system from unexpected behavior.

In Books, this validation takes place when the user clicks the Submit button. That might be a good solution for small pages, but it's an imposition on bigger ones. Have you ever been miffed by pages that alerted you a problem in the first input filled *after* you've filled a few hundred more? To be user-friendly, we'll provide feedback after every input field. That's where AJAX enters the game.

JSF offers a set of components that usually will be translated (rendered) into HTML components. Some people believe this is an unnecessary abstraction layer. Why code <h:inputText .../> where HTML expects <input type = "text .../>? The answer is quite simple: a JSF tag might be handled by a different rendering engine. For example, a PDF renderer might translate the inputText into an interactive text field. JSF tags are a kind of domain-specific language (DSL) to create different formats.

If we only need to render HTML, we might omit a DSL and code our pages directly using HTML, enriched with JSF information. (Chapter 5 offers a short introduction into this kind of coding.) We'll develop two versions of the registration: one using the traditional JSF tags and the second using mainly HTML tags. And, of course, we have to consider security. To prevent the user from injecting HTML code, we have to correctly escape the output. A JSF tag will handle that automatically for us.

Listing 24-3 shows the first raw version of the registration form, and Figure 24-1 shows the extract.

Listing 24-3. Registration Form

```
1    <h:form>
2
3       <div class="inputPart">
4         <h:outputLabel for="firstName"
5                        value="#{msg.lblFirstName}"
6                        styleClass="label"/>
7         <h:message id="msgFirstName" for="firstName"
8                    styleClass="errorMessage"/>
9         <h:inputText id="firstName"
10                     value="#{register.accountRequest.firstName}"
11                     styleClass="inputFull"/>
12      </div>
13
14      <div class="inputPart">
15        <h:outputLabel for="lastName"
16                       value="#{msg.lblLastName}"
17                       styleClass="label"/>
18        <h:message id="msgLastName"
19                   for="lastName"
20                   styleClass="errorMessage"/>
21        <h:inputText id="lastName"
22                     value="#{register.accountRequest.lastName}"
23                     styleClass="inputFull"/>
24      </div>
25
```

```
26    <div class="inputPart">
27      <h:outputLabel for="loginName"
28                     value="#{msg.lblLoginName}"
29                     styleClass="label"/>
30      <h:message id="msgLoginName"
31                 for="loginName"
32                 styleClass="errorMessage"/>
33      <h:inputText id="loginName"
34                   value="#{register.account.loginName}"
35                   styleClass="inputFull"/>
37    </div>
38
39    <div class="inputPart">
40      <h:outputLabel for="email"
41                     value="#{msg.lblEmail}"
42                     styleClass="label"/>
43      <h:message id="msgEmail"
44                 for="email"
45                 styleClass="errorMessage"/>
46      <h:inputText id="email"
47                   value="#{register.accountRequest.email}"
48                   styleClass="inputFull"/>
49    </div>
50
51  <div class="inputPart">
52    <h:outputLabel for="password"
53                   value="#{msg.lblPassword}"
54                   styleClass="label"/>
55    <h:message id="msgPassword"
56               for="password"
57               styleClass="errorMessage"/>
58    <h:inputSecret id="password"
59                   styleClass="inputFull"/>
60  </div>
61
```

```
62  <div class="inputPart">
63    <h:outputLabel for="repeatPassword"
64                    value="#{msg.lblRepeatPassword}"
65                    styleClass="label"/>
66    <h:message id="msgRepeatPassword"
67               for="repeatPassword"
68               styleClass="errorMessage"/>
69    <h:inputSecret id="repeatPassword"
70                   value="#{register.password}"
71                   styleClass="inputFull"/>
72  </div>37
73      <div class="buttonBar">
74        <h:commandButton value="#{msg.btnRegister}"
75                         action="#{register.register()}"
76                         styleClass="button"/>
77      </div>
78
79    </h:form>
```

First name
Michael

Last name
Müller

Login name
mike

Email address
michael.mueller@mueller-bruehl.de

Password
·········

Repeat password
·········|

Register

Figure 24-1. *Extract of registration form*

In this form we have a couple input fields, each embedded in its own `div`, together with a label and a message. For example, take a look at the first name (lines 3–12). We start with the label (lines 4–6). After that label, a message (lines 7 and 8) will be displayed in case of error. Finally, we have the appropriate input field where the user can key in the information (lines 9–11).

For the password fields, we use `inputSecret` in place of `inputText`. This renders a secret input field that displays dots for every character, hiding the real input. Apart from that, it's used like the other input fields.

As mentioned, error messages will be displayed in case of validation error. If a form is created like this, validation only takes place when the user clicks the Register button.

Looking at this code, some questions may arise:

- How can we perform the validation?

- How can we provide immediate feedback after entering each value?

- All input parts look similar—is it possible to predefine and reuse such a structure?

- How do we process the password?

The next few chapters answer these questions.

Summary

This chapter introduced Alumni, a social media application that depends on user input. That means we need all the dialogs to be fault-tolerant and to provide immediate feedback.

Alumni is mainly built up by different software modules for GUI, business logic, and data. An independent microservice manages the user both for Alumni and for the authentication. This chapter introduced interesting parts of the required POMs, with special care given to Java EE 8.

Developing a registration form like we developed forms for Books would seem tedious and brings up questions of how it could be done better.

CHAPTER 25

Validation

Before JSF transfers data into the model, the raw data has to be converted and validated. A short overview of *bean validation* was given in Chapter 15. As stated there, JSF offers its own validation specification besides bean validation. Although bean validation is the newer technique, it's not a replacement for the older JSF validation—sometimes it's very handy to use this "old" validation.

This chapter covers different kinds of validation.

Bean Validation

Bean validation uses special constraints that are applied to the fields or accessors by annotations. Some of these were mentioned in earlier chapters, when describing the Book entity in Books. You can get a table of these constraints as part of the Java EE 8 tutorial (`https://javaee.github.io/tutorial/bean-validation.html`). A full description of the bean validation is also available at `http://beanvalidation.org`.

To further our discussion, Listing 25-1 shows an excerpt of the Account entity used for the registration process.

Listing 25-1. Data Model for the Registration

```
01   @Entity
02   @Table(name = "Account")
03   public class Account implements Serializable {
04
05     // <editor-fold defaultstate="collapsed" desc="Property Id">
06     @Id
07     @Column(name = "id")
08     private byte[] _id = UuidUtil.toBytes(UUID.randomUUID());
09
```

© Michael Müller 2018
M. Müller, *Practical JSF in Java EE 8*, https://doi.org/10.1007/978-1-4842-3030-5_25

```
10      public String getId() {
11         return HashUtils.byte2hex(_id);
12      }
13      // </editor-fold>
14
15      // <editor-fold defaultstate="collapsed" desc="Property Status">
16      @Column(name = "status")
17      private AccountStatus _status = AccountStatus.New;
18
19      public AccountStatus getStatus() {
20         return _status;
21      }
22
23      public void setStatus(AccountStatus status) {
24         _status = status;
25      }
26      // </editor-fold>
27
28      // <editor-fold defaultstate="collapsed" desc="Property LoginName">
29      @Column(name = "loginName")
30      private String _loginName;
31
32      @Size(min = 1, max = 50)
33      public String getLoginName() {
34         return _loginName;
35      }
36
37      public void setLoginName(String loginName) {
38         _loginName = loginName;
39      }
40      // </editor-fold>
41
```

```
42    // <editor-fold defaultstate="collapsed" desc="Property FirstName">
43    @Column(name = "firstName")
44    private String _firstName = "";
45
46    @Size(min = 1, max = 50)
47    public String getFirstName() {
48      return _firstName;
49    }
50
51    public void setFirstName(String firstName) {
52      _firstName = firstName;
53    }
54    // </editor-fold>
55
56    // <editor-fold defaultstate="collapsed" desc="Property LastName">
57    @Column(name = "lastName")
58    private String _lastName;
59
60    @Size(min = 1, max = 50, message = "{validation.lastname.size}")
61    public String getLastName() {
62      return _lastName;
63    }
64
65    public void setLastName(String lastName) {
66      _lastName = lastName;
67    }
68    // </editor-fold>
69
70    // <editor-fold defaultstate="collapsed" desc="Property Email">
71    @Column(name = "email")
72    private String _email = "";
73
```

```
74      @Size(min = 6, max = 100)
75      public String getEmail() {
76        return _email;
77      }
78
79      public void setEmail(String email) {
80        _email = email;
81      }
82      // </editor-fold>
83    }
```

Besides the id, this excerpt shows some—but not all—fields that correspond to the appropriate input fields of the UI. The names must be from 1–50 characters in length. The email has to follow a special pattern, which is enforced by a regular expression (covered later in this chapter). The size of the email is restricted to 100 characters.

Note   There are stories of impossible registration because the system validated a minimum length of 3, but the valid name (as far as I remember, this can occur with some African names) was only 1 character long.

JSF automatically invokes bean validation. Behind the scenes, there's a lot to do: JSF must discover whether bean validation is used and invoke it if needed. The essence of this invocation is shown in Listing 25-2, a short code snippet that demonstrates the principle.

Listing 25-2. Programmatic Invocation of Bean Validation

```
1   @Inject private Account _account;
2
3   Validator validator = Validation.buildDefaultValidatorFactory()
4                                    .getValidator();
5   Set<ConstraintViolation<Accountt>> violations =
6                                    validator.validate(_account);
```

This snippet only shows how to check the violations and assign them to a set. What JSF performs behind the scenes is much more than this.

If JSF discovers one or more constraint violations, it will generate the appropriate messages and rerender the current page to display them. The data isn't transferred to the model, and whatever should happen when the user clicks the Register button won't be executed.

Bean validation offers an option to annotate a customized message:

```
1    @Size(min = 1, max = 50,
2     message = "Length of first name must be between {min} and {max}
characters")
```

You may want to develop an international application. By the approach shown here, it's possible to customize the message, but not to localize it. You do that by creating a ValidationMessages.properties file and its localized variants (for example, ValidationMessages_de.properties) in the default package. In this file, you can override the default values or create your own customized messages, including their localized variants.

Creating a Customized Message

1. (Optional) In the project tree, select the Other Sources/src/ main/resources folder.

2. To create a properties file using NetBeans, choose New File (or press Ctrl+N). The New File dialog opens (Figure 25-1).

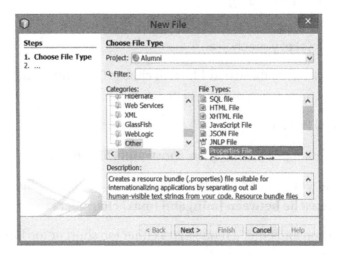

Figure 25-1. *New File dialog*

3. In the dialog, choose the category Other and then Properties File.

4. Click Next.

5. In the Name field, enter **ValidationMessages**.

6. If you did step 1, the folder should be prepopulated with src\
   main\resources. Otherwise, enter this value or browse to the
   desired folder.

7. Click Finish. NetBeans creates the properties file for you.

8. Right-click the properties file and choose Customize. NetBeans
   opens the Customizer dialog, shown in Figure 25-2.

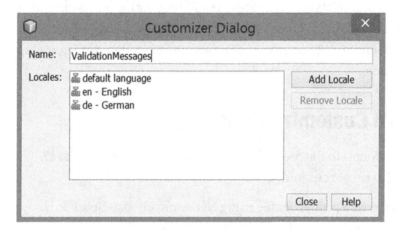

Figure 25-2. *Customizer dialog*

9. Add locale(s) of your choice.

10. Right-click any of these new files and choose Open (not Edit).
    NetBeans opens the properties editor with all locales.

11. Click New Property.

12. For Key, enter **javax.validation.constraints.Size.message**.

13. For Value, enter your customized message. For example, **The
    length must be between {min} and {max} characters**.

14. Run the app and enter a name that's either too short or too long.
    JSF displays the customized message.

Details of Customized Messages

So, how can you determine that magic key? And how do you create other customized messages for the same constraint (on other fields or getters)? You'll find the answer in this book—or by browsing the Java source code. Using NetBeans, place the cursor on the @Size annotation and invoke press Ctrl+B (Ctrl+Enter if you're using Eclipse). This is a shortcut for Go To Declaration. NetBeans opens Size.java in its editor, shown in Listing 25-3.

Listing 25-3. Size.java (Excerpt)

```
1   [...]
2   public @interface Size {
3     [...]
4     public String message()
5                   default "{javax.validation.constraints.Size.message}";
6
7     public int min() default 0;
8
9     public int max() default 2147483647;
10    [...]
11  }
```

Here you'll find the declaration of message with a default value. Look at the properties min and max. Both are public and may be referenced in the value of the message if placed in the message within curly braces.

With that knowledge, we can create different keys at different locations. See Listing 25-4.

Listing 25-4. Customized Message with Customized Key

```
1   @Size(min = 3, max = 50, message = "{validation.lastname.size}")
2   public String getLastName() {
3     return _lastName;
4   }
```

Watch out for the curly braces, which indicate the key. Without them, the message would be treated as plain text. The curly braces are not part of the key. In ValidationMessages.properties, we now can add the key validation.lastname.size and a value like this:

```
The length of LastName must be between {min} and {max} characters.
```

Null Handling

Bean validation offers two constraints to handle null (@Null) or non-null (@NotNull) values. Before conversion, all UI input is treated as strings by JSF. Thus, an empty input field is an empty string, which is something else than null. You may instruct JSF to treat empty strings as null in the web.xml file. See Listing 25-5.

Listing 25-5. Context Parameter to Treat Empty Input as null

```
1  <context-param>
2    <param-name>
3      javax.faces.INTERPRET_EMPTY_STRING_SUBMITTED_VALUES_AS_NULL
4    </param-name>
5    <param-value>true</param-value>
6  </context-param>
```

Because it's always good to avoid nulls, I recommend not using this option. If an empty input isn't allowed, define a minimum length or set the attribute required to true. See Listing 25-6.

Listing 25-6. required Attribute (Including Customized Message)

```
1  <h:inputText id="lastName"
2               value="#{register.accountRequest.lastName}"
3               required="true"
4               requiredMessage="#{msg.msgValueRequired}"
5               styleClass="inputFull">
```

Validation Method

The validation method is one of JSF's own validation features. By defining the Facelets (JSF page), it's possible to add the attribute `validator`, which takes the name of a method to validate the input, as in Listing 25-7.

Listing 25-7. Add `validator` to Markup

```
1    <h:inputText id="email"
2                 value="#{register.accountRequest.email}"
3                 required="true"
4                 requiredMessage="#{msg.msgValueRequired}"
5                 validator="#{register.checkEmail}"
6                 styleClass="inputFull">
```

In line 5, the method `checkEmail` of the `Register` bean is called. Three parameters are passed to this method: The `FacesContext`, the `Uicomponent`, and the converted value as object, which you have to cast to the appropriate type. See Listing 25-8.

Listing 25-8. `validator` Method to Check the Email

```
1    public void checkEmail(FacesContext context,
2                           UIComponent component,
3                           Object value) {
4       String address = (String) value;
5       if (!address.matches(
6          "(\\w[a-zA-Z_0-9+-.]*\\w|\\w+)@(\\w(\\w|-|\\.)*\\w|\\w+)\\.
           [a-zA-Z]+"))\
7       {
8          String msg = Helper.getMessage("errEmail");
9          throw new ValidatorException(new FacesMessage(msg));
10      }
11   }
```

In the case of a converting problem, the validator method throws a ValidatorException, which takes a message of your choice. JSF will collect all messages (there may be exceptions from other components) and display them while rerendering the page, if you've defined appropriate message tags within the page. If you missed such a message tag, JSF will display all messages when you define the development stage in the web.xml file (see Chapter 6).

Validator

Besides specifying a validation method, you may declare a validator with a special tag. Such a validator has to be inserted into the desired component, as in Listing 25-9.

Listing 25-9. validateLength

```
1    <h:inputText id="lastName"
2                    value="#{register.accountRequest.lastName}"
3                    styleClass="inputFull">
4        <f:validateLength minimum="3" maximum="50"/>
5    </h:inputText>
```

Listing 25-9 demonstrates this in line 4. validateLength is a predefined validator that performs the same validation that we did before using bean validation with the @Size constraint.

If you want to override or localize the messages, you can put the desired keys into your messages.properties file. For the length validator, the key is javax.faces.Length.

JSF comes with a couple of predefined validators. For a list, see the JSF core library section in Appendix C. You can also define your own validators. Your validator needs to implement Validator and override the validate method. It will be registered by a @FacesValidator annotation, as shown in Listing 25-10. I assume the remaining part of that class is really self-explanatory. Listing 25-11 demonstrates the usage of our validator (line 4).

Listing 25-10. Custom validator

```
1    @FacesValidator(value = "EmailValidator")
2    public class EmailValidator implements Validator {
3
4        @Override
```

```
 5      public void validate(FacesContext context, UIComponent component,
 6                              Object value) throws ValidatorException {
 7         if (value == null) {
 8            return;
 9         }
10         if (!isValidEmail("" + value)) {
11            String msg = Helper.getMessage("msgNoEmail");
12            throw new ValidatorException(new FacesMessage(msg));
13         }
14      }
15
16      public static boolean isValidEmail(String address) {
17         return address.matches(
18            "(\\w+|\\w(\\w|[+-.])*\\w)@(\\w+|\\w(\\w|[-.])*\\w)\\.
               [a-zA-Z]+");
19      }
20   }
```

Listing 25-11. Usage of Custom Validator

```
1   <h:inputText id="email"
2                value="#{register.accountRequest.email}"
3                styleClass="inputFull">
4      <f:validator validatorId="EmailValidator"/>
5   </h:inputText>
```

Multi-Component Validation

On the registration page, a password is queried from the user. To prevent a typo, the user has to reenter the password a second time. The validator needs to check the second input against the first one. This is a kind of *multi-component* validation.

JSF 2.3 introduced a multi-component validation. It's not a special JSF validation feature but is built on standard bean validation.

Usually every field must be validated before it's transferred to the data model. To perform the multi-component validation, we may need access to the value of another field of the model. But this field also will be transferred into the model only if it could be validated before. In other words, we need a validation to transfer a field into the model and we need the value inside the model to perform the validation. A kind of deadlock.

JSF uses a simple trick: the data model is temporarily copied, and this copy receives the new values before the validation takes place. If the copy could be validated, then the values are pushed to the data model.

Multi-component validation needs to be configured within web.xml, as shown in Listing 25-12.

Listing 25-12. Context Parameter within web.xml to Enable Multi-Component Validation

```
01  <context-param>
02      <param-name>javax.faces.validator.ENABLE_VALIDATE_WHOLE_BEAN</param-name>
03      <param-value>true</param-value>
04  </context-param>
```

We need to define different validation groups within our data model—for example, entity. JSF allows definition of different validation groups in the validateBean tag. Suppose we want the user to repeat his email. In the page representation, we define two fields, belonging both to the default validation group and to a special validation group for the multi-component validation. Here, this special group is de.muellerbruehl.demo. RepeatedEntryConstraint. You may declare any interface you like to use as the group name.

Assigning an input field to multiple validation groups isn't a new feature. But JSF 2.3 introduced the new tag validateWholeBean, which must be placed after all the input fields. This is where the new action takes place—see lines 23–25 in Listing 25-13).

Listing 25-13. Example of Repeated Input (Must be Placed in an h:form)

```
1 <?xml version='1.0' encoding='UTF-8' ?>
2 <!DOCTYPE html>
3 <html xmlns="http://www.w3.org/1999/xhtml"
4       xmlns:h="http://xmlns.jcp.org/jsf/html"
5       xmlns:f="http://xmlns.jcp.org/jsf/core">
6   <h:body>
7     <h:form>
```

```
8
9        <div>
10         <h:outputLabel value="Enter email"/>
11         <h:inputText id="email1" value="#{emailBean.email1}"/>
12         <h:message id="msgEmail1" for="email1"/>
13       </div>
14
15       <div>
16         <h:outputLabel value="Repeat email"/>
17         <h:inputText id="email2" value="#{emailBean.email2}"/>
18         <h:message for="emailValidator"/>
19       </div>
20
21       <h:commandButton value="check" actionListener="null"/>
22
23       <f:validateWholeBean value="#{emailBean}"
24                            validationGroups="de.muellerbruehl.demo.
                             RepeatedEntryConstraint"
25                            id="emailValidator"/>
26
27     </h:form>
28   </h:body>
29 </html>
```

The preceding listing creates a form with two input fields labled "Enter email" and "Repeat email." The first one contains an h:message, which is assigned directly to it, whereas the message tag that's placed nearby the second input field is assigned for the validateWholeBean tag. This validator will validate both input fields. If they differ, a "Both input fields must match" message will be displayed just after the second input. The validation will be performed when the user clicks the check button (line 21). This button performs no special action—the only purpose of this form is to show how multi-field validation works.

In this example, we check whether an email is entered the same twice. We might also check a password repetition. To create a more generic validator, we don't create an EmailValidator but a RepeatedEntryValidator. This validator will receive a copy of our data model—here, an instance of the class EmailBean (line 23). With the generalization in mind, the validator will accept an interface RepeatedValueHolder. The duty of this interface is to provide the two input fields. See Listing 25-14.

Listing 25-14. Interface RepeatedValueHolder

```
1 public interface RepeatedEntryHolder {
2
3   String getValue1();
4
5   String getValue2();
6 }
```

The validator needs to implement a ConstraintValidator, which takes two arguments (Listing 25-15, line 2): our constraint definition and our value holder.

Listing 25-15. Validator

```
1 public class RepeatedEntryValidator
2         implements ConstraintValidator<RepeatedEntryConstraint,
          RepeatedEntryHolder> {
3
4   @Override
5   public void initialize(RepeatedEntryConstraint constraintAnnotation) {
6   }
7
8   @Override
9   public boolean isValid(RepeatedEntryHolder other,
10          ConstraintValidatorContext context) {
11    return other.getValue1().equals(other.getValue2());
12  }
13
14 }
```

The ConstraintValidator interface forces us to implement two methods, for initialization (initialize, lines 4-6) and validation (isValid, lines 8-12). Because we don't need to initialize our validator, the first method implementation remains empty. The validation is really simple: we just return whether both values are equal.

Next we need to define our constraint. Each constraint needs to host three attributes, as shown in Listing 25-16. (For more, see `https://javaee.github.io/javaee-spec/javadocs/javax/validation/Constraint.html`.)

Listing 25-16. RepeatedEntryConstraint

```
1 @Constraint(validatedBy = RepeatedEntryValidator.class)
2 @Documented
3 @Target(TYPE)
4 @Retention(RUNTIME)
5 public @interface RepeatedEntryConstraint {
6
7   String message() default "Both input fields must match";
8
9   Class<?>[] groups() default {};
10
11   Class<? extends Payload>[] payload() default {};
12 }
```

Line 1 defines which validator this constraint is validated by.

For the three attributes, we only provide a simple value for the message (line 7). Instead of providing a literal, as in this simple example, it may be better to provide a key to a localizable string.

The last part of our validation puzzle is the backing bean for our page, as shown in Listing 25-17.

Listing 25-17. EmailBean

```
1 @Named
2 @RequestScoped
3 @RepeatedEntryConstraint(groups = RepeatedEntryConstraint.class)
4 public class EmailBean implements RepeatedEntryHolder, Cloneable {
5
6   //<editor-fold defaultstate="collapsed" desc="Property Email1">
7   private String _email1 = "";
8
9   @NotNull
```

```
10    @Pattern(regexp = "(\\w+|\\w(\\w|[+-.])*\\w)@(\\w+|\\w(\\w|
      [-.])*\\w)\\.[a-zA-Z]+",
11            message = "This is not a valid email")
12    public String getEmail1() {
13      return _email1;
14    }
15
16    public void setEmail1(String email1) {
17      _email1 = email1;
18    }
19    //</editor-fold>
20
21    //<editor-fold defaultstate="collapsed" desc="Property Email2">
22    private String _email2 = "";
23
24    @NotNull
25    public String getEmail2() {
26      return _email2;
27    }
28
29    public void setEmail2(String email2) {
30      _email2 = email2;
31    }
32    //</editor-fold>
33
34    //<editor-fold defaultstate="collapsed" desc="Implement
      RepeatedEntryHolder">
35    @Override
36    public String getValue1() {
37      return _email1;
38    }
39
40    @Override
41    public String getValue2() {
42      return _email2;
43    }
```

```
44   //</editor-fold>
45
46   //<editor-fold defaultstate="collapsed" desc="Implement Cloneable">
47   @Override
48   protected Object clone() throws CloneNotSupportedException {
49     EmailBean other = (EmailBean) super.clone();
50     other.setEmail1(this.getEmail1());
51     other.setEmail2(this.getEmail2());
52     return other;
53   }
54   //</editor-fold>
55 }
```

This class is annotated by our constraint (line 3). Because we use this interface for the group name, too, its class is declared for groups again (line 4). Remember, we might have used a different interface for the group name.

The bean implements both RepeatedEntryHolder and Clonable. We need the first for passing into the validator—otherwise, the validator would have needed to accept an instance of the EmailBean class, which prevents generalization. Remember, validation in JSF takes place *before* the data is transferred into the model (backing bean). Multi-field validation takes place in a copy of the object, which is why we need to clone it. There's no need to copy the email fields because JSF will set them within the clone to the current input fields.

As I hope you can see, this is a lot of effort for just validating a field the user needs to repeat. In my opinion, such effort is only worthwhile if the validation needs to perform more than just comparing two fields. Because I didn't use the password comparison for this explanation, you can guess that I've chosen a different approach for comparing the passwords in Alumni. In other words, we won't use the built-in multi-validation for such a simple scenario.

Self-Made

The backing bean for the registration refers to an account that contains the target password field. This password will be compared to another field that will be placed in the form before the account's password. This first password field is held by the backing bean.

The inputSecret for the password repetition refers to the checkPassword method of this bean: validator="#{register.checkPassword}". See Listing 25-18.

Listing 25-18. Excerpt of the Registration Bean

```
1    private Account _account = new Account();
2
3    public Account getAccount() {
4      return _account;
5    }
6
7    public void setAccount(Account account) {
8      this._account = account;
9    }
10
11   String _password;
12
13   public String getPassword() {
14     return _password;
15   }
16
17   public void setPassword(String password) {
18     _password = password;
19   }
20
21   public void checkPassword(FacesContext context,
22           UIComponent component,
23           Object value) {
24     if (_password != null && !_password.equals("" + value)) {
25       String msg = Helper.getMessage("msgPasswordMismatch");
25       throw new ValidatorException(new FacesMessage(msg));
27     }
28 }
```

For the password check, our validator needs to compare the value of the second entry with the first one. Because the data isn't transferred to the model yet (it will be after the successful validation), we need to compare the raw values of the input component.

In the solution given, the raw value is compared to the password field, which needs to be transferred to the bean before. This is what AJAX, the topic of the next chapter, is used for.

Without using AJAX, we also need to retrieve the raw value of the first password field. We'll get it out of the component tree, as shown in Listing 25-19.

Listing 25-19. Example of Multi-Component Validation

```
1    public void checkPassword(FacesContext context, UIComponent
     component, Obj\
2   ect value) {
3      UIViewRoot root = context.getViewRoot();
4      String targetId = component.getNamingContainer().getClientId() +
       ":passw\
5   ord";
6      Object password = ((HtmlInputSecret) root.findComponent(targetId))
7               .getValue();
8      if (!password.equals("" + value)) {
9        String msg = Helper.getMessage("msgPasswordMismatch");
10       throw new ValidatorException(new FacesMessage(msg));
11     }
12  }
```

This method shown in Listing 25-19 replaces the one in Listing 25-18.

Summary

Even though JSF has offered its own validation since the early days, it's now possible to use Java EE's bean-validation feature. JSF invokes bean validation automatically if the data model is annotated with validation constraints. Since JSF 2.3 (Java EE 8), a multi-component validation based on bean validation groups is available. It needs a lot of boilerplate code, so it's best used if you need complex validations. Simply comparing two fields for identical values might be implemented easier without this new feature.

CHAPTER 26

AJAX Components

In a normal request, the browser queries for a whole page. By contrast, AJAX (Asynchronous JavaScript and XML) is commonly used to query only small portions of data with a special object called the XMLHttpRequest. That object is used to query data in the background (asynchronous) while the page is still displayed. Depending on the response, parts of the page might be rerendered. In JSF, this is called a *partial request*.

When the term was first used, the response was some XML data. Nowadays, the most preferred format for the response's payload is a JSON string, which is more compact than an XML document. Or, if desired, a developer might send plain text as payload. But the technique behind the scenes is still called AJAX.

Using AJAX for Immediate Feedback

AJAXifying a dialog can help improve the user experience. For example, the content of each single input component may be sent to the server and provide an immediate feedback to the user. Although AJAX can also be useful for smaller dialogs, such as the category editor of Books, I'll introduce AJAX for JSF by way of the registration form.

JSF offers a special tag, <f:ajax>. One way to AJAXify a component is to embed this tag into the component. In the case of the registration form, we simply put it into the <h:inputText> elements, as shown in Listing 26-1.

Listing 26-1. Registration Form, AJAXified (Excerpt)

```
1   <h:form>
2
3     <div class="inputPart">
4       <h:outputLabel for="firstName"
5                      value="#{msg.lblFirstName}"
6                      styleClass="label"/>
```

© Michael Müller 2018
M. Müller, *Practical JSF in Java EE 8*, https://doi.org/10.1007/978-1-4842-3030-5_26

```
 7        <h:message id="msgFirstName" for="firstName"
 8                   styleClass="errorMessage"/>
 9        <h:inputText id="firstName"
10                     value="#{register.account.firstName}"
11                     styleClass="inputFull">
12          <f:ajax render="@this msgFirstName"/>
13        </h:inputText>
14      </div>
15
16      <div class="inputPart">
17        <h:outputLabel for="lastName"
18                       value="#{msg.lblLastName}"
19                       styleClass="label"/>
20        <h:message id="msgLastName"
21                   for="lastName"
22                   styleClass="errorMessage"/>
23        <h:inputText id="lastName"
24                     value="#{register.account.lastName}"
25                     styleClass="inputFull">
26          <f:ajax render="@this msgLastName"/>
27        </h:inputText>
28      </div>
29
30      <div class="inputPart">
31        <h:outputLabel for="email"
32                       value="#{msg.lblEmail}"
33                       styleClass="label"/>
34        <h:message id="msgEmail"
35                   for="email"
36                   styleClass="errorMessage"/>
37        <h:inputText id="email"
38                     value="#{register.account.email}"
39                     styleClass="inputFull">
40          <f:ajax render="@this msgEmail"/>
41        </h:inputText>
42      </div>
```

```
43
44     <div class="buttonBar">
45       <h:commandButton value="#{msg.btnRegister}"
46                          action="#{register.register()}"
47                          styleClass="button"/>
48     </div>
49
50   </h:form>
```

This form contains three AJAXified elements (see lines 12, 26, and 40). The render attribute tells JSF which components should be rendered when the data is sent back from the server. @this is a special keyword that refers to the surrounding (parent) component. msgXXX is the name of the associated message.

When the user leaves an input field, JSF invokes an asynchronous request and sends the content of this field to the server. This value will be converted, validated, and if validation succeeded, transferred to the model. Then the server sends back the new content of the two mentioned components (each @this and the message) to render. Doing so, we provide immediate feedback to the user, similar to a desktop application.

Using the ajax tag is quite simple and hides away all the JavaScript code. JSF completely handles the server side, so no special programming is needed.

The form shows a very basic use of the <f:ajax> tag, which almost uses some default values. For example, we omit the event and the component on which this request executes. By default, the parent component of <f:ajax> is executed (sent to the server) during its change event. The default event depends on the component's type. If the component holds a value (such as inputText, selectOneMenu, and so on), then the default is onChange. For components that are clicked, like buttons or links, it defaults to onClick.

All these defaults might be changed. Let's assume we want to act on the repeatPassword field's onBlur event and execute both password fields:

```
<f:ajax event="blur" execute="@this password" render="msgRepeatPassword"/>
```

We'll go over these and other options and attributes when we discuss more complex forms.

Besides nesting this tag into a component's tag, it's possible to nest one or more components inside the `<f:ajax>` tag, as seen in Listing 26-2.

Listing 26-2. AJAX as Parent for Other Components

```
01 <f:ajax>
02   <component1/>
03   <component2/>
04   ...
05 </f:ajax>
```

Instead of using the `ajax` tag, you might use the JSF JavaScript API—for example, if implementing a form using HTML-friendly markup, or when you like to combine the partial request with other scripts, such as performing some JavaScript validation and sending the partial request afterwards.

Listing 26-3 shows an example of an HTML-friendly markup, omitting the JSF tags.

Listing 26-3. AJAX with HTML-Friendly Markup

```
<input type="input"
       jsf:value="#{register.password}"
       onchange="jsf.ajax.request(this, event);"/>
```

HTML uses onchange to react on the change event. In JSF's `ajax` tag, the on prefix is omitted.

Depending on the requirements, it's possible to receive and process the response directly via JavaScript without using the simplicity of the `ajax` tag. See Listing 26-4.

Listing 26-4. Skeleton for a Self-Made AJAX Response Handler

```
1   <script>
2   function handleAjax(data) {
3     var status = data.status;
4
5     switch (status) {
6       case "begin":
```

```
 7            // start of the Ajax request
 8            break;
 9
10      case "complete":
11            // Ajax response is completed
12            break;
13
14      case "success":
15            // Ajax response is processed and HTML DOM updated
16            alert(data.responseText);
17            break;
18    }
19  }
20
21  jsf.ajax.addOnEvent(handleAjax);
22  </script>
```

Listing 26-4 shows the principle of such a handler. Line 21 registers the handleAjax function to the onEvent handler. Now this function will be called several times with its current status: at the start of the request (line 6), when the response is completed (line 10), and just after the HTML DOM has been updated after successfully processing the response (line 14). In this example we simply alert the response's text.

Using the JavaScript approach might be helpful for special requirements. I mention it here for completeness. (Within the Java EE 8 tutorial, there's one page about JavaScript AJAX, at https://javaee.github.io/tutorial/jsf-ajax010.html.) We'll use the JSF ajax tag.

Listing 26-1 showed basic use of the ajax tag only. Besides defining the elements that will be rendered during the response, we can define the event to react on or the GUI elements that will be processed by invoking their setters on the server side. We can also define a *listener*—a method that will be invoked on the server side. I'll explain such features later in this book when they're used for Alumni.

Summary

AJAX can be used to send partial requests to the server. Because only small parts of the page are used in such a request-respond cycle, the communication usually performs quickly. This technique allows transfer of a single field into the data model and/or provides immediate feedback to the user.

AJAXifying a JSF application is as simple as adding the `<f:ajax>` tag to a component. Due to defaults, this is sufficient in many cases. For more complete control, the application developer may add attributes to override the defaults.

A partial request might be initiated by a script, too. JSF offers an appropriate library.

CHAPTER 27

Building Composite Components

Remember the questions at the end of Chapter 24? Is it possible to predefine and reuse such similar input structures? This chapter shows how to build such components.

Before JSF 2.0, you could still create your own components. These custom components follow a special convention to programmatically implement behavior with Java code. Sometimes that's useful to create components with completely new behavior.

Beginning with JSF 2.0, a new feature was introduced: *composite components*. With this feature you simply use Facelets to compose reusable components of existing elements—you can treat them as kind of lightweight custom components.

Transform into a Composition

In the registration form, we use a label, input field, and message for almost every data field. The goal is to transform this coherent series of components into a composition—a composite component.

Listing 27-1 takes a look at the input part for firstName.

Listing 27-1. Input Part for firstName

```
1    <div class="inputPart">
2      <h:outputLabel for="firstName"
3                     value="#{msg.lblFirstName}"
4                     styleClass="label"/>
5      <h:inputText id="firstName"
6                   value="#{register.account.firstName}"
7                   styleClass="inputMedium">
```

© Michael Müller 2018
M. Müller, *Practical JSF in Java EE 8*, https://doi.org/10.1007/978-1-4842-3030-5_27

```
8              <f:ajax render="@this msgFirstName"/>
9            </h:inputText>
10           <h:message id="msgFirstName" for="firstName"
11                      styleClass="errorMessage"/>
12         </div>
```

This is composed of a label, an AJAXified input field, and a message, all nested within a div. The same structure applies to lastName. Email is similar but contains an additional validator. We'll focus on the names first to create a simple version of a reusable composite component.

Now let's treat the part shown in Listing 27-1 as a component. It displays a label and offers an input field for a variable. If we want to use it for the last name, we have to exchange these two values from outside of this component. Both the ajax and the message tags are used inside the component only. There's no need to pass some value from the outside into these tags.

If we want to convert this snippet into a component, we need to define something to pass the label text as well as the input variable into. We need to define an interface with two attributes. For the interface definition of composite components, JSF offers some special tags from the composite library. Usually the related namespace http://xmlns. jcp.org/jsf/composite would be assigned to the alias cc.

Besides the interface, Listing 27-1 would become the implementation. We need to replace the concrete expressions with the two defined within the interface. Because the ids aren't related to concrete values anymore, we may choose some generalized names.

Whew! It seems there's a lot to do. But even though it may sound complicated, it's only a little change, as demonstrated by the code of this component, shown in Listing 27-2.

Listing 27-2. Input Part as Composite Component

```
1    <?xml version='1.0'  encoding='UTF-8'  ?>
2    <html xmlns="http://www.w3.org/1999/xhtml"
3          xmlns:cc="http://xmlns.jcp.org/jsf/composite"
4          xmlns:h="http://xmlns.jcp.org/jsf/html"
5          xmlns:f="http://xmlns.jcp.org/jsf/core">
6
7    <!-- INTERFACE -->
8    <cc:interface>
9      <cc:attribute name="label"/>
```

```
10        <cc:attribute name="value"/>
11     </cc:interface>
12
13     <!-- IMPLEMENTATION -->
14     <cc:implementation>
15       <div class="inputPart">
16         <h:outputLabel for="input"
17                         value="#{cc.attrs.label}"
18                         styleClass="label"/>
19         <h:inputText id="input"
20                       value="#{cc.attrs.value}"
21                       requiredMessage="#{msg.msgValueRequired}"
22                       styleClass="inputMedium">
23           <f:ajax render="@this msgInput"/>
24         </h:inputText>
25         <h:message id="msgInput" for="input" styleClass="errorMessage"/>
26       </div>
27     </cc:implementation>
28   </html>
```

Within the <cc:implementation> tag, you'll find the transformed code snippet. It really looks similar. But instead of concrete values referring to the label and input field, we now use #{cc.attrs.XXX}, where XXX represents each an attribute of the interface.

Although the HTML is ready, we still have to perform some more (simple) tasks to use this component. First of all, JSF looks for components in certain places. Remember the resources folder under the webapp folder? We have to place the component into this or another valid resources location. Let's create a subfolder called components and save our file into that location. As a name for our component, we'll choose LabeledText.

So far, we've prepared the component. Now let's use it. First we have to reference our component file by a special namespace: http://xmlns.jcp.org/jsf/composite. We need to append the folder we used to store our components under the resources. We've chosen components, so we have to add that. And, as usual for a namespace declaration, we have to use an alias. I've chosen mm for my components. So, the whole namespace declaration becomes this:

```
xmlns:mm="http://xmlns.jcp.org/jsf/composite/components"
```

Listing 27-3 shows our page and shows how to use our component.

Listing 27-3. Refactored Page That Uses Composite Components

```
1   <?xml version='1.0' encoding='UTF-8' ?>
2   <!DOCTYPE html>
3   <ui:composition xmlns:ui="http://xmlns.jcp.org/jsf/facelets"
4                   template="/common/alumniTemplate.xhtml"
5                   xmlns:h="http://xmlns.jcp.org/jsf/html"
6                   xmlns:c="http://java.sun.com/jsp/jstl/core"
7                   xmlns:f="http://xmlns.jcp.org/jsf/core"
8                   xmlns:mm="http://xmlns.jcp.org/jsf/composite/components">
9
10     <ui:define name="content">
11       <h1>Register</h1>
12
13       <h:form>
14
15         <mm:LabeledText label="#{msg.lblFirstName}"
16                         value="#{register.accountRequest.firstName}"  />
17         <mm:LabeledText label="#{msg.lblLastName}"
18                         value="#{register.accountRequest.lastName}"  />
19
20         [other markup omitted for brevity]
21
22       </h:form>
23     </ui:define>
24   </ui:composition>
```

The preceding listing shows how to use our component for both the first name and the last name input parts. All we need to do is to reference the component by the namespace alias plus the filename we've chosen (lines 15–18) and then to each pass two values by the names we've defined in the interface. The code became quite short and concise. Each component (firstName, lastName) needs just 2 lines instead of the 12 lines we needed before as seen in Listing 27-2. Really nice, isn't it?

Enable Child Element for the Composition

Next we have to tackle the `email` input component. In addition to the parts we've used so far, we have to consider the validator. One possible solution would be to define a validator inside our component. But there are a couple of different validators that might be used to validate an input. To consider all of them could result in messy code, with conditions to display none or just one of them. It would be more flexible if we just could nest a validator or other components into our `labeledText` as we do with other components. See Listing 27-4.

Listing 27-4. Use Component `LabeledText`

```
1    <mm:LabeledText label="#{msg.lblEmail}"
2                       value="#{register.accountRequest.email}">
3        <f:validator validatorId="EmailValidator" for="input"/>
4    </mm:LabeledText>
```

In Listing 27-4, I simply nested the validator into `labeledText` as we nested the validator into the `inputText` tag of the original registration form. Yet if we run the application with this code in the registration, the validator wouldn't be invoked.

Why not? Imagine a composite component composed of a couple of input elements—a common scenario. For which of these elements is the validator for? Yes, we used an id `input` for the internal `inputText`. As with a local variable in a Java method, we can't reach the internal element from outside. Rather, we have to define a kind of forwarding of the validator to the desired internal element. And that's what `editableValueHolder` is for. As its name suggests, this tag links to the internal component that's used to hold the value. But more than that, it may point to multiple targets:

```
<cc:editableValueHolder  name="input"/>
```

`name` is the name we need to use in the `for` of the validator. Defining targets, we can redirect from an "outside name" to the internal component(s):

```
<cc:editableValueHolder name="input" targets="input"/>
```

If we omit the `targets` attribute, it defaults to the same as defined for `name`. So, the preceding code is semantically the same as before. But we may use a different name:

```
<cc:editableValueHolder name="email" targets="input"/>
```

305

This defines a name that can be used outside the component and its internal target(s). Now we have to declare for="email" within the validator. In most JSF tutorials or code snippets, you'll find the editableValueHolder nested into the <cc:interface> tag. But you can also place it within <cc:implementation>. I recommend doing that because it enables more variable usage.

Take a look at the Facelets fragment in Listing 27-5.

Listing 27-5. Use id for Composite Component

```
1    <mm:LabeledText id="myId" label="#{msg.lblEmail}"
2                       value="#{register.accountRequest.email}">
3      <f:validator validatorId="EmailValidator" for="myId"/>
4    </mm:LabeledText>
```

We've defined an id for our element. And as usual we used this id at the for attribute of the validator. Until now, we can't use it this way because our editableValueHolder has the name "email" and that's what we need to use. Can't we use the component's id as name of the editableValueHolder? The good news is yes, that's possible if we use it within the implementation. The EL has two predefined variables pointing to the id: either #{cc.attrs.id} or simply #{cc.id}. See Figure 27-6.

Listing 27-6. Component LabeledText Using Variable Id for editableValueHolder

```
1    <?xml version='1.0' encoding='UTF-8' ?>
2    <html xmlns="http://www.w3.org/1999/xhtml"
3          xmlns:cc="http://xmlns.jcp.org/jsf/composite"
4          xmlns:h="http://xmlns.jcp.org/jsf/html"
5          xmlns:f="http://xmlns.jcp.org/jsf/core">
6
7      <!-- INTERFACE -->
8      <cc:interface>
9        <cc:attribute name="label"/>
10       <cc:attribute name="value"/>
11     </cc:interface>
12
```

```
13    <!-- IMPLEMENTATION -->
14    <cc:implementation>
15      <cc:editableValueHolder name="#{cc.id}" targets="input"/>
16      <div class="inputPart">
17        <h:outputLabel for="input"
18                       value="#{cc.attrs.label}"
19                       styleClass="label"/>
20        <h:message id="msgInput" for="input" styleClass="errorMessage"/>
21        <h:inputText id="input"
22                     value="#{cc.attrs.value}"
23                     requiredMessage="#{msg.msgValueRequired}"
24                     styleClass="inputMedium">
25          <f:ajax render="@this msgInput"/>
26        </h:inputText>
27      </div>
28    </cc:implementation>
29  </html>
```

Using the component, the final register form would become quite short.
See Listing 27-7.

Listing 27-7. Register Form Using the Composite Component (Excerpt)

```
1    <?xml version='1.0' encoding='UTF-8' ?>
2    <!DOCTYPE html>
3    <ui:composition xmlns:ui="http://xmlns.jcp.org/jsf/facelets"
4                    template="/common/alumniTemplate.xhtml"
5                    xmlns:h="http://xmlns.jcp.org/jsf/html"
6                    xmlns:c="http://java.sun.com/jsp/jstl/core"
7                    xmlns:mm="http://xmlns.jcp.org/jsf/composite/
                      components"
8                    xmlns:f="http://xmlns.jcp.org/jsf/core">
9
10   <ui:define name="content">
11     <h1>Register</h1>
12
```

```
13        <h:form>
14
15            <mm:LabeledText label="#{msg.lblFirstName}"
16                            value="#{register.accountRequest.firstName}"  />
17            <mm:LabeledText label="#{msg.lblLastName}"
18                            value="#{register.accountRequest.lastName}"/>
19
20            <mm:LabeledText id="email" label="#{msg.lblEmail}"
21                            value="#{register.accountRequest.email}">
22              <f:validator validatorId="EmailValidator" for="email"/>
23            </mm:LabeledText>
24
25            [other fields omitted for brevity]
26
27            <div class="buttonBar">
28              <h:commandButton value="#{msg.btnRegister}"
29                               action="#{register.register()}"
30                               styleClass="button"/>
31            </div>
32
33        </h:form>
34      </ui:define>
35    </ui:composition>
```

Pass In Validation Method

For the multi-component validation of the password fields, Alumni uses a validation method (see Chapter 25). This simple approach can't be moved into a general validator because it needs to know about another password field. Because we can't use a child component for validation as we did for the email, we need to pass in a reference to the validation method to the composite component.

The principle should be like passing the value of the input field. See Listing 27-8.

Listing 27-8. Principle to Pass in a Validation Method (Malfunction)

```
1    <cc:interface>
2      <cc:attribute name="value"/>
3      <cc:attribute name="validator"/>
4    </cc:interface>
5
6    <cc:implementation>
7      ...
8      <h:inputSecret id="input"
9                     value="#{cc.attrs.value}"
10                    validator="#{cc.attrs.validator}"
11                    ...>
12      ...
13    </h:inputText>
14    ...
15   </cc:implementation>
```

Don't try the preceding code—it can demonstrate the goal, but it doesn't work. In line 2 we define an attribute (value) to transfer a simple string into the component. Let's assume we want to pass in an object of the Account class, which is more complex than a simple string. We need to inform JSF about the fully qualified type of this object. As a rule of thumb, use the fully qualified class when you need it in Java code too, or if you need to import the class to omit the package name:

```
<cc:attribute name="account" type="de.muellerbruehl.alumni.business.dto.
Account">
```

To pass in a method, we also need to inform JSF. In this case, we need to add a method signature with the appropriate attribute:

```
<cc:attribute name="validator"
        method-signature="void validate(
        javax.faces.context.FacesContext,
        javax.faces.component.UIComponent,
        Object)"/>
```

We also need to declare the return type and the parameter types. This is done the standard Java way for a file without imports. So, we need to pass the fully qualified class names for non-simple objects. As method name, we're free to choose any valid name—it doesn't matter.

Normally in the interface section we can reuse the attribute names of the internal components. But for `validator`, we need to choose a different name to get it to work. I called it `validationMethod`.

Ubiquitous Input Component

To get a ubiquitous input component, we have to add some more attributes that can be passed from the outside. Listing 27-9 shows the complete `LabeledSecretValidate` composite component of Alumni. It's a sibling of `LabeledTextValidate` with an additional attribute, `redisplay`, which is specific to `inputSecret`.

Listing 27-9. Complete Composite Component `InputSecretValidate`

```
01    <?xml version='1.0' encoding='UTF-8' ?>
02    <html xmlns="http://www.w3.org/1999/xhtml"
03          xmlns:cc="http://xmlns.jcp.org/jsf/composite"
04          xmlns:h="http://xmlns.jcp.org/jsf/html"
05          xmlns:f="http://xmlns.jcp.org/jsf/core">
06
07      <!-- INTERFACE -->
08      <cc:interface>
09        <cc:attribute name="label" />
10        <cc:attribute name="value"/>
11        <cc:attribute name="required" default="true"/>
12        <cc:attribute name="componentStyleClass" default="inputPart"/>
13        <cc:attribute name="labelStyleClass" default="label"/>
14        <cc:attribute name="textStyleClass" default="inputMedium"/>
15        <cc:attribute name="messageStyleClass" default="errorMessage"/>
16        <cc:attribute name="readonly" default="false"/>
17        <cc:attribute name="disabled" default="false"/>
```

```
18        <cc:attribute name="redisplay" default="false"/>
19        <cc:attribute name="renderElement" default="@this"/>
20        <cc:attribute name="validationMethod"
21                       method-signature="void validate(
22                       javax.faces.context.FacesContext,
23                       javax.faces.component.UIComponent,
24                       Object)"/>
25        <cc:actionSource name="input"/>
26    </cc:interface>
27
28    <!-- IMPLEMENTATION -->
29    <cc:implementation>
30      <cc:editableValueHolder name="#{cc.id}" targets="input"/>
31
32      <div class="#{cc.attrs.componentStyleClass}">
33
34        <h:outputLabel for="input"
35                       value="#{cc.attrs.label}"
36                       styleClass="#{cc.attrs.labelStyleClass}"/>
37
38        <h:inputSecret id="input"
39                       value="#{cc.attrs.value}"
40                       validator="#{cc.attrs.validationMethod}"
41                       required="#{cc.attrs.required}"
42                       requiredMessage="#{msg.msgValueRequired}"
43                       readonly="#{cc.attrs.readonly}"
44                       disabled="#{cc.attrs.disabled}"
45                       redisplay="#{cc.attrs.redisplay}"
46                       styleClass="#{cc.attrs.textStyleClass}">
47          <f:ajax event="change" render="#{cc.attrs.renderElement}
             msgInput"/>
48        </h:inputSecret>
49
```

```
50              <h:message id="msgInput"
51                         for="input"
52                         styleClass="#{cc.attrs.messageStyleClass}"/>
53
54          </div>
55
56      </cc:implementation>
57   </html>
```

Watch out for the interface section: if needed, can define reasonable defaults for the attributes. If you don't need a different value than this default, you might omit that attribute within the HTML file which uses this component.

You may ask why the component names end with Validate. If we don't pass in a validation method, no validation takes place, and no value is transferred to the model, even though we use AJAX here. We either need to pass in a dummy validation method (with an empty body) or implement a special handling of the absent method. In such a case, we have to omit the validator property. Such handling would inflate the component, so Alumni uses two more components, LabeledText and LabeledSecret, without the ability to pass in a validation method.

Summary

When a couple of components are used together in a similar manner, they might be composed into a reusable composite component. A composite component consists of an (optional) interface and an implementation. This chapter demonstrated how to transform existing code into such components.

Special attention is needed to allow child components for a composite component. We need to define which internal component(s) act as editable value holder.

The interface defines the attributes that can be passed into the composite. For nontrivial types, JSF needs to be informed about the attribute's type or, in the case of a method, about the method signature.

Finally, this chapter showed a reusable ubiquitous input component.

CHAPTER 28

Secure Passwords

Access to special areas of Alumni will be restricted to members only. That means we need to restrict access to authorized persons only. During the registration process, we ask the user to enter a password that we store together with the account entity.

Because Alumni is exposed to the web, there's a potential risk that somebody might tamper with the system. Passwords need special protection—they should never be stored in plain text format. Although there is no such things as 100% protection against *crackers* (malicious hackers—there are nice hackers), it's possible to store passwords in a reasonably safe way by following these guidelines:

- Strongly encrypt all passwords

- Grant no access to any decrypted passwords

- Use an algorithm that takes some time to calculate

- Calculate different hashes even though two users may have chosen the same password

- Use an algorithm to verify the password that takes almost the same time regardless of password length

Hash

Encryption without any possible decryption can be achieved by a hash function. A *hash* is the output of a hash function that maps text (or other data) of arbitrary size to an output string of a fixed size. A cryptographic useful hash function will produce an output that differs in almost all characters even if the input only has little changes. A hash function is a one-way function: you may calculate the hash from the text but you cannot calculate the text from the hash. Different input may produce the same hash. This situation is called a *collision*. A good hash function will produce as few collisions

© Michael Müller 2018
M. Müller, *Practical JSF in Java EE 8*, https://doi.org/10.1007/978-1-4842-3030-5_28

as possible. A purist may claim that a hash is something other than an encryption, but it still calculates an encrypted value. By choosing the right algorithm, we can reduce the risk of retrieving the same hash for two different passwords. For example, if you use Secure Hash Algorithm (SHA), say, SHA-512, the risk for such a collision tends to zero. Implementing such a hash function is quite easy, as you can see in Listing 28-1.

Listing 28-1. Simple Encryption (Hashing) of a Password

```
1    public static byte[] getSHAHash(String secret) {
2      try {
3        MessageDigest md = MessageDigest.getInstance("SHA");
4        byte[] digest = md.digest(secret.getBytes("utf-8"));
5        return digest;
6      } catch (UnsupportedEncodingException | NoSuchAlgorithmException ex) {
7        Logger.getLogger("HashUtils").log(Level.SEVERE, null, ex);
8        throw new RuntimeException(ex);
9      }
10   }
```

The strategy would be to store a hash into the database. That way, even if an unauthorized person gets access to the database, they can't read the passwords, only the hashes. But using a simple algorithm as shown in the preceding listing isn't advisable. There are some drawbacks we have to consider. If the hash algorithm tends to have lots of collisions, then it might become easier to produce the same hash as stored in the password hash table without knowing the correct password. SHA-1 for example is treated as being not really secure, even if only a few known huge documents produce the same hash. Other algorithms like MD5 are much less secure. But this obvious issue isn't the only problem.

Security Issues and Mitigation

A cracker might try to start a brute force attack by sending a massive amount of different password combinations until they hit the right one. The simple hash is calculated very fast, and the attacker can try many passwords in a short period of time. One thing we can do is slow down the process of user authentication and authorization. If the whole turnaround takes approximately 0.5–1.0 second, that wouldn't hinder the user. But it dramatically slows down the attacker.

Tip   *Authentication:* Is this the right user? *Authorization:* Which rights does this user have?

Suppose a cracker has stolen the hashes. If he knows which algorithm is used to calculate them, he can use a brute force attack against the hashes. Again, we need to slow down the process to prevent the cracker from finding valid passwords. We can delay the user authentication at any point in the process, but now the only chance is to use a hashing algorithm that takes a long time. Pure SHA is much too fast for this.

If the cracker finds a valid password, and the hash is used by more than one user, the cracker gains access to multiple accounts. To prevent that, we need to generate a different hash for different users, even if they've chosen the same password. You can do this by "salting" the password. Suppose you have a string salt with a random value. You can calculate the hash by adding that salt to the password, like this:

```
byte[] hash = getSHAHash(salt + secret)
```

Because we need the salt to calculate the correct hash, we need to store the salt somewhere. That might be within the same table where we store the password hash.

For a given password, the hash function always calculates the same hash. Thus, it would be possible to store phrases and their hashes. Then you can look up the password by querying the database with a hash. Such tables are known as *rainbow tables* and are available online for download from several sources (a search for "rainbow tables download" will list a lot of URLs). A salted password offers protection against such rainbow tables, too.

The user enters the password using the browser. But the database with the hashes resides somewhere else on a server. That means the password needs to be transferred from a browser to a server. To protect the password during transport, it is essential to choose a secure transport layer, such as Transport Layer Security (TLS), a cryptographic protocol for communication security. In conjunction with a certificate, an application server or upstream HTTP server can use HTTPS. Configuring the server is beyond this book's scope.

Password Algorithm

Putting all this together, Alumni uses the Password-Based Key Derivation Function 2 (PBKDF2) algorithm, as illustrated in Listing 28-2.

Listing 28-2. Revised Encryption (Hashing) of a Password

```
1   public static byte[] hashPassword(String password, byte[] salt,
2                                     int iterations, int keyLength) {
3     try {
4       SecretKeyFactory skf = SecretKeyFactory.
5          getInstance("PBKDF2WithHmacSHA512");
6       PBEKeySpec spec = new PBEKeySpec(password.toCharArray(), salt,
7                                       iterations, keyLength);
8       SecretKey key = skf.generateSecret(spec);
9       return key.getEncoded();
10    } catch (NoSuchAlgorithmException | InvalidKeySpecException ex) {
11      Logger.getLogger("HashUtils").log(Level.SEVERE, null, ex);
12      throw new RuntimeException(ex);
13    }
14  }
```

By setting the iterations to a high value, the calculation is slowed by additional rounds of calculation. On my development computer, a value of around 100,000 iterations will take 0.5 seconds. Using a value of 100,047 or a similar unexpected number of iterations won't affect the felt time but produces a different hash. Such numbers are used more rarely than big even numbers, which further helps improve security.

The delay depends on your machine, so don't copy this exact value. You need to figure out the best value for your machine.

KeyLength determines the length of the output. Alumni uses a key length of 1024, which is 1024 bits / 8 = 128 bytes.

This sketched-out approach might not meet the high requirements of a banking application, but it's fine for a social application like Alumni. (If you want to read more about this, check out the interesting article "Secure Password Storage" at http://goo.gl/Spvzs.)

Besides securely storing the password, the password also has to be checked during user authentication. Usually, comparing two values will fail at the first difference. If two strings are either different at the first or the last character, the comparison for the latter case would take a bit longer. This fact might help a cracker to guess a password. Later on, when we perform the user authentication and authorization, we'll compare the hash byte by byte to its end without shortcutting this process.

Summary

Most parts of Alumni are restricted to members only. A common way to perform user authentication is with a user-password combination. This chapter discussed some aspects of securing passwords. A password must never be stored in plain text format, but should be encrypted with a one-way encryption. Calculation of this hash needs to take some time to protect against brute force attacks. This chapter discussed the algorithm used for this purpose in Alumni, but without going into detail on the strength or weakness of passwords themselves, like password length, use of special characters, and so on.

CHAPTER 29

Data Facade

For Books, we used a simple service to store an entity. Each service derived an abstract service class and provided the class of the given entity. Although this approach was quite easy, it needed a concrete service for each entity.

Alumni is a bigger application, and it uses many entities. Some entities are related and can be grouped together. During the registration process, for example, Alumni creates an Account object. A message is sent to the user who follows an activation link. After this activation, the account is activated. We want to access the Account as well as related entities through one class, called a *facade*.

Abstract Data Service

Although Alumni uses one facade to access one or more related entities, we need a couple of facades to access different kinds of data. For convenience, all these facades are derived from the same abstract service. See Listing 29-1.

Listing 29-1. Abstract Service Class to Access Entities

```
1   public abstract class AbstractService {
2
3     @PersistenceContext(unitName = "AlumniPU")
4     private EntityManager _em;
5
6     protected <T> T read(Object id, Class<T> entityClass) {
7       return _em.find(entityClass, id);
8     }
9
```

© Michael Müller 2018
M. Müller, *Practical JSF in Java EE 8*, https://doi.org/10.1007/978-1-4842-3030-5_29

```
10    protected <T> T save(T entity) {
11      T merge = _em.merge(entity);
12      return merge;
13    }
14
15    protected void delete(Object entity) {
16      if (isAttached(entity)) {
17        _em.remove(entity);
18      } else {
19        _em.remove(_em.merge(entity));
20      }
21    }
22
23    protected <T> T find(Class<T> entityClass, Object id) {
24      return _em.find(entityClass, id);
25    }
26
27    protected <T> T findFresh(Class<T> entityClass, Object id) {
28      Map<String, Object> hints = new HashMap<>();
29      hints.put("javax.persistence.cache.retrieveMode", "BYPASS");
30      return _em.find(entityClass, id, hints);
31    }
32
33    protected <T> List<T> findAll(Class<T> entityClass) {
34      CriteriaQuery cq = _em.getCriteriaBuilder().createQuery();
35      cq.select(cq.from(entityClass));
36      return _em.createQuery(cq).getResultList();
37    }
38
39    protected <T> List<T> findRange(Class<T> entityClass, int[] range) {
40      return findRange(entityClass, range[0], range[1]);
41    }
42
```

```
43    protected <T> List<T> findRange(Class<T> entityClass, int from,
      int to) {
44      CriteriaQuery cq = _em.getCriteriaBuilder().createQuery();
45      cq.select(cq.from(entityClass));
46      javax.persistence.Query q = _em.createQuery(cq);
47      q.setMaxResults(to - from + 1);
48      q.setFirstResult(from);
49      return q.getResultList();
50    }
51
52    protected <T> int count(Class<T> entityClass) {
53      CriteriaQuery cq = _em.getCriteriaBuilder().createQuery();
54      Root<T> rt = cq.from(entityClass);
55      cq.select(_em.getCriteriaBuilder().count(rt));
56      javax.persistence.Query q = _em.createQuery(cq);
57      return ((Long) q.getSingleResult()).intValue();
58    }
59
60    protected boolean isAttached(Object entity) {
61      return _em.contains(entity);
62    }
63
64    protected void clearCache() {
65      _em.flush();
66      _em.getEntityManagerFactory().getCache().evictAll();
67    }
68
69  }
```

Compared with the earlier approach with Books, the main difference is that we don't pass the entity class into the constructor. Instead, for some accesses we need to provide the appropriate class of an entity (line 6 type var entityClass) to implement a generic access to entities of a certain class.

Concrete Facade

Now we can create some methods to access different entities through the same facade. The excerpt in Listing 29-2 demonstrates this.

Listing 29-2. AccountingService as Facade to a Couple of Entities (Excerpt)

```
01    @ApplicationScoped
02    @Transactional
03    public class AccountService extends AbstractService {
04
05      public Account saveAccount(Account account) {
06        return save(account);
07      }
08
09      public List<Account> findAllAccounts() {
10        return findAll(Account.class);
11      }
12
13      public Account findAccount(byte[] id) {
14        return find(Account.class, id);
15      }
16
17      public Account createAccount(Account account) {
18        if (emailExists(account.getEmail())) {
19          throw new IllegalArgumentException("createAccount, email exists:
"
20                          + account.getEmail());
21        }
22        account.setLoginName(deriveUniqueLoginName(account));
23        account.setStatus(AccountStatus.New);
24        return save(account);
25      }
26
27      ...
28
```

```
29    public boolean activateAccount(String accessKey) {
30      try{
31        Account account = findAccountByAccessKey(accessKey);
32        account.setStatus(AccountStatus.Active);
33        save(account);
34        return true;
35      }catch(Exception ex){
36        LOGGER.log(Level.WARNING, ex.getMessage());
37        return false;
38      }
39    }
40
41    private Account findAccountByAccessKey(String accessKey) {
42      String jpql = "select a from Account a where a._accessKey =
          :accessKey";
43      TypedQuery<Account> query = getEntityManager().createQuery(jpql,
          Account.class);
44      query.setParameter("accessKey", HashUtils.hex2byte(accessKey));
45      try {
46        return query.getSingleResult();
47      } catch (Exception ex) {
48        throw new IllegalArgumentException("Unknown accessKey: " +
          accessKey);
49      }
50    }
51
52    public void deleteAccount(String id) {
53      String jpql = "DELETE FROM Account a WHERE a._id = :id";
54      Query query = getEntityManager().createQuery(jpql);
55      query.setParameter("id", HashUtils.hex2byte(id));
56      query.executeUpdate();
57      clearCache();
58    }
59
60  }
```

As you can see, this concrete facade either simply delegates to the abstract facade or adds more complex functions like findAccountbyAccessKey. Although a new instance might be saved by the saveAccount method (line 5), there's a special method to create an account starting at line 17. This method checks whether the email exists to ensure that each email can be assigned to one account only. The login name might be updated during account creation to ensure a unique login name. Last but not least, the account status is set to new. This indicates a nonactivated account. Login is possible for activated accounts only.

Starting at line 52, there's a delete method. It deletes an account that is identified by its id without any need to load it into memory beforehand.

For brevity's sake, Listing 29-2 doesn't show the whole class.

Account Entity

Account takes all information collected in the registration form and adds a creation date. If the user doesn't activate his account during a defined period beginning with that date, we'll prune this account. See Listing 29-3.

Listing 29-3. Entity Accounting

```
01   @Entity
02   @Table(name = "Account")
03   public class Account implements Serializable {
04
05     private static final long serialVersionUID = 1L;
06     private static final int KEY_LEN = 1024;
07     private static final int ROUNDS = 100_021;
08
09     // <editor-fold defaultstate="collapsed" desc="Property Id">
10     @Id
11     @Column(name = "id")
12     private final byte[] _id = makeUuidAsBytes();
13
14     public String getId() {
15       return HashUtils.byte2hex(_id);
16     }
```

```
17      // </editor-fold>
18
19      // <editor-fold defaultstate="collapsed" desc="Property Key">
20      @Column(name = "accessKey")
21      private final byte[] _accessKey = makeUuidAsBytes();
22
23      public String getAccessKey() {
24        return HashUtils.byte2hex(_accessKey);
25      }
26      // </editor-fold>
27
28      // <editor-fold defaultstate="collapsed" desc="Property Status">
29      @Column(name = "status")
30      private AccountStatus _status = AccountStatus.New;
31
32      public AccountStatus getStatus() {
33        return _status;
34      }
35
36      public void setStatus(AccountStatus status) {
37        _status = status;
38      }
39      // </editor-fold>
40
41      // <editor-fold defaultstate="collapsed" desc="Property LoginName">
42      @Column(name = "loginName")
43      private String _loginName;
44
45      @Size(min = 1, max = 50)
46      public String getLoginName() {
47        return _loginName;
48      }
49
```

```
50      public void setLoginName(String loginName) {
51        _loginName = loginName;
52      }
53      // </editor-fold>
54
55      // <editor-fold defaultstate="collapsed" desc="Property FirstName">
56      @Column(name = "firstName")
57      private String _firstName = "";
58
59      @Size(min = 1, max = 50)
60      public String getFirstName() {
61        return _firstName;
62      }
63
64      public void setFirstName(String firstName) {
65        _firstName = firstName;
66      }
67      // </editor-fold>
68
69      // <editor-fold defaultstate="collapsed" desc="Property LastName">
70      @Column(name = "lastName")
71      private String _lastName;
72
73      @Size(min = 1, max = 50, message = "{validation.lastname.size}")
74      public String getLastName() {
75        return _lastName;
76      }
77
78      public void setLastName(String lastName) {
79        _lastName = lastName;
80      }
81      // </editor-fold>
82
```

```
83      // <editor-fold defaultstate="collapsed" desc="Property Email">
84      @Column(name = "email")
85      private String _email = "";
86
87      @Size(min = 6, max = 100)
88      public String getEmail() {
89        return _email;
90      }
91
92      public void setEmail(String email) {
93        _email = email;
94      }
95      // </editor-fold>
96
97      // <editor-fold defaultstate="collapsed" desc="Property
        LastChanged">
98      @Temporal(javax.persistence.TemporalType.TIMESTAMP)
99      @Column(name = "lastChanged")
100   private Date _lastChanged = new Date();
101
102   public Date getLastChanged() {
103     return _lastChanged;
104   }
105
106   public void setLastChanged(Date lastChanged) {
107     _lastChanged = lastChanged;
108   }
109
110   @PreUpdate
111   private void tagLastChanged() {
112     _lastChanged = new Date();
113   }
114   // </editor-fold>
115
```

```
116    // <editor-fold defaultstate="collapsed" desc="Property Created">
117    @Temporal(javax.persistence.TemporalType.TIMESTAMP)
118    @Column(name = "created")
119    private Date _created = new Date();
120
121    public Date getCreated() {
122      return _created;
123    }
124
125    public void setCreated(Date created) {
126      _created = created;
127    }
128    // </editor-fold>
129
130    // <editor-fold defaultstate="collapsed" desc="Property Password">
131    @Column(name = "password")
132    private byte[] _passwordHash;
133
134    public void setPassword(String password){
135      _passwordHash = obtainPasswordHash(password);
136    }
137
138    public boolean checkPassword(String password) {
139      return _status == AccountStatus.Active
140              && Arrays.equals(obtainPasswordHash(password),
                  _passwordHash);
141    }
142
143    private byte[] obtainPasswordHash(String password) {
144     byte[] passwordHash = HashUtils.hashPassword(password, makeSalt(),
145              ROUNDS, KEY_LEN);
146      return passwordHash;
147    }
148
```

```
149    private byte[] makeSalt() {
150      byte[] salt = new byte[32];
151      System.arraycopy(_id, 0, salt, 0, 16);
152      System.arraycopy(_accessKey, 0, salt, 16, 16);
153      return salt;
154    }
155    // </editor-fold>
156
157 }
```

Just a reminder: The comments for editor-fold are specific to NetBeans and allow for collapsing (folding) the source code.

Alumni doesn't use a sequential number as primary key (as Books does), but a UUID converted into a byte array. Because this id will never be changed for a given account, it's assigned during its declaration (line 12). A second UUID is used to create an access key, which is used to activate the account. Both id and access key are used as salt for the password (see Chapter 28 for more on salting passwords). Each is built with 16 bytes, so the total length of the salt is 32 bytes, which is fine for the password encryption.

Two timestamps are used to indicate the creation time as well as the last change. The lastChanged is tagged before any update due to the @PreUpdate annotation.

Lines 131–154 show the password handling. When the password is passed in, its hash is calculated and stored in the appropriate field. This hash will be stored in the database. The password has no getter; instead, checkPassword is used to verify whether the password (as provided during login) matches the hash.

Summary

Each access to the database is performed through a data façade, which offers an interface to a couple of methods to access a group of related data. This facade is used to hide the details of the data access. For different kinds of data, Alumni offers a couple of facades that are derived from an abstract facade.

This chapter also showed details of the data that's stored, updated, and deleted using the facade. The password is encrypted once it's passed to the entity and will never be stored with its original value.

CHAPTER 30

Activation Mail

In Alumni, once the Account is created, we send an activation mail to the user, which contains a link with a universally unique identifier (UUID). If the user follows this link, the account will be activated and become ready for use.

Config Mail Properties by Code

The sending of the email is performed by an application scoped class called the Mailer. Within this class, some hardcoded properties are collected into a map. In the final version, a JavaMail session will be our choice to retrieve the config from (see the next section).

Listing 30-1. Mailer (with Hardcoded Properties for Demonstration)

```
01    @Dependent
02    public class Mailer implements Serializable {
03
04      protected static final Logger LOGGER = Logger.getLogger("Mailer");
05
06      public boolean sendMail(String to, String subject, String body) {
07        List<Recipient> recipients = new ArrayList<>();
08        recipients.add(new Recipient(to, RecipientType.TO));
09        return sendMail("mailer@alumni-web.de", recipients, subject, body);
10      }
11
12      public boolean sendMail(String from, List<Recipient> recipients,
13              String subject, String body, String... files) {
14        try {
15          Properties properties = obtainConfig();
```

331

© Michael Müller 2018
M. Müller, *Practical JSF in Java EE 8*, https://doi.org/10.1007/978-1-4842-3030-5_30

```
16          Session session = Session.getDefaultInstance(properties);
17          MimeMessage message = composeMessage(session, from, recipients,
18                   subject, body, files);
19          Transport.send(message, from, "secret");
20          return true;
21        } catch (MessagingException ex) {
22          LOGGER.log(Level.SEVERE, "Mailer failed: {0}", ex.getMessage());
23          return false;
24        }
25      }
26
27      private Properties obtainConfig() {
28        Properties properties = System.getProperties();
29        properties.put("mail.transport.protocol.rfc822", "smtps");
30        properties.put("mail.smtps.host", "smtp.strato.de");
31       properties.put("mail.smtps.port", 465);
32        properties.put("mail.smtps.auth", true);
33        return properties;
34      }
35
36      private MimeMessage composeMessage(Session session,
37              String from,
38              List<Recipient> recipients,
39              String subject,
40              String body,
41              String[] files) throws MessagingException {
42        MimeMessage message = new MimeMessage(session);
43        for (Recipient recipient : recipients) {
44          message.addRecipient(recipient.getType(),
45                  new InternetAddress(recipient.getEmail()));
46        }
47        message.setSubject(subject);
48        message.setContent(getMultipartBody(body, files));
49        message.setFrom(new InternetAddress(from));
50        return message;
51      }
```

```
52
53    private Multipart getMultipartBody(String body, String[] files)
54            throws MessagingException {
55      MimeBodyPart messageBodyPart = new MimeBodyPart();
56      messageBodyPart.setText(body);
57      Multipart multipart = new MimeMultipart();
58      multipart.addBodyPart(messageBodyPart);
59      for (String file : files) {
60        addAttachment(multipart, file);
61      }
62      return multipart;
63    }
64
65    private static void addAttachment(Multipart multipart, String filename)
66            throws MessagingException {
67      if (filename.isEmpty()) {
68        return;
69      }
70      MimeBodyPart messageBodyPart = new MimeBodyPart();
71      DataSource source = new FileDataSource(filename);
72      messageBodyPart.setDataHandler(new DataHandler(source));
73      File file = new File(filename);
74      messageBodyPart.setFileName(file.getName());
75      multipart.addBodyPart(messageBodyPart);
76    }
77
78  }
```

JavaMail is part of the Java Enterprise Edition (EE). Thus, there's no need to refer to the JavaMail jar directly. All we have to do is to add the right dependency for Java EE to the POM.

Without this dependency, the IDE can't add the required imports. NetBeans offers a Maven search for unsatisfied imports. We need to add the following:

```
import javax.mail.Message;
```

Place the cursor at the end of that line and press Alt+Enter. NetBeans offers a Maven search dialog, shown in Figure 30-1.

Figure 30-1. *Maven search dialog*

Choose `javax:javaee-api` in the Matching Artifacts field. NetBeans will add the dependency to the POM. Using a different IDE, you may add the dependency manually. See Listing 30-2.

Listing 30-2. Dependency for JavaMail (and Other Parts of the Java EE API)

```
1  <dependency>
2    <groupId>javax</groupId>
3    <artifactId>javaee-api</artifactId>
4    <version>8.0</version>
5    <type>jar</type>
6  </dependency>
```

Once that dependency is included, NetBeans can fix the missing imports (Ctrl+Shift+I).

Let's examine the code: line 1 shows the @Dependent annotation. This declares a CDI eligible bean whose lifecycle depends on the bean where it's injected to.

For sending the activation mail, Alumni uses the method sendMail, which starts at line 6. It simply sends an email, which is composed of a subject and body, to one recipient.

We may need to attach files or add other recipients. sendMail delegates to an overloaded version of this method, which takes some more parameters (line 12 in Listing 30-1). It might be nice to replace so many parameters with a mail information object that carries all the information. Because the final version of the Mailer needs one fewer parameter, it may be okay as is.

To create a message we need a session. Such a session is created by passing mail server–specific properties to its factory method (line 16). These properties are collected into a map by the obtainConfig method (line 27). Within this method, some hardcoded properties are collected into a map. In the final version, a JavaMail Session will be our choice to retrieve the config from.

Alumni uses a secured protocol version, so we set the protocol to SMTPS. Next, we set some SMTPS parameters according to the mail server. The properties mail.smpts.XXX correspond to the chosen protocol. You can read a full description of the API at https://javaee.github.io/javaee-spec/javadocs/javax/mail/package-summary.html.

Once sendMail obtains a session, it composes the message (lines 17 and 18) and sends the mail (line 19). Here we're providing a secret password. If no password is needed, we may set the sender with a property and pass the message only to the Transport.send method.

Mail Session

As mentioned earlier, a hardcoded configuration isn't a good choice here. Maybe you need to distinguish between development and production, or need different configurations on different production systems. Alumni uses a JavaMail session defined at GlassFish/Payara, as shown in Figure 30-2. Assuming you're running the server locally, admin pages are available at the address `https://localhost:4848`. If you use NetBeans, you alternatively open the admin console via the context menu of your server in the Services tree view. In the admin console, choose Resources ➤ JavaMail Sessions ➤ New to create a session.

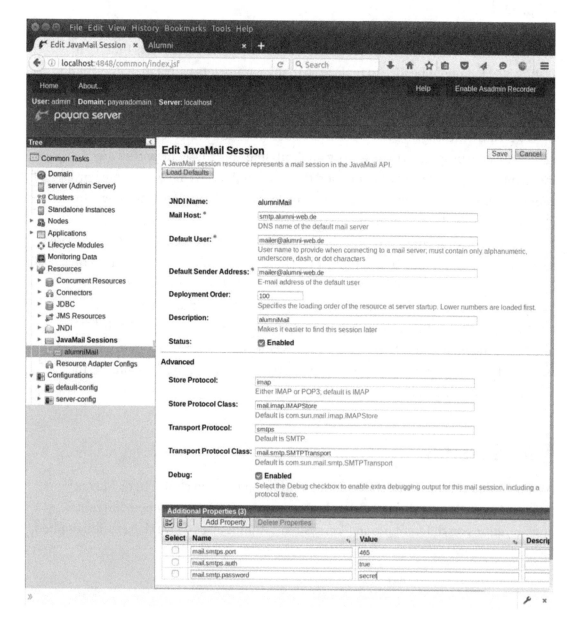

Figure 30-2. *JavaMail session in GlassFish/Payara*

Alternatively, you might create a `glassfish-resources.xml` file (or let NetBeans create it in the proper place), which resides in the `WEB-INF` folder. See Listing 30-3.

Listing 30-3. `glassfish-resources.xml`

```
01   <!DOCTYPE resources PUBLIC
02   "-//GlassFish.org//DTD GlassFish Application Server 3.1 Resource
     Definitions//EN"
03   "http://glassfish.org/dtds/glassfish-resources_1_5.dtd">
04   <resources>
05     <mail-resource debug="true"
06                    enabled="true"
07                     from="mailer@alumni-web.de"
08                     host="smtp.strato.de"
09                    jndi-name="alumniMail"
10                    object-type="user"
11                    store-protocol="imap"
12                    store-protocol-class="com.sun.mail.imap.IMAPStore"
13                    transport-protocol="smtps"
14                    transport-protocol-class="mail.smtp.SMTPTransport"
15                    user="mailer@alumni-web.de">
16       <description>alumniMail</description>
17       <property name="mail.smtps.port" value="465"/>
18       <property name="mail.smtps.auth" value="true"/>
19       <property name="mail.smtps.password" value="secret"/>
20     </mail-resource>
21   </resources>
```

This session can be injected by a traditional `@Resource` annotation, as shown in Listing 30-4. Since JSF 2.3, it's been available via `@Inject`. There's no need to collect the config properties because they're defined outside the code, as shown in Listing 30-5. So you can change the config without changing the code just by changing the parameters using the admin console.

Take a look at the interesting parts of the final `Mailer` class, which is reduced in size as we remove the `from` parameter of `sendMail`. See Listing 30-4.

Listing 30-4. `Mailer` Using an Injected Session (Excerpt)

```
01      @Resource(lookup = "alumniMail")
02      private Session _session;
03
04      public boolean sendMail(List<Recipient> recipients,
05              String subject, String body, String... files) {
06        try {
07          MimeMessage message = composeMessage(recipients,
08                  subject, body, files);
09          String user = _session.getProperty("mail.user");
10          String password = _session.getProperty("mail.smpt.password");
11          Transport.send(message, user, password);
12          return true;
13        } catch (MessagingException ex) {
14          LOGGER.log(Level.SEVERE, "Mailer failed: {0}", ex.getMessage());
15          return false;
16        }
17      }
18
19      private MimeMessage composeMessage(List<Recipient> recipients,
20              String subject,
21              String body,
22              String[] files) throws MessagingException {
23        MimeMessage message = new MimeMessage(_session);
24        for (Recipient recipient : recipients) {
25          message.addRecipient(recipient.getType(),
26                  new InternetAddress(recipient.getEmail())));
27        }
```

```
28      message.setSubject(subject);
29      message.setContent(getMultipartBody(body, files));
30      String from = _session.getProperty("mail.from");
31      message.setFrom(new InternetAddress(from));
32      return message;
33    }
```

Send Activation

When the user clicks the Register button, Alumni creates a new account with a status of new. I'll explain this later in relation to login. Login will be possible once the account is activated (that is, status = *active*).

In order to send an activation mail to the user, we need an email template to which we'll add information such as username and an activation link. This template will be created by the admin using a simple JSF-based web form and will be stored in a table of the database. It consists of an id, a name (as a kind of human readable identifier), a subject, and a body. Remember to store a template version for every language you want to support.

When I showed the Mailer, I concentrated on the sendMail functionality. In Alumni, the Mailer delegates to an instance of the class MailService (not shown here), which is used to access the mail templates. Within such a template, we use names within curly braces as placeholders that are replaced before sending. The body of the activation mail might look like this:

Hello {firstName},
In order to complete your registration, please click the following link
{link}.

Sending the activation mail becomes straightforward: retrieve a mail template (line 4 of Listing 30-5), build subject and body by replacing the placeholders (lines 5–9), and send the mail (line 10). The most complicated part is to build the URL that replaces one of the placeholders (lines 13—30).

Listing 30-5. Register User (Excerpt)

```
01    @Inject private Mailer _mailer;
02
03    private void sendMail(String accessKey) {
04      MailTemplate template = _mailer.findTemplateByName(TemplateName.
          ActivationMail);
05      String subject = template.getSubject();
06      String body = template
07              .getBody()
08              .replace("{firstName}", _account.getFirstName())
09              .replace("{link}", getUrl(accessKey));
10      _mailer.sendMail(_account.getEmail(), subject, body);
11    }
12
13    private String getUrl(String key) {
14      HttpServletRequest request = obtainServletRequest();
15      try {
16        URL url = new URL(request.getScheme(),
17                request.getServerName(),
18                request.getServerPort(),
19                request.getContextPath() + Page.Activate.url() +
                "?key=" + key);
20        return url.toString();
21      } catch (MalformedURLException ex) {
22        Logger.getLogger(Register.class.getName()).log(Level.SEVERE, null, ex);
23        return "";
24      }
25  }
```

```
26
27    private HttpServletRequest obtainServletRequest() {
28       FacesContext context = FacesContext.getCurrentInstance();
29       return (HttpServletRequest) context.getExternalContext().getRequest();
30    }
```

Usually, we navigate to pages in the application. Such a path will be automatically appended to the context path. But for the activation mail, we need to send the user a complete URL (URI), including the domain name (or for development, the server's name) and the context path. This URL is built in lines 16–20. If your server is operating on a standard HTTP port (port 80, or 430 for HTTPS), you can omit the port number.

Once a user receives this activation mail, they follow the link.

Summary

With JavaMail, you have an API for handling emails that you can use either in Java SE or Java EE. It's included in Java EE, so there's no need to add an extra reference to the POM within a Java EE project.

JavaMail requires some properties to configure the transport, including mail server, protocol, and more. This chapter showed such properties with a hardcoded solution. Even better, these properties are set outside the application. A Java EE-compliant server offers the ability to define a mail session via its console or a `.properties` file. That's how Alumni uses the mail functionality to send activation mails or other info to the user.

CHAPTER 31

Scheduled Tasks

If a user doesn't activate their account, we'll get an *orphaned* registration (or account). We have to clean up the database periodically, and what works better for periodically jobs than a timer? This is where scheduled tasks come into play. Because timers can be very sensitive to errors within the same thread, we'll do this scheduling asynchronously.

Scheduler

Timers are available within Enterprise Java Beans (EJBs). Alumni uses a central class to invoke timed events: the Scheduler class, annotated as @Singleton. Any method that should be invoked by a timer will be annotated with @Schedule. See Listing 31-1.

Listing 31-1. Scheduler Class

```
1   @Singleton
2   public class Scheduler {
3
4     @Inject DatabaseCleaner _dbCleaner;
5
6     @Schedule(hour = "*/1")
7     private void cleanDatabase() {
8         _dbCleaner.cleanAccountRequests();
9     }
10  }
```

Line 6 shows a schedule for every hour. The server will create an appropriate timer. If we write hour = "1", the timer will fire once a day, at 1 o'clock. Using the asterisk and a number after the slash, */n stands for every *n* hours (you can also use minutes, seconds, and so on). An asterisk on its own stands for "doesn't care." So, if we want to

© Michael Müller 2018
M. Müller, *Practical JSF in Java EE 8*, https://doi.org/10.1007/978-1-4842-3030-5_31

schedule a task every ten seconds, the hours and minutes "don't care." We annotate the method like this:

```
@Schedule(hour = "*", minute = "*", second = "*/10")
```

The DatabaseCleaner class is used to bundle a couple of database-cleaning task starters. At first glance, this class does nothing but delegate to the register service and log in case of error. See Listing 31-2.

Listing 31-2. DatabaseCleaner Class

```
1    @Stateless
2    public class DatabaseCleaner {
3
4      @Inject private AccountService _registerService;
5
6      public void cleanAccountRequests() {
7        try {
8          _registerService.deleteOldAccountRequests();
9        } catch (Exception ex) {
10         Logger.getLogger(Scheduler.class.getName())
11                 .log(Level.SEVERE, null, ex.getMessage());
12       }
13     }
14
15   }
```

Once a timer is created, the application server ensures that it will be triggered. If the server goes down, that won't stop the timer: after a reboot, the server restores all timers. After any downtime, the server tries to catch up on everything.

Delete Query

Using the Java Persistence API (JPA), people become acquainted with CRUD (create, read, update, delete) operations: persist, find, merge, and remove. To delete a single entity, you usually use the remove(entity) method. With this approach, you first have to load the entity and then pass it as a parameter to the remove method. It's only suitable when you want to delete an entity that was loaded into memory before for some other reason.

But why should you load an entity if you only want to delete it? I know people who dislike JPA because of that. However, JPA offers more than the well-known CRUD operations. For example, there's executeUpdate(), which you can use for other SQL-like operations. We use it to delete all requests that are older than one day. We'll have to calculate this date. Although the new LocalDate is very handy, we can't use it here. We need the old-fashioned Date. Or at least we need to convert a LocalDate into that type (the good news about JPA 2.2 is that defining an entity, you might use the Java 8 date API). See Listing 31-3.

Listing 31-3. AccountService Class (Excerpt)

```
01    public void deleteOldAccountRequests() {
02      String jpql = "DELETE FROM Account a "
03              + "WHERE a._created < :date and a._status = :status";
04      Query query = getEntityManager().createQuery(jpql);
05      Date deleteBefore = new Date();
06      query.setParameter("date", getDateWithDayOffset(-1));
07      query.setParameter("status", AccountStatus.New);
08      query.executeUpdate();
09    }
10
11    public Date getDateWithDayOffset(int offset) {
12      return new Date(System.currentTimeMillis()+ offset*24*60*60*1000);
13    }
```

Now if we start the application, the application server will create a timer; every hour, the cleaning operation will be called. And in case of an error, the error will be logged. So far, everything seems to work fine.

 Provoke an error

But let's enforce an exception. We're going to provoke an error.

Modify the jpql statement: WHERE a.createdXXX < :date. Note that appending the three Xs makes the field name invalid. Change the time to be invoked every 5 seconds (you don't want to have to wait for hours).

Then start the application and observe the server log.

As you might have expected, the server reports an error:

```
Info:   Error during transaction processing
java.lang.IllegalArgumentException: An exception occurred while creating a
query in EntityManager:
Exception Description: Problem compiling [DELETE FROM Account a WHERE
a._createdXXX < :date and a._status = :status].
[28, 41] The state field path 'a._createdXXX' cannot be resolved to a
valid type.
```

But after the second attempt to invoke the database cleaner, the timer stops, and the server logs the following:

```
Info: EJB5119:Expunging timer [...] after [2] failed deliveries
```

As reported in the log, the timer stops. This happens even though we catch the error. This apparent strange behavior is by design with EJB. Usually our code would be correct, but imagine the database server is down unexpectedly. After some time it comes back up and is running again. We want our scheduled server to operate on the database again, but by this time the timer might be expunged.

How can we solve this problem? Catching the exception isn't an option, as we just showed. Luckily, there *is* a simple solution: the timer won't be expunged if the exception occurs in a different thread.

Becoming Asynchronous

If we want to trigger long-running tasks, it might be great to start without waiting for results.

The recent version of Java EE supports *asynchronous method calls*: the method is invoked in a different thread, and control immediately returns to the caller. All you need to do is to declare the method that's called by the timer as Asynchronous by using the appropriate annotation, as shown in Listing 31-4.

Listing 31-4. Asynchronous Method

```
1    @Asynchronous
2    public void cleanAccountRequests() {
3        ...
4    }
```

Even though the deletion task we defined is very short, it gets its benefit from the Asynchronous call: the timer won't stop any more due to the error in the jpql statement. Besides running asynchronous, we'll get a stable timer.

Summary

This chapter provided a lean introduction into scheduled events. Java EE supports timed events by simply adding the @Schedule annotation to a method. The first use in Alumni is a periodically database-cleaning process that uses a delete query. Thus, there's no need to load any entity before it becomes deleted. Timers are vulnerable to exceptions, even though this exception might be caught. Using an Asynchronous method call helps to increase the timer's stability.

CHAPTER 32

Authentication and Authorization

Sometimes it's crucial to protect an application or data against unauthorized access. Although Alumni offers some public pages, most are restricted to members. The system will grant access to certain features for well-known users only. Luckily, the application server provides some security features, like authentication and authorization, and controls access to parts of the program with the concept of user roles.

Container-provided security isn't specific to JSF. It's part of the HTTP handling and can be used by a simple servlet too. Before integrating it into Alumni, let's go over some basic information about security.

Security Basics

To grant a user access to a secured application, you first have to authenticate the user. The user must tell the system who they are. This might be done by providing a username ("it's me") and a password ("you can verify that it's really me, by checking some secret information that only we share"). Alternative authentication techniques include the use of identity cards, certificates, fingerprints, and so on. In this book, we focus on usernames and passwords.

Once the system has authenticated the user, it authorizes the user, deciding whether to let them access the whole application or only parts of it, depending on security status. This is realized by assigning one or more different *roles* to the user. Depending on the role, access to the application is controlled.

© Michael Müller 2018
M. Müller, *Practical JSF in Java EE 8*, https://doi.org/10.1007/978-1-4842-3030-5_32

Let's recap:

1. System offers a login (such as a form) to query username and password.

2. User provides this information.

3. System verifies this information. If there is no match, login is aborted.

4. System determines roles and grants access depending on these roles.

Using container-provided security, step 1 might be realized in (at least) three ways:

- The user's web browser displays a simple input dialog. The appearance and client-side data handling are determined by the browser. There's no further action required by the developer. This mode is called *basic authentication*.

- The developer provides an HTML form for the two input fields and buttons to submit or reset. These fields may be integrated in a web page with the look and feel of the application. The names of the input fields and the actions have to strictly follow a convention. This mode is called *form-based authentication*.

- The developer uses a pre-arranged JSF form. On the server side, the application calls the container's login method. This is called *programmatic authentication*.

The username and password have to be sent from client to server. It doesn't make any difference whether the password is sent as plain (clear) text or as hashed digest (which might be configured in a server property): if someone captures this data, they might try to use it to gain access. Thus, a common recommendation is to use a secure transport protocol such as TSL/SSL. Users may identify such a secure protocol by the `https://` protocol part of a URL—the *s* stands for security.

For step 3 of the authentication/authorization process, the server must check the input (username/password) against information stored somewhere. This is realized by so-called security *realms*. Usually, one or more realms are predefined at your server. GlassFish, for example, provides a couple of realms. We'll discuss two of them: fileRealm (user info stored in a file) and jdbcRealm (user info stored in a database). Last but not least, we'll talk about a self-programmed (custom) realm.

Even though these security realms are sometimes implemented in a similar way, they're still vendor specific. Terminology conventions may differ, too. Some call it *realm*, others say *domain, zone*, and so on. The same applies to other terminology in this context, such as *group, role, principal, right*, and so on.

To overcome this confusion, a standard has been created: Java Authentication Service Provider Interface for Containers (JASPIC, JSR 196). Although the definition of JASPIC started more than a decade ago, proprietary realms are still prevalent. With Java EE 6, this started to change, and it seemed JASPIC became a kind of first-class citizen. Anyway Java EE 7 didn't introduce as much as needed, and there's an ongoing standardization process (JSR 375) that builds on top of JSAPIC and JACC (Java Authorization Service Provider Contract for Containers). This Java Security API is partially scheduled for Java EE 8 and will be completed with Java EE 9. We'll use its reference implementation, Soteria, later on for simpler access than with plain JASPIC.

We'll start with the HTTP authentication and its realms. The Java Authentication and Authorization Service (JAAS) was integrated into Java 2 SDK 1.4. (To read more about this, check out `https://docs.oracle.com/javase/8/docs/technotes/guides/security/jaas/JAASRefGuide.html`.) Keep in mind vendor-specific implementations when I write about realms. I'll focus on GlassFish and NetBeans, and you may have to transform some info into your environment.

For example, NetBeans offers some special editors to configure container-based security. I'll discuss this as well as the resulting configuration, which usually is pure XML.

Basic Authentication and fileRealm

To secure Alumni, we need to add a security constraint to `web.xml`. Open this file in your editor. Using NetBeans, choose on your project tree `Web Pages, WEB-INF, web.xml`. NetBeans opens this file by default in the source view. To get an overview, switch to the Security tab. Doing so alters the view and allows you to easily read or define security settings. See Figure 32-1.

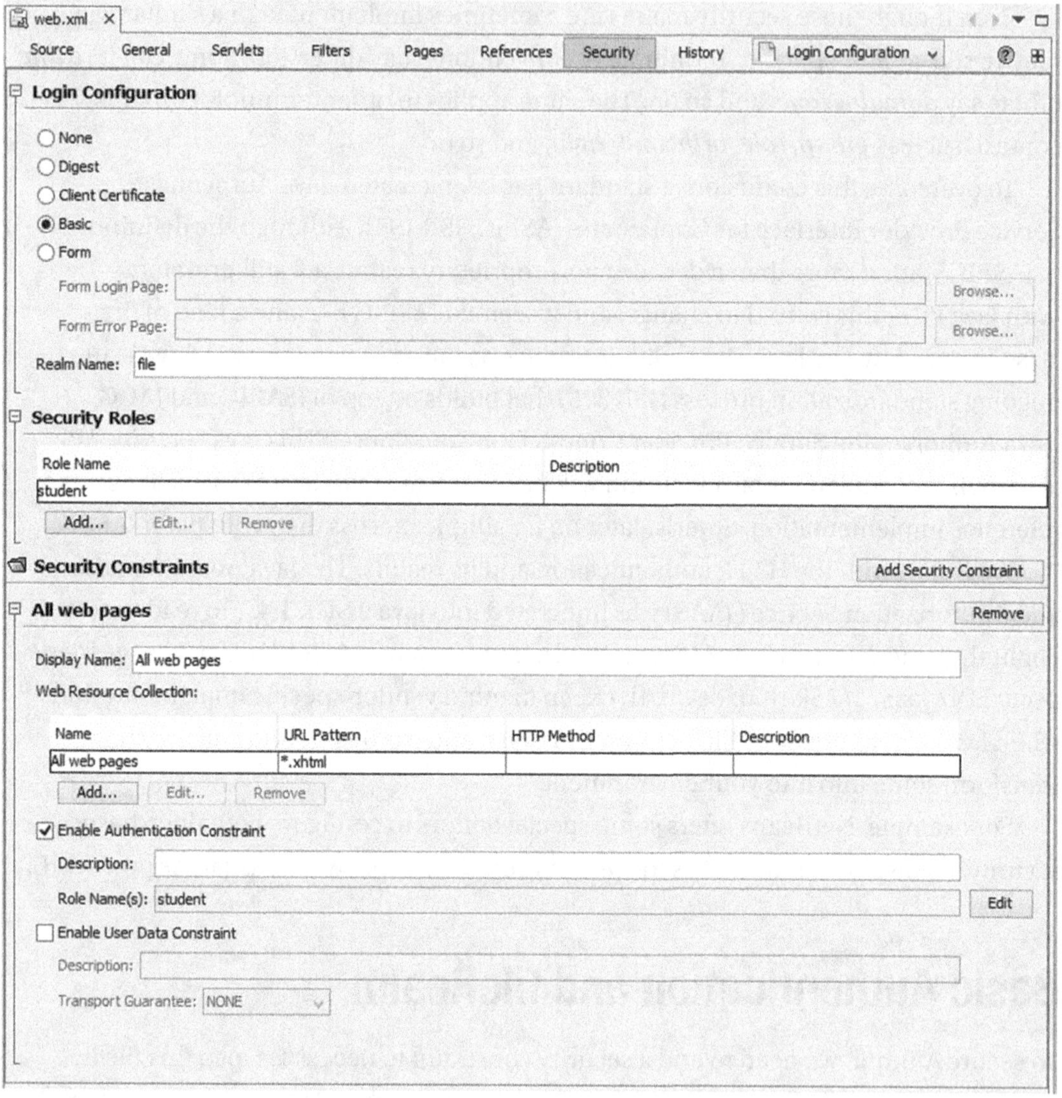

Figure 32-1. *Security tab for* web.xml.

At the top, note the different Login Configurations. As mentioned, I'll cover Basic and
Form in this tutorial. From the users' point of view, Digest is almost the same as Basic:
both present a small input dialog in the browser where the user can enter username and
password. Under the hood, a *digest* (hash value) is derived from the password. Thus,
no clear text is sent to the server. But this isn't really a security feature. If the digest were
captured by some criminal it would have almost the same effect as if the password were
captured. So, you must encrypt the connection itself using SSL (Secure Socket Layers)

or its modern successor TLS (Transport Layer Security). Using either will result in an HTTPS connection.

The Form login configuration will display the specified form to query the credentials. This allows you to customize the process.

The Client Certificate login configuration is based on SSL and a server certificate in conjunction with a client certificate.

To proceed with the basic authentication, choose Basic and enter **file** in the Realm Name field. This info isn't checked by NetBeans, so be sure to enter an existing realm name. Refer to your application server to figure out which values are valid. Because I'm using GlassFish for this tutorial, *file* is a valid realm name. A file realm (a.k.a. domain, zone, and so on) is available for most app servers.

Next, go to Security Roles and add two roles. Call them **member** and **admin**. You can define as many roles as you like. This might be useful for applications where you need to distinguish between different access levels like admin, normal user, manager, service, and so on. For the full version of Alumni, we need a couple of roles too, but for this first demonstration, there's no need to define more roles yet.

The next step to configure web.xml is to add security constraints. Click Add Security Constraint to add one. The display name is optional and for your convenience. We'll use *member access* here. The display name is very useful, if you have to deal with lots of different constraints.

Now add a web resource collection (see Figure 32-2). Give it a name and provide a URL pattern. /**member**/* applies to all pages of the member folder. Click OK to return to the Security tab.

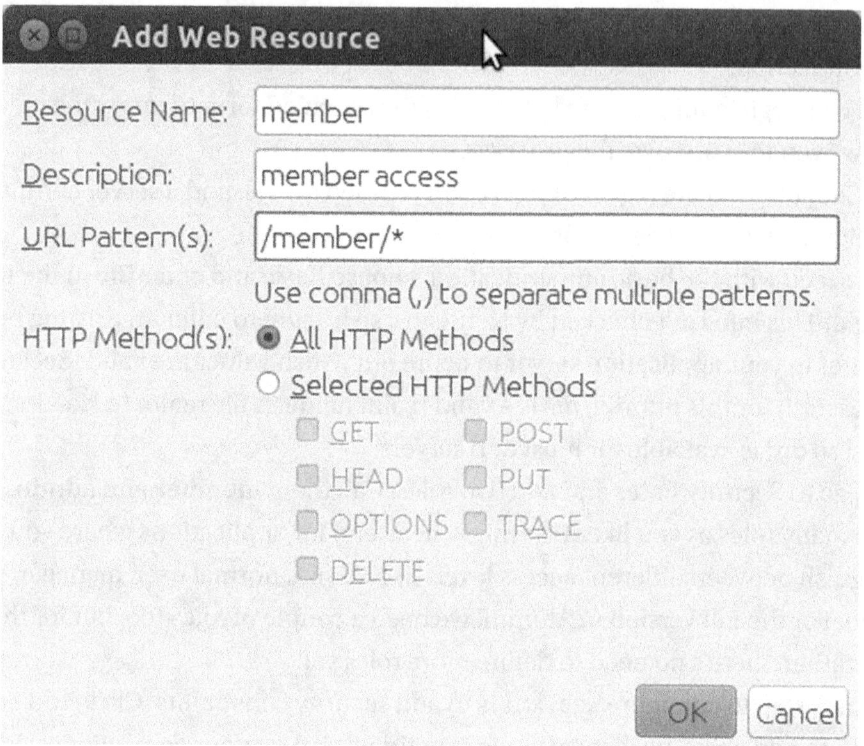

Figure 32-2. *Add web resource*

We want to restrict access to members of a given role, so check Enable Authentication Constraint and edit Role Name. Choose both *member* and *admin*, the roles we defined earlier. This establishes a requirement for authorization, whereas Enable User Data Constraint forces a requirement for the transport layer.

Now create a second security constraint that grants access to the admin pages for members of the admin role only.

No NetBeans available? Or maybe you prefer to edit an XML file directly? Let's take a look at that. Using NetBeans, choose the Source tab. Your web.xml should look similar to Listing 32-1.

Listing 32-1. security-constraint Section in web.xml

```
1   <?xml version="1.0" encoding="UTF-8"?>
2   <web-app version="3.1" xmlns="http://xmlns.jcp.org/xml/ns/javaee"
3       xmlns:xsi="http://www.w3.org/2001/XMLSchema-instance"
4       xsi:schemaLocation="http://xmlns.jcp.org/xml/ns/javaee
```

```
 5      http://xmlns.jcp.org/xml/ns/javaee/web-app_3_1.xsd">
 6
 7
 8      [... omitted entries...]
 9
10      <security-constraint>
11          <display-name>member access</display-name>
12          <web-resource-collection>
13              <web-resource-name>member</web-resource-name>
14              <description>member access</description>
15              <url-pattern>/member/*</url-pattern>
16          </web-resource-collection>
17          <auth-constraint>
18              <description>Member pages are available to all roles
                </description\>
19
20              <role-name>member</role-name>
21              <role-name>admin</role-name>
22          </auth-constraint>
23      </security-constraint>
24      <security-constraint>
25          <display-name>admin access</display-name>
26          <web-resource-collection>
27              <web-resource-name>admin</web-resource-name>
28              <description>admin access</description>
29              <url-pattern>/admin/*</url-pattern>
30          </web-resource-collection>
31          <auth-constraint>
32              <description>Admin pages are restricted to people of the
                admin role only</description>
33
34              <role-name>admin</role-name>
35          </auth-constraint>
36      </security-constraint>
37      <login-config>
```

```
38              <auth-method>BASIC</auth-method>
39              <realm-name>file</realm-name>
40          </login-config>
41          <security-role>
42              <description/>
43              <role-name>member</role-name>
44          </security-role>
45          <security-role>
46              <description/>
47              <role-name>admin</role-name>
48          </security-role>
49      </web-app>
```

Locate the tags security-constraint, login-config, security-role, and their children. This is the result of the configuration made earlier. Thus, the intent of these tags should be clear. If you know these tags, it can be faster to edit the XML file directly. To apply more than these constraints, add a sibling. Within one constraint, you can add further web resource collections. And you may restrict it to one or more dedicated HTTP methods, as shown in Listing 32-2.

Listing 32-2. Dedicated HTTP Method Example

```
1   <web-resource-collection>
2       <web-resource-name>All web pages</web-resource-name>
3       <description/>
4       <url-pattern>*.xhtml</url-pattern>
5       <http-method>PUT</http-method>
6       <http-method>POST</http-method>
7   </web-resource-collection>
```

<login-config> is where you need to apply changes if you choose a different authentication, such as Form, or a different realm. Changing the method usually doesn't affect the security constraint(s) or role(s), so I won't explain this again when we move to a different realm or authentication method.

To test the security behavior, we create three simple web pages, each within the folders admin, member, and public. Always give it the name test.xhtml. For this simple test, we don't need any JSF-specific tag. Just place some text in the page to identify the folder. Listing 32-3 shows my test page within the admin folder.

Listing 32-3. Simple Test Page

```
1   <?xml version='1.0' encoding='UTF-8' ?>
2   <!DOCTYPE html PUBLIC "-//W3C//DTD XHTML 1.0 Transitional//EN"
3       "http://www.w3.org/TR/xhtml1/DTD/xhtml1-transitional.dtd">
4   <html xmlns="http://www.w3.org/1999/xhtml">
5       <head>
6           <title>Admin Test Page</title>
7       </head>
8       <body>
9           <h1>Admin Page</h1>
10      </body>
11  </html>
```

Now what happens if you start the application and navigate to these pages? First try the public page http://localhost:8080/Alumni/public/test.xhtml or its TLS counterpart https://localhost:8181/Alumni/public/test.xhtml. If you haven't installed your own validated certificate, the latter uses a self-signed certificate of the GlassFish server, so your browser will moan about an untrusted certificate. Because you know it's your server, you can accept it. The connection will be fully encrypted.

Your browser will display the page as expected. But if you try to navigate to the test page in the member oder admin folder, this behavior changes: your browser will display a small login dialog to query username and password, as shown in Figure 32-3.

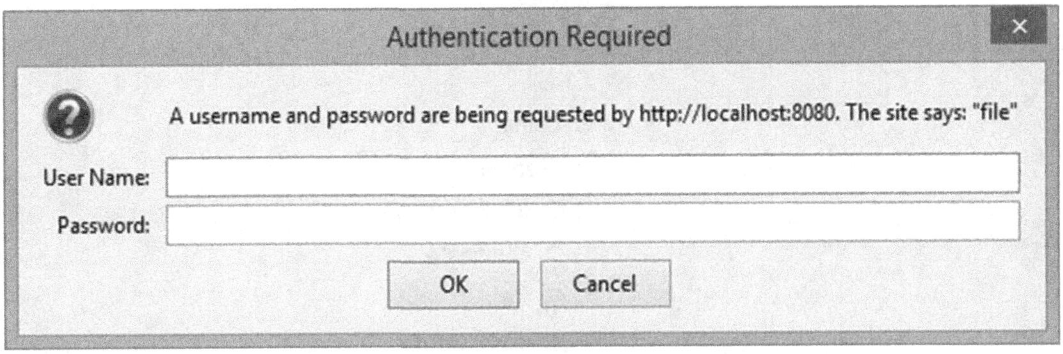

Figure 32-3. *Login dialog for basic authentication*

Enter some credentials, press Enter (or click OK), and this dialog will be re-displayed until (depending on your browser) you enter a valid username/password combination. But we have no user defined, so the only choice is to cancel. You'll get a *401 – Unauthorized* page displayed by the browser. The application is secured now.

Want to let in some user? Okay, let's define them.

Open the GlassFish admin console. Ensure GlassFish is running (it will be started with your app). Using NetBeans, open the Services view (Ctrl+5), choose Servers, and open the context menu of your GlassFish. Choose View Domain Admin Console. Alternatively, go to `http://localhost:4848/` in your browser.

In the Navigation pane, choose Configurations ➤ server-config ➤ Security ➤ Realms ➤ file, as shown in Figure 32-4.

Figure 32-4. *GlassFish Configurations tree*

GlassFish displays the Edit Realm page. Click Manage Users ➤ New. Now enter some credentials as shown in Figure 32-5. Confirm by clicking OK.

New File Realm User

OK   Cancel

Create new user accounts for the currently selected security realm.

* Indicates required field

Configuration Name: server-config

Realm Name:	file
User ID: *	mike
	Name can be up to 255 characters, must contain only letters, digits, underscore, dash, or dot characters
Group List:	admin
	Separate multiple groups with colon
New Password:	••••
Confirm New Password:	••••

Figure 32-5. *GlassFish User Editor (for file realm)*

For the test, you can enter two different users, one for group member and the other for group admin. As the Realm name suggests, your user information will be stored in a file, which is located in your domain/config folder and called keyfile. You can open it with a text editor. The content should be similar to the following:

```
1    guest;{SSHA256}c6/mlRhM7djvO1PY+eA1tF6plcQ/3IROXeCwOO6ZTLtkF+dqmg2Erw==;\
2    student
```

Each line is built up by three columns: Username, password, and group(s). For technical reasons the group is shown in line 2. For protection, the password is stored as an encrypted hash value. See Chapter 28 if you need a refresher on secure passwords. With this in mind, the file realm might be used for applications only where weak security is sufficient.

If you start the application, you still can't log in. Do you remember web.xml dealing with roles and GlassFish storing groups? Although we used the same names (member and admin), these are two slightly different objects. What's missing is a mapping from group (or principal) to role. That's a task specific to GlassFish.

For this mapping, you need a glassfish-web.xml (or sun-web.xml) file. You'll have to create one if it doesn't exist yet. Using NetBeans, choose New ➤ Other ➤ GlassFish ➤ GlassFish Descriptor to create this file. Or create it manually in the WEB-INF folder.

In the Security tab, enter information as shown in Figure 32-6.

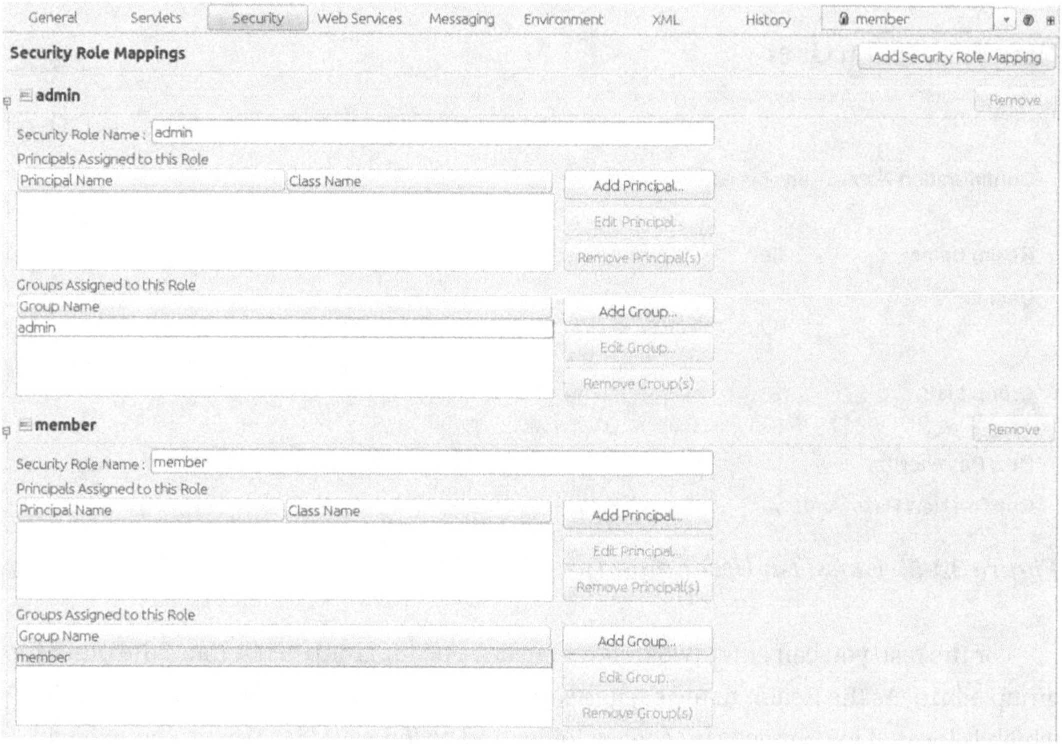

Figure 32-6. *NetBeans security editor*

The information you entered in the Security Role Mappings box simply adds the lines in Listing 32-4 to the file. If you prefer, you can edit them directly in XML mode.

Listing 32-4. Map One Group to Each Role

```
1    <security-role-mapping>
2      <role-name>admin</role-name>
3      <group-name>admin</group-name>
4    </security-role-mapping>
5    <security-role-mapping>
6      <role-name>member</role-name>
7      <group-name>member</group-name>
8    </security-role-mapping>
```

You can map a couple of groups to one role, as shown in Listing 32-5.

Listing 32-5. Map Multiple Groups to a Role

```
1   <security-role-mapping>
2     <role-name>member</role-name>
3     <group-name>admin</group-name>
4     <group-name>member</group-name>
5   </security-role-mapping>
```

This configuration maps both groups `member` and `admin` to the role `member`.

You can also map a user (`principal`) directly to a role: {lang="XML", title="map groups and members to a role"}:

```
1   <security-role-mapping>
2     <role-name>admin</role-name>
3     <group-name>admin</group-name>
4     <principal-name>muellermi</principal-name>
5   </security-role-mapping>
```

If there's no need for this flexible mapping, you can switch it off. In GlassFish, choose Configurations ➤ server-config ➤ Security check ➤ Default Principal To Role Mapping. Now a group is directly mapped to a role (group name = role name)—no need for a dedicated mapping. But beware: this affects only applications deployed after changing this setting! Usually users and roles will fit the requirements. There's no need for variant groups. So, I recommend using this setting.

Now if you start the application, login to Alumni is possible.

Form Login

Now that we've addressed basic login with simple file realm, let's move on and change the authentication method. Remember, this book is about web development with JavaServer Faces. All I've showed for container-based security so far is technology that's entirely independent from JSF. The same applies to simple form login. But it's possible to embed this into some JSF techniques. And, further on, programmatic login is done using JSF.

For the form-based login, we have to change our web.xml slightly. Besides changing the authentication method, we have to declare two pages, one for the login and one failure page (which might be the same) .

So, replace Listing 32-6 with Listing 32-7.

Listing 32-6. Config for Basic Authentication

```
1   <login-config>
2       <auth-method>BASIC</auth-method>
3       <realm-name>file</realm-name>
4   </login-config>
```

Listing 32-7. Config for Form Authentication

```
1   <login-config>
2       <auth-method>FORM</auth-method>
3       <realm-name>file</realm-name>
4       <form-login-config>
5           <form-login-page>/public/login.xhtml</form-login-page>
6           <form-error-page>/public/loginError.xhtml</form-error-page>
7       </form-login-config>
8   </login-config>
```

Listing 32-8 shows a short login page.

Listing 32-8. Simple Login Page

```
1   <?xml version='1.0' encoding='UTF-8' ?>
2   <!DOCTYPE html PUBLIC "-//W3C//DTD XHTML 1.0
3       Transitional//EN" "http://www.w3.org/TR/xhtml1/DTD/xhtml1-
        transitional.d\
4   td">
5   <html xmlns="http://www.w3.org/1999/xhtml"
6         xmlns:h="http://xmlns.jcp.org/jsf/html">
7       <h:head>
8           <title>Login</title>
9       </h:head>
```

```
10      <h:body>
11          <form method="POST" action="j_security_check">
12              Username: <input type="text" name="j_username" />
13              Password: <input type="password" name="j_password" />
14              <br />
15              <input type="submit" value="Login" />
16          </form>
17      </h:body>
18  </html>
```

Because this book is mainly about JSF, I used the NetBeans commands New ➤ JSF Page to create a stub. But the heart of this page is pure HTML—the form with the method POST and the action j_security_check. This name is fixed, as are the names for the user (j_username) and password (j_password) fields. If you like, you can insert this form into a full-fledged JSF page. Or you can embed this login form into a JSF component to make it more reusable. Remember to use this standard HTML form to define the action; its JSF counterpart doesn't know about defining a special action.

Listing 32-9 shows an example error page, but you can use any page. Here I used some simple JSF without any backing bean. It simply informs the user about the authentication failure and offers a navigation button back to the login page.

Listing 32-9. Example Login Error Page

```
1   <?xml version='1.0' encoding='UTF-8' ?>
2   <!DOCTYPE html PUBLIC "-//W3C//DTD XHTML 1.0 Transitional//EN"
3       "http://www.w3.org/TR/xhtml1/DTD/xhtml1-transitional.dtd">
4
5   <html xmlns="http://www.w3.org/1999/xhtml"
6         xmlns:h="http://xmlns.jcp.org/jsf/html">
7       <h:head>
8           <title>Login Error</title>
9       </h:head>
10      <h:body>
11          <div>
12              <h:outputText value="Sorry, you could not be authenticated."/>
13          </div>
```

```
14              <div>
15                  <h:button outcome="/public/login.xhtml" value="Try again."/>
16              </div>
17          </h:body>
18      </html>
```

Start your app, and it should use form authentication. If you try to access a page that needs authentication, the system redirects you to the login page. After you enter valid credentials, the system will open the requested page. But after login to the member's page with user John (who has member access only), try to navigate to the admin folder. As you might expect, you'll receive an unauthorized message, because you need admin access. The system won't redirect you to the login page because you're already logged in. The automated redirect is only available if the user isn't logged in. Usually this is what your intention is.

But what do you do to secure your computer? Do you log in as a normal user for your daily work and use a separate login for administrative tasks? Using Linux, this separate login might be root, and you perform a su or sudo on this kind of operating system. So, you might have two accounts with different access levels for an application like Alumni, too. In that case, you need a chance to login as a different user (without closing and reopening your browser). To tackle this, we need a logout functionality. Unfortunately, the HTTP authentication doesn't provide a logout facility. But luckily, instead of using the predefined fields and actions as shown before, we can use a programmatic login as well as a programmatic logout.

Programmatic Login

I think this programmatic login I just mentioned is much more interesting. It lets us create our own form. The login is done within its backing bean. Let's try it (Listing 32-10).

Listing 32-10. JSF Form for Programmatic Login

```
1   <?xml version='1.0' encoding='UTF-8' ?>
2   <!DOCTYPE html PUBLIC "-//W3C//DTD XHTML 1.0
3       Transitional//EN" "http://www.w3.org/TR/xhtml1/DTD/xhtml1-
        transitional.d\
```

```
4    td">
5    <html xmlns="http://www.w3.org/1999/xhtml"
6            xmlns:h="http://xmlns.jcp.org/jsf/html">
7        <h:head>
8            <title>Login</title>
9        </h:head>
10       <h:body>
11           <h:form>
12               <div>
13                   <h:outputLabel for="userName" value="User"/>
14                   <h:inputText id="userName" value="#{login.userName}"
15                                required="true"
16                                requiredMessage="Please enter username"/>
17               </div>
18               <div>
19                   <h:outputLabel for="password" value="Password"/>
20                   <h:inputSecret id="password" value="#{login.password}"
21                                  required="true"
22                                  requiredMessage="Please enter password"/>
23               </div>
24               <div>
25                   <h:commandButton action="#{login.login}" value="Login"/>
26               </div>
27           </h:form>
28       </h:body>
29   </html>
```

Listing 32-10 shows a fully fledged JSF page, and it's up to you to design it as you like. Username and password fields are mandatory now, guaranteed by the use of the required property, and are stored into two properties of the backing bean. If the user clicks the Login button, the login action is performed. For this kind of login, no change to web.xml is necessary. See Listing 32-11.

Listing 32-11. Login Method for Programmatic Login

```
1   public String login() {
2       FacesContext context = FacesContext.getCurrentInstance();
3       HttpServletRequest request = (HttpServletRequest) context
4                                                   .getExternalContext().
                                                    getRequest();
5
6       try {
7           request.login(_userName, _password);
8       } catch (ServletException e) {
9           context.addMessage(null, new FacesMessage("Login failed."));
10          return "/public/loginError";
11      }
12      return "/member/index";
13  }
```

First, you have to obtain the HttpServletRequest and then delegate the login by calling its login method. Quite simple, isn't it? If the login fails, a ServletException exception is thrown. I simply created a FacesMessage, which will be displayed in the user's browser. Instead of returning /public /loginError, it's possible to return an empty string. Doing so, the login form will be redisplayed with the failure message (don't forget to add a message tag to this page). Although this method doesn't care about the <form-error-page> tag of web.xml, you can't omit this tag. It's still required, but its content doesn't care.

You may have recognized one important difference compared to the so-called form-based login: as before, the login page is displayed when you try to navigate to a protected page. Using form login, the page you tried to navigate to is called. Using the programmatic login, the page that's returned by the login method is the target of our navigation. So, we can force the user to a specific entry page. Usually that's what we want to do. To keep the behavior of the form-based login, we need to store the target page before opening the login dialog and call it on successful login.

Programmatic Logout

As mentioned earlier, to change the user, we need to log out first. We do that by calling the `logout` method of the servlet request, as shown in Listing 32-12.

Listing 32-12. Logout Method for Programmatic Logout

```
1   public void logout() {
2       FacesContext context = FacesContext.getCurrentInstance();
3       HttpServletRequest request = (HttpServletRequest) context
4                                              .getExternalContext().
                                               getRequest();
5       try {
6           request.logout();
7       } catch (ServletException e) {
8           context.addMessage(null, new FacesMessage("Logout failed."));
9       }
10  }
```

You only need to place a command link to this method somewhere on the page, as in Listing 32-13.

Listing 32-13. Call Logout Method

```
1   <h:commandLink action="#{login.logout}" value="Logout"/>
```

Next I'll show you how to exchange the password store. At first, we'll move on to JDBCRealm, which lets you store your username and password information in a database.

jdbcRealm

Okay, we've secured our JSF web application by using a JSF form. The user information is still stored in a flat text file. But as I said, your application server provides more. Let's move on to GlassFish's JDBCRealm, which allows you to store the user information in the database.

In your application you may provide a registration form where the user enters their username, some other data, and a password. You may store this data all together in a table named account. Or you might store the credentials in a separate table called user, for example. Feel free to persist the data as it's relevant to your application. You might store the password as clear text (not recommended—use only for testing purpose) or hashed by a well-known algorithm like SHA-256. All the container needs is access to a table (or view) that contains the username and password in one row.

To access this table from your application and from the JDBCRealm, you need to set up a connection pool and an appropriate JDBC resource. Besides the user table, a second one is used to access the user's role. A column for the username is needed, plus a second one for the group. A user may be member in a couple of groups. If a user is assigned to exactly one group, you can store this information in the same table as the password.

Let's set up the realm. Open the GlassFish console and choose Configurations ➤ server-config ➤ Security ➤ Realms. See Figure 32-7.

Figure 32-7. GlassFish configuration

GlassFish displays an overview of existing realms. Click New to create a new one. The New Realm dialog opens, as shown in Figure 32-8.

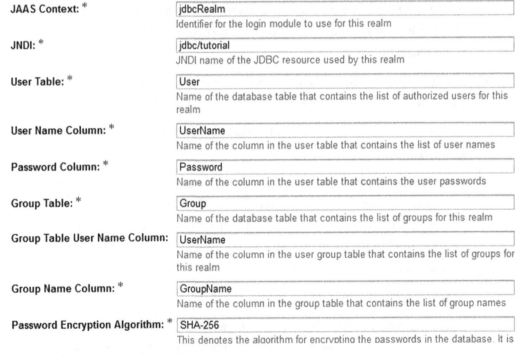

Figure 32-8. *New realm dialog of GlassFish*

Here are some pointers on filling out the dialog:

- Provide a name of your choice. This name will be referenced in your `web.xml` configuration.

- Choose JDBCRealm from the Class Name drop-down list.

- For JAAS Context, enter **jdbcRealm**.

- For JNDI, enter the name you've chosen for your JDBC resource.

- For User Table, provide the name of the table where you store the credentials.

- For User Name Column, enter the column name where you store the username.

- For Password Column, enter the column name where you store the password.

- For Group Table, provide the name where you store the group information. If a user can be in exactly one group and you store the group information in the same table as the credentials, enter the same name here.

- Group Table User Name Column column provides the same username as the User Table, even though its name may be different.

- For Group Name Column, enter the column name that contains the group name.

- Password Encryption Algorithm: As stated before, you can store your password as plain text or encrypted. It's highly recommended that you use encryption. Choose the algorithm you use. Remember, MD5 or SHA1 are known to be insecure, so choose SHA-256 or SHA-512, for example.

- Digest Algorithm: Provide the same algorithm.

- Encoding: You can store the encrypted password as a hex string or base 64 encoded. This property defines the encoding (Hex or Base64).

- Charset: Choose the charset you use to store the password. You may use UTF-8.

Store your config by clicking OK. If you prefer to configure GlassFish by editing a config file, open the file YourGlassFishRoot/glassfish/domains/yourDomain/config/ domain.xml. Locate the tag security-service and add the auth-realm, as shown in Listing 32-14. (Note that [...] indicates text omitted for brevity.) This tag appears twice, for default and active config!

Listing 32-14. domain.xml (Excerpt)

```
1    [...]
2    <security-service activate-default-principal-to-role-mapping="true">
3      <auth-realm classname="com.sun.enterprise.security.ee.auth.realm.jdbc.JDBC\
4    Realm"
5              name="jdbcRealm">
6        <property name="jaas-context" value="jdbcRealm"></property>
7        <property name="encoding" value="Hex"></property>
8        <property name="password-column" value="Hash"></property>
9        <property name="datasource-jndi" value="jdbc/tutorial"></property>
10       <property name="group-table" value="Group"></property>
11       <property name="charset" value="UTF-8"></property>
12       <property name="user-table" value="User"></property>
13       <property name="group-name-column" value="GroupName"></property>
14       <property name="digestrealm-password-enc-algorithm" value="SHA-256">
15       </property>
16       <property name="group-table-user-name-column" value="UserName">
17       </property>
18       <property name="digest-algorithm" value="SHA-256"></property>
19       <property name="user-name-column" value="UserName"></property>
20     </auth-realm>
21    [...]
22    </security-service>
23    [...]
```

Make sure you stopped your GlassFish before editing this file and restart it afterwards.

Once we've defined the realm (and stored some credentials and groups into the tables), the only thing to do is to edit the security configuration in web.xml. All you have to do is exchange the realm. Replace the file with JDBCRealm, as shown in Figure 32-9.

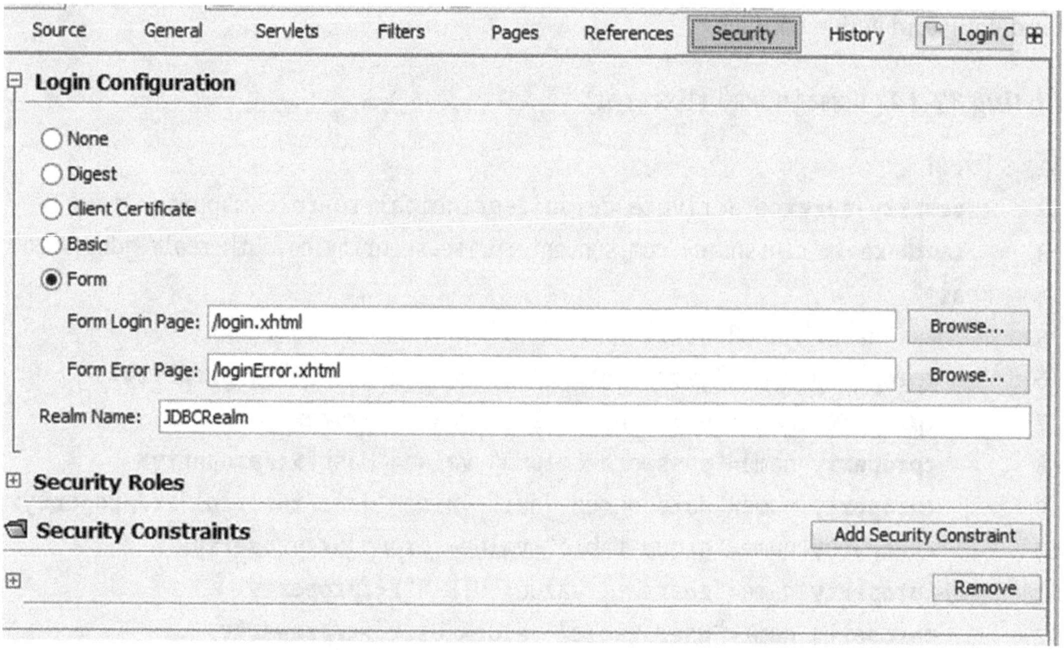

Figure 32-9. *NetBeans Security*

Or do it within the XML view NetBeans offers to you (other IDEs might offer the XML view only):

```
1   <realm-name>JDBCRealm</realm-name>
```

That's it.

Custom Realm

Remember the requirements for secure passwords?

- We need an algorithm that takes some time to calculate to protect from brute force attacks (or at least reduce their chance of success). JDBCRealm lets you determine the algorithm.

- We need to add a salt to every password to protect against rainbow tables. JDBCRealm fails on this requirement.

Here's where a custom realm comes into play. It enables the developer to save the passwords in any store with any algorithm. Such a custom realm might be vendor specific. The realm in Listing 32-15 was developed for the GlassFish server. You can check to see whether it's applicable to your server. First, we need to derive a custom realm from AppservRealm.

Listing 32-15. Custom Realm for Alumni

```
01   public class AlumniRealm extends AppservRealm {
02
03     @Override
04     public String getAuthType() {
05       return "alumniRealm";
06     }
07
08     @Override
09     public String getJAASContext() {
10       return "alumniRealm";
11     }
12
13     @Override
14     public Enumeration getGroupNames(String username) {
15       List<String> groups = new ArrayList<>();
16       groups.add("member");
17       groups.add("admin");
18       return Collections.enumeration(groups);
19     }
20
21   }
```

We need to override three methods. For AuthType and JAASContext, this realm simply returns its name. This is necessary to identify this realm in the server's configuration.

The intention of GroupNames is to provide all possible groups of the solution. For demonstration purposes and simplicity's sake, all the names are coded within the method. This might be okay for an authentication realm that's used for a certain application. Even better, you might define the group names within some properties, or get it from a database.

Next, we need a `LoginModule`, which needs to be derived from `AppservPasswordLoginModule`. See Listing 32-16.

Listing 32-16. Custom Realm for Alumni

```
01   public class LoginModule extends AppservPasswordLoginModule {
02
03     @Override
04     protected void authenticateUser() throws LoginException {
05       if (!(_currentRealm instanceof AlumniRealm)) {
06         throw new LoginException("Unexpected realm: "
07                 + _currentRealm.getClass().getSimpleName());
08       }
09
10       String[] groups = obtainPermittedGroups(_username, _passwd);
11       if (groups.length > 0) {
12         commitUserAuthentication(groups);
13       }
14     }
15
16   String[] obtainPermittedGroups(String userName, char[] passwd) {
17       ...
18       return groups;
19     }
20
21   }
```

In the login module, we first check whether the current realm is the expected custom realm. _currentRealm (with the leading underscore, as I do throughout this book) is a field within the parent method. If it's not of the expected type, we throw an exception.

In line 10 we call the method, which returns an array of permitted group names. If the authentication fails, this method doesn't return any group name. Otherwise, we call `commitUserAuthentication` by passing in this array.

Within `obtainPermittedGroups`, we need to check the user credentials and determine the permitted groups. I omitted the concrete implementation in Listing 32-16,
but will show it in the next chapter. Instead, in Listing 32-17, I present a poor implementation to give you a first impression of what needs to be happen here. You can use such a
fake method to test the realm without needing to implement a real user/password check
at this time.

Listing 32-17. Poor Implementation of the Authentication (Fake Method)

```
01    String[] obtainPermittedGroups(String userName, char[] passwd) {
02      List<String> groupList = new ArrayList<>();
03      String password = new String(passwd);
04      if ("muellermi".equals(userName) && "secret".equals(password)) {
05        String[] groups = new String[2];
06        groups[0] = "member";
07        groups[1] = "admin";
08        return groups;
09      }
10      return new String[0];
11    }
```

Create a simple Java project named `AlumniRealm` that contains the two classes. I'm
using the package `de.muellerbruehl.alumnirealm` for these classes. The project simply
needs to build a `jar` file. Now we need to deploy the resulting `jar` into the `lib` folder of
your GlassFish domain. Before you copy this file, make sure your server is down.

Next, locate the config folder of your GlassFish domain—for example,
`GlassFishRoot/glassfish/domains/domain1/config`. Edit the `login.conf` file. Here we
need to add the new realm, as shown in Listing 32-18.

Listing 32-18. Line to Be Added to `login.conf`

```
01    alumniRealm {
02      de.muellerbruehl.alumnirealm.LoginModule required;
03    };
```

In the same folder, edit the `domain.xml` file too. Here you need to add the
authentication realm in the `<security-service>` tag, as shown in Listing 32-19.

Listing 32-19. `domain.xml` (Excerpt)

```
1 ...
2   <security-service>
3     <auth-realm classname="de.muellerbruehl.alumnirealm.AlumniRealm"
4     name="alumniRealm"></auth-realm>
5     ...
6   </security-service>
7 ...
```

If you don't want to edit `domain.xml` directly, you can start your server and open the admin console. Using the object tree, open Configurations ➤ server-config ➤ Security ➤ Realms and click New. Then provide the following information, as shown in Figure 32-10.

- *Name:* `alumniRealm`

- *Class name:* `"de.muellerbruehl.alumnirealm.AlumniRealm"`
  `name="alumniRealm"`

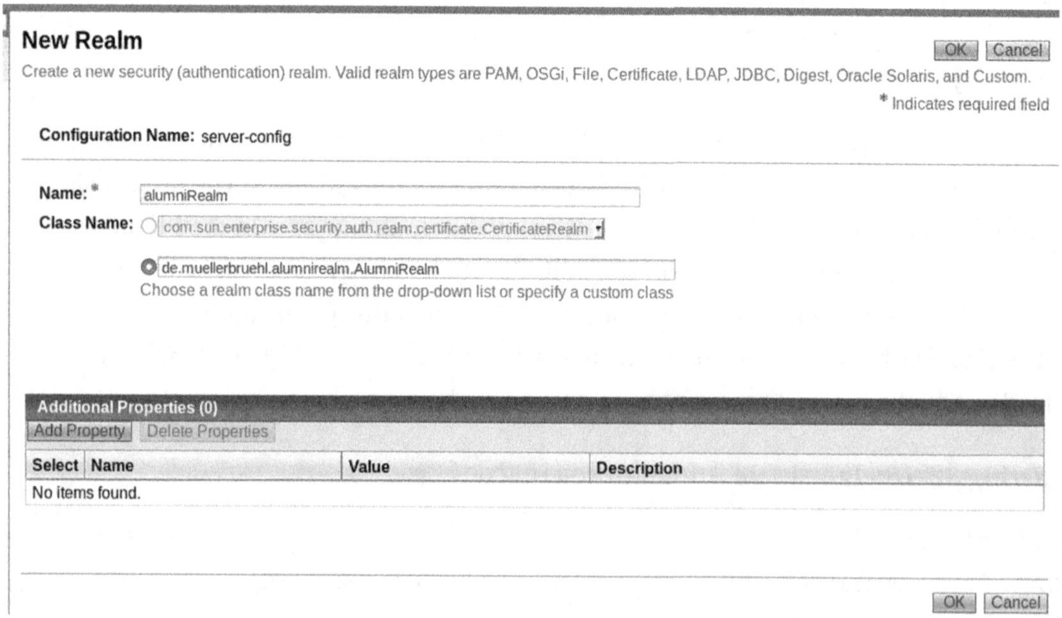

Figure 32-10. `web.xml` (Excerpt)

The custom realm is ready to use.

All we need is to configure the application (within its `web.xml` file) to use it:

```
<realm-name>alumniRealm</realm-name>
```

Summary

Java EE supports security features like user authentication and authorization out of the box. The servlet specification defines a couple of different modes to query the user credentials, like basic or form.

Although basic isn't useful for most scenarios, the form-based mode might be used to redirect a non-logged-in user to a login form. The most flexible method for login is the programmatic login. Here, it's up to the developer to embed the login into an appropriate page.

Depending on the application server, the application developer may choose from several authentication realms (zones, domains, and so on). GlassFish, for example, offers a fileRealm as well as a JDBCRealm. To enforce a strong password policy, the developer may need a realm that enables him to use his own identity store. Here, a custom realm comes into play.

In the next chapter, I'll demonstrate how this custom realm interacts with the identity store.

CHAPTER 33

Account Handling

If you'll recall from Chapter 32's custom realm, I left the `obtainPermittedGroups` method empty and promised to describe it later. To authenticate the user, the custom realm needs to check the user's credentials, which are stored in an `account` object. Or in terms of the database, stored in the `account` table. If we add a data access class to the realm, we need to access the account within Alumni, too.

Thinking about the DRY principle (*don't repeat yourself*) raises the question of whether it's possible not to use the same code in two distinct places. We want to write the code to access an account only once and then reuse it in different places. Should we write a library that might be used by Alumni as well as the custom realm? Or should the custom realm call the appropriate data access of Alumni? Both solutions have their drawbacks, especially the latter, which forces the realm to know about Alumni. Would it be possible to run that `account` object independently?

The good news is: yes it is.

Micro Service

Creating, retrieving, and deleting a user account as well as setting its state and login will be handled by a small application that runs independently from both Alumni and the custom realm. Usually such a unit would be called a *service*. You can develop and deploy such a service independently from the other units. In the domain of web development, we usually use two kinds of services:

- WS* services that communicate using SOAP

- Services based on the REST architectural style

SOAP (`www.w3.org/TR/soap/`) is a protocol standard for the communication of web services in the WS* family. Usually SOAP is tunnelled via HTTP. *SOAP* originally stood for Simple Object Access Protocol, but today only the acronym is used. There are simpler protocols available.

379

© Michael Müller 2018
M. Müller, *Practical JSF in Java EE 8*, https://doi.org/10.1007/978-1-4842-3030-5_33

We're talking about the WS* family because these kinds of service use the Web Services Description Language (WSDL). (You can read more about WSDL at `www.w3schools.com/xml/xml:wsdl.asp`.) When web services became popular in conjunction with service oriented architecture (SOA) in the early 2000s, they often were used in combination with a kind of registry, which could be used to look up a catalog of services. From the point of view of the application using a WS* service, it could be treated as a kind of remote method invocation. Calling such a service is as easy as calling a local method. We can pass parameters and receive a result object. Personally, I often use WS* services, but within Alumni, I've chosen to follow a REST-like style, which usually is more lightweight.

Today, we're talking about micro services. Often people misunderstand this term. A *micro service* is not a "small" service. It's an application that offers a complete set of associated functions with high cohesion. Its functionality is available with a public interface and can be reached via the network. A micro service stands on its own; it doesn't need the overhead of any supporting components like a registry (for example, as designed for WS* services).

This definition restricts a micro service to neither a special protocol nor to a special architecture. If we omit the supporting infrastructure, a WS* service might act as a micro service.

The other popular kind of services includes the ones that follow the REST architectural style. Of course, there are more kinds of services, but the two I'm talking about in this chapter are the most important in the domain of web development.

Note   *REST*, by the way, is short for *REpresentational State Transfer* and was described by Roy Thomas Fielding in his dissertation "Architectural Styles and the Design of Network-based Software Architectures," which you can read at `www.ics.uci.edu/~fielding/pubs/dissertation/top.htm`.

Within REST, a resource is represented by an identifier. Using HTTP as transfer medium, a resource is identified by a URI. Actions on such a resource are associated with HTTP methods like POST, GET, PUT, or DELETE. Usually POST is used to create an object, GET to read it, PUT to update, and DELETE to delete it. Thus, all the well-known CRUD operations can be supported.

For more on REST and the HTTP methods, you might read "Using HTTP Methods for RESTful Services" (`www.restapitutorial.com/lessons/httpmethods.html`) or "RESTFUL API tutorial" (`https://restfulapi.net/http-methods/`). Lots of other articles and good books are available, too. Discussing all the fundamentals of RESTful services goes far beyond this book.

Let's assume we want to handle customers. A list of customers might be accessed by `<baseAddress>/customers` using the `GET` method. The same address using the `POST` method and passing the data for a customer will create a new customer and return its id. A `GET` to `<baseAddress>/customers/<id>` (where `<id>` represents the appropriate id) will retrieve the customer, whereas the same address in conjunction with the `DELETE` method deletes it.

Java EE includes the Java API for RESTful Web Services (JAX-RS). The current version Java EE 8 includes RAX-RS 2.1, which has been defined as JSR370 (`https://jcp.org/en/jsr/detail?id=370`).

For Alumni, the access to the account information is handled by a micro service based on JAX-RS.

Account Service

Many older JSF applications (including mine, in the beginning) tended to become monolithic. Compiling and deploying a growing application takes a growing amount of time. Such a monolith becomes harder to maintain, so it's better to compose the whole application using a set of smaller parts. We might integrate a couple of independent JSF apps using *portlets* (see the portlet specification, JSR 362, at `https://jcp.org/en/jsr/detail?id=362`). Or we can design a couple of JSF apps to interact seamlessly by sharing a session. Or we can call services.

Let's look at how *Alumni* handles its accounts. The address to reach its API will be `http://<server:port>/AccountService/Accounts`. Alumni might call this address with the `POST` method and pass some account data to create a new account. In contrast to the customer example mentioned earlier, I inserted an additional `id` sub-path to access a specific account (I hope RESTful purists won't hurt me). This allowed me to add other sub-branches for the specific functions of enabling login and disabling an account.

ACCOUNTS API DOCUMENTATION

An account may have one of four different states:

- New

- Active

- Inactive

- Retired

Creating an account will initially set the status to *new*. If the user activates their account within three days from creation, the status will be set to *active*—otherwise, the account will be removed (deleted from the database).

If, and only if, the account is in the active state, the user may

- Log in to their account

- Update account information

- Delete their account

DELETE may remove the account from the database or set the account's status to the status *retired* and remove essential information identifying the user (name, email, and so on).

This behavior depends on the data that's linked to this account. If some data has to be kept as information within the system, then the account remains anonymized in the retired state. Otherwise, it's completely removed from the database.

If, and only if, the account is in an active state, the administrator can make it *inactive*. This might be done to temporarily disable an account, for example while investigating a case of abusing the account. Then the administrator might switch the status back to active.

For this kind of reason, the account service (AlumniAccount) offers this API:

AlumniAccount/api/account

- POST: Create an account.

- Returns 409 conflict if the database contains an account with the given email.

- Returns 201 created if the account could be created. If the given loginName existed in the database, the system will change the loginName to a unique one.

AlumniAccount/*api/account/{id}*

- GET: Retrieve account.

AlumniAccount/*api/account/{id}*

- PUT: Update account.

AlumniAccount/*api/account/{id}*

- DELETE: Delete account (either anonymize and set to retired or totally remove from DB).

AlumniAccount/*api/account/activate/{id}*

- PUT: Set account status to active.

AlumniAccount/*api/account/login/{loginName}/{password}*

- GET: Return a list of groups, if the user is allowed to log in.

Although AccountService is a separate web application, it derives its project object model (POM) from Alumni.

NetBeans supports the creation of RESTful services out of the box. You can choose to create a new RESTful web service from pattern, database, or entity. If you want to create it from an entity class, for example, NetBeans creates a class for the data access as well as the service and its configuration. Usually this is a good starting point for your further development.

To configure the REST service, we need a class that derives from `Application`. Add the @ApplicationPath annotation with the path to your REST API. This path will be appended to the application's context path. I simply use `api`.

Within our class, we need to override the `getClasses` method, which returns all classes we want to expose for the service. If you use NetBeans to create your REST service, the configuration class contains an `addRestResourceClasses` method to add the service classes. Don't alter this method because it's been generated and will be administered by NetBeans if you add or remove REST service classes. See Listing 33-1.

Listing 33-1. REST Service Configuration

```
01   @javax.ws.rs.ApplicationPath("api")
02   public class ApplicationConfig extends Application {
03
04     @Override
05     public Set<Class<?>> getClasses() {
06       Set<Class<?>> resources = new java.util.HashSet<>();
07       addRestResourceClasses(resources);
08       return resources;
09     }
10
11     private void addRestResourceClasses(Set<Class<?>> resources) {
12       resources.add(de.muellerbruehl.alumniaccount.rest.AccountService.
         class);
13     }
14
15   }
```

In that listing, we only add one Service class. Let's take a look at it in Listing 33-2.

Listing 33-2. AccountService (Excerpt)

```
01   @Path("/account")
02   public class AccountService {
03
04     @Context private UriInfo context;
05
06     @POST
07     @Consumes(MediaType.APPLICATION_JSON)
08     @Produces(MediaType.APPLICATION_JSON)
09     public Response createAccount(Account account) {
10       try {
11         AccountFacade.getInstance().createAccount(account);
12         URI path = context.getAbsolutePath().resolve(account.getId());
13         return Response.created(path).entity(account.getAccessKey()).build();
14       } catch (IllegalArgumentException ex) {
```

```
15        return Response.status(Status.CONFLICT).build();
16      } catch (Exception ex) {
17        return Response.notAcceptable(null).build();
18      }
19    }
20
21    @GET
22    @Path("{id}")
23    @Produces(MediaType.APPLICATION_JSON)
24    public Account getAccount(@PathParam("id") String id) {
25      Account account = AccountFacade.getInstance().findAccount(id);
26      return account;
27    }
28    ...
29  }
```

In line 1, there is a Path annotation. This declares the relative path within our API. The full path is a combination of protocol, server, port, context path, API path as configured, and last but not least the relative path to the account resource. Thus the full path to access the AccountService on a local machine would be http://localhost:8082/AlumniAccount/api/account. You may wonder why the port differs from the usual 8080. I operate this service on its own application server. (Yes, it's possible to Docker-ize it, but that's beyond this book's scope.)

The excerpt contains two methods: createAccount takes an account via API and passes it to the AccountFacade, which performs some checks and persists the account. In line 4, we've got a UriInfo object injected. We'll use it to create a path for our response in case of successful creation. Within this response, we return the newly created id of the account.

If the new (not yet existing) account comes with an email that exists in the account table, an IllegalArgumentException will be thrown. Once we catch it here (line 14), we return an HTTP error code 409 (conflict). In any other case, we return a not-acceptable state.

When a client calls this method, it doesn't need to pass an object of the Account class like the server uses. All data of the client's account is converted to its JSON representation. On the server side, the data is converted to an object in the server's Account class. This conversion works because both classes use the same getter and setter names. Although the password of the client's account comes as clear text (as entered by the user), the server's password is hashed within its setter. That's because we only want to store encrypted passwords in the data base.

To protect the password during transport, we need to use a secure transport protocol such as TLS between the browser and our application server. If we assume that both our application server and the AccountService reside on the same network behind a firewall, then we don't need to secure the transport between both servers. That's why the service is available at a non-secured (http:) URI.

The second method, getAccount, accepts an id and retrieves the appropriate account from the database. Look at line 22: here the path is surrounded by curly braces. That means "expect a variable id as part of the URI." Within the method signature we refer this part of the path to assign its value to the parameter. Because we annotated this method with @GET, it reacts only to the HTTP GET method.

Now if we keep the path but change the HTTP method, we can implement a DELETE method, as shown in Listing 33-3.

Listing 33-3. AccountService (Excerpt: DELETE)

```
01      @DELETE
02      @Path("{id}")
03      public void delete(@PathParam("id") String id) {
04          AccountFacade.getInstance().deleteAccount(id);
05      }
```

If we need more than one variable, we simply add it to the path. For the login, the relative path contains the literal login and two variables for login name and password. If the user can be authenticated, the login method returns all the groups the user belongs to. That's what our custom realm needs to proceed. See Listing 33-4.

Listing 33-4. AccountService (Excerpt: login)

```
01      @GET
02      @Produces(MediaType.APPLICATION_JSON)
03      @Path("login/{loginName}/{password}")
04      public String login(@PathParam("loginName") String loginName,
05              @PathParam("password") String password) {
06          try {
07              Account account = AccountFacade.getInstance()
```

```
08                    .findAccountByName(loginName);
09            if (!account.checkPassword(password)) {
10              return "";
11            }
12            return AccountFacade.getInstance().retrieveRoles(account.getId());
13          } catch (IllegalArgumentException ex) {
14            LOGGER.log(Level.INFO, ex.getMessage());
15          }
16          return "";
17        }
```

Testing

Testing a web application can be a challenge. Usually developers test their units of code with the aid of a unit test framework, but lots of a web application's functionality relies on other modules or other Java EE technologies. We can mock away parts of the application to isolate our unit under test.

Sometime we can't mock away anything. If we need features provided by the container, it becomes hard to write a test with a simple test framework. Besides Selenium, which automates the browser, we might use Arquillian (http://arquillian.org). In conjunction with ShrinkWrap, only those parts of an application needed for the test are packed together into a web archive. Arquillian launches an embedded app server with the reduced system to perform the test. This approach might be combined with a unit test framework.

Luckily, testing an isolated micro service doesn't require such an effort. Besides unit testing single classes, we can write a small REST client and use the test framework to call our service's methods. Indeed, this isn't unit testing—it's integration testing.

Listing 33-5 shows a short excerpt of my tests for the AccountService.

Listing 33-5. Integration Test of the AccountService (Excerpt)

```
01      @Test
02      public void createAndDeleteAccount() {
03        AccountClient client = new AccountClient();
04        Account account = createAccount();
```

```
05        Response postJson = client.createAccount(account);
06        assertEquals(201, postJson.getStatus());
07
08        String path = postJson.getLocation().getPath();
09        String id = path.substring(path.lastIndexOf("/") + 1);
10        assertEquals("testclient", client.getAccount(id).getLoginName());
11        client.deleteAccount(id);
12        assertEquals(null, client.getAccount(id));
13    }
```

Summary

Both Alumni and the custom realm use account management. To avoid dependencies from the realm to the application, we sourced out the account management into its own application. Such an application that focuses on a solitary business case is known as a micro service.

Java EE supports two different kinds of web services out of the box:

- WS* services

- RESTful services

We implemented AccountService as an independent RESTful service based on the JAX-RS functionality. JAX-RS supports easy access to the information the client sends via an HTTP request. We can extract information out of the URI by defining path patterns, or we can access data sent via header—for example, POST data.

To test this service, we create an appropriate client and use a unit test framework to call the service methods.

CHAPTER 34

Classroom Chat (WebSockets)

Alumni is built for former pupils or students who join one or more classes. They may communicate within each class. The application supports two different kinds of communication: messaging and chat.

Using the messaging feature, the user can select a couple of recipients, write the message, and send it. By clicking the Send button, the message is stored to a table. Some metadata, including a link to that message, is stored for every recipient. They may log in at any time and open their message box to read the messages. This kind of communication is usually used for asynchronous communication between individuals. It is realized by techniques described already in earlier chapters, so I won't dive further into its implementation.

A chat, on the other hand, is used for *synchronous* communication. You can compare chatting with speaking in a room: all people in that room can listen to the words at the time of speaking, assuming there is no considerable delay and people are able to hear. We often use the term *chat room*, a colloquial synonym for a shared communication channel. When any user writes a message, it's displayed immediately to all users in the same chat room. For this to work, either the client needs to pull new information every few milliseconds or the server needs to push the information. So far, we've used HTTP concept: the client initiates the communication, the server sends the answer, and the communication terminates until the next request. Pure HTTP can be used to implement this *pull* concept, but it's not hard to imagine the huge amount of traffic that approach can generate. So we need another technique that allows us to implement the *push* approach.

When someone enters a chat room, it's nice for them to be able to easily get a sense of the ongoing discussion. Alumni stores a few of the latest messages and shows them to a user entering the chat room as a kind of replay.

© Michael Müller 2018
M. Müller, *Practical JSF in Java EE 8*, https://doi.org/10.1007/978-1-4842-3030-5_34

HTTP Protocol and Alternatives

HTTP is one of the Internet protocols that all current browsers support. HTTP (short for HyperText Transfer Protocol) is the standard for Internet browsing. As its name suggests, it was developed to transfer text from a server to a client. This text can contain hyperlinks to other texts. HTTP was standardized by the World Wide Web Consoritum (W3C), and you can read more about this at `www.w3.org/Protocols/`.

HTTP is a stateless request-response protocol: a client sends a request to the server. The server sends a response to the client and terminates the connection. For every requested resource, a new connection is needed. For example, if a web page contains some text and three images, then a total of four requests is needed.

Because every request is initiated by the client, normally it's not possible to push information from server to client at any time. There are some workarounds, such as *deferred answers*: the server delays its response until certain information is available and then sends the answer. After that, the connection is closed, and the server needs a new request before it can *push* more information.

Although widespread, HTTP has a few other limitations, so some alternatives and extensions have been developed to overcome these restrictions.

HTTP/2 (`https://tools.ietf.org/html/rfc7540`) lets the client request resources more effectively because this protocol allows multiple concurrent exchanges on the same connection. It allows the server to preemptively push chunks of data using the same client-side initiated connection. For a page with three images, the server answers the client's request by sending the page content and pushing the three images. This boosts the performance, but it's still not what we need to realize a chat. HTTP/2 became standardized by the Internet Engineering Task Force (IETF) in 2015 and became part of the Java Enterprise Edition starting with version 8 (Java EE 8).

Server Sent Events (SSE) provide a way to really push information from the server to the client. The core protocol is still HTTP: as with vanilla HTTP, the connection is requested by the client. The server keeps the connection and is able to push chunks of information in so-called *events*.

SSEs provide a real server push and are part of Java EE 8, too, but it's one-way communication only, from server to client. To create a chat with SSE, we can AJAXify an input field to send the user's input to the server. Then we push this message to all clients in the chat room. Because SSE is realized on top of JAX-RS, we need to introduce some other techniques that differ a bit from the usual JSF way. So SSE isn't used to realize Alumni's chat room either.

WebSockets (https://html.spec.whatwg.org/multipage/web-sockets.
html#network) represent a different approach to establishing a server push. The
WebSocket protocol enables a real bidirectional communication between two peers.
It was standardized by the IEFT in 2011. Like SSE, its specification is part of the HTML
living standard.

This technique seems to fit best for the chat room, so Alumni uses the WebSocket
protocol. WebSocket became part of Java EE 7 and is supported by JSF 2.3 or newer,
which is part of Java EE 8. Although the WebSocket protocol is directly supported by JSF,
it's implemented more like a pure server push. To take advantage of the full bidirectional
support, Alumni doesn't use WebSocket's support of JSF. I'll show you an alternative
implementation with JSF's WebSocket feature later in this book.

WebSocket

Technically, the WebSocket protocol is initiated as an upgrade of an HTTP request.
This implies that a connection needs to be initiated by a client. Once the WebSocket
connection is established after this upgrade request, both partners act as peers. The
connection becomes a full-duplex communication. Every peer can send data at any time.

The bidirectional communication isn't the only advantage of this protocol. Because
the connection stays active, it doesn't need to be initiated again and again for every
chunk of information. That saves a couple of bits and increases performance.

The switchover from HTTP to WebSocket is initiated by the WebSocket Opening-
Handshake-Request, which starts like Listing 34-1.

Listing 34-1. WebSocket Opening-Handshake-Request (Excerpt)

```
1   GET /endpoint HTTP/1.1
2   Host: mueller-bruehl.de
3   Connection: Upgrade
4   upgrade: websocket
5   ...
```

GET /endpoint refers to an endpoint of the WebSocket server. endpoint isn't a
fixed term but the name of the endpoint you want to connect to. Implementing a chat
application, that might be GET /chat. Implementing such an endpoint is essential.

I don't want to dive really deep into the protocol. If you're interested in such details, I recommend you read the spec. Check out the resources I already mentioned or the detailed overview on Wikipedia.

Endpoint

First, I'll demonstrate how to create a WebSocket endpoint with NetBeans. Begin by creating a fresh web project. Then add a new file (Ctrl+N). In the New File dialog, choose WebSocket Endpoint, as shown in Figure 34-1.

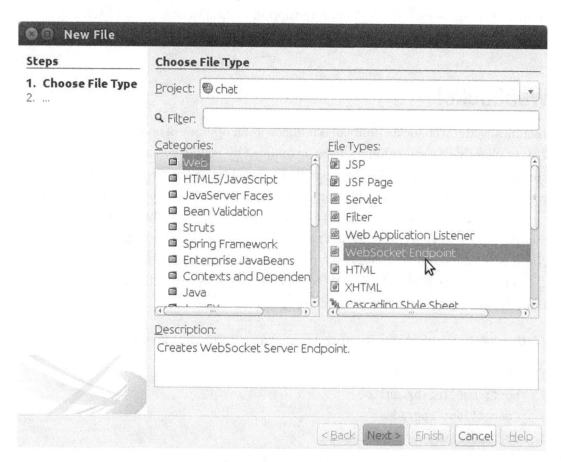

Figure 34-1. *New File wizard, WebSocket endpoint*

Click Next to provide a class name, package name, and endpoint name. After confirming with Finish, NetBeans creates a skeleton class for you, as shown in Listing 34-2.

Listing 34-2. Generated Skeleton Class for WebSocket Communication

```
 1   package de.muellerbruehl.chat;
 2
 3   import javax.websocket.OnMessage;
 4   import javax.websocket.server.ServerEndpoint;
 5
 6   /**
 7    *
 8    * @author mmueller
 9    */
10   @ServerEndpoint("/chat")
11   public class Chat {
12
13     @OnMessage
14     public String onMessage(String message) {
15       return null;
16     }
17
18   }
```

The @OnMessage annotated method is invoked when this endpoint receives data on its connection. Here we need to implement the desired behavior. Before describing Alumni's chat room, I'm going to explain the use of WebSockets step by step using a small example application.

Simple Chat

First, I'll describe the smallest possible chat I could write with JSF and WebSockets so far. JSF is only used to handle some elements within the browser. In such small applications, that might be also handled with pure HTML/JavaScript, but this book is about Java EE and JSF, so we're going to learn about using WebSockets in Java EE.

This paragraph offers a step-by-step tutorial with NetBeans. If the IDE of your choice is a different one, it should be possible for you to transfer the steps. Or give NetBeans a try. You'll need to install the NetBeans Java EE (or the all) bundle.

From the NetBeans menu, choose File ➤ New Project (or press Shift+Ctrl+N) to open the New Project window. Choose Maven ➤ Web Application and click Next, as shown in Figure 34-2.

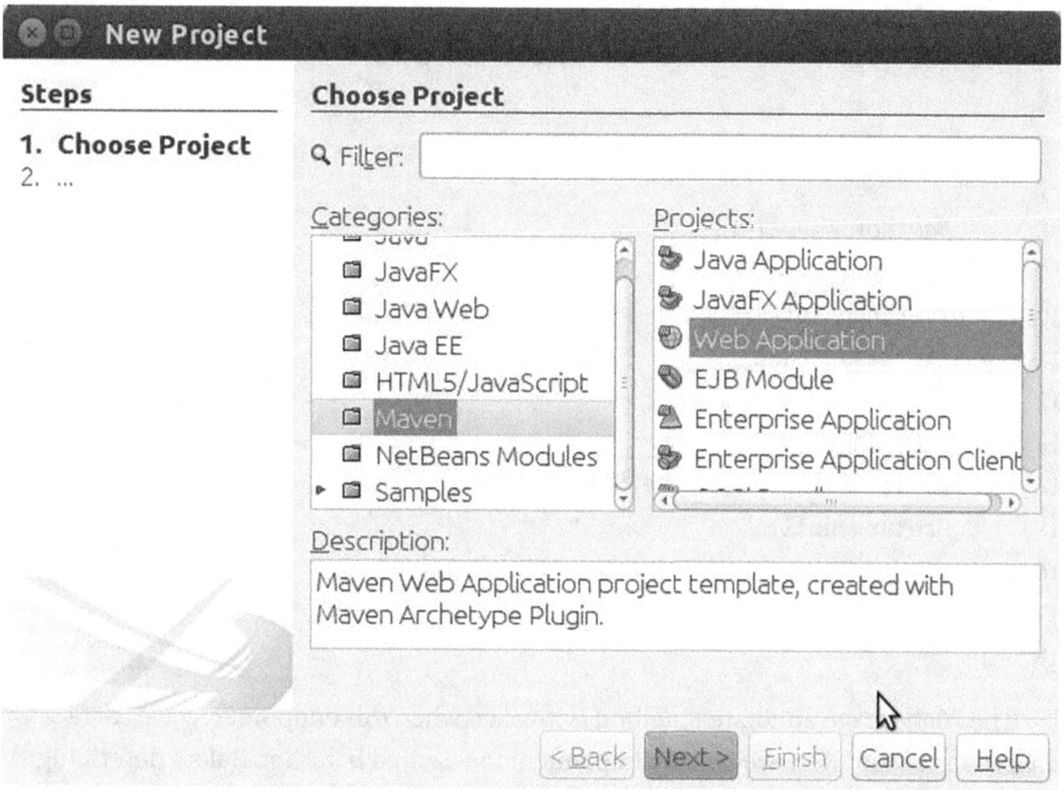

Figure 34-2. New Project wizard

In the next screen, provide a project name (**SimpleChat**), and in the last screen choose GlassFish (or Payara if installed) as the application server. Then finish the wizard.

Once NetBeans creates the project for you, right-click the project and open the Project Properties dialog. Add the JavaServer Faces framework, as shown in Figure 34-3.

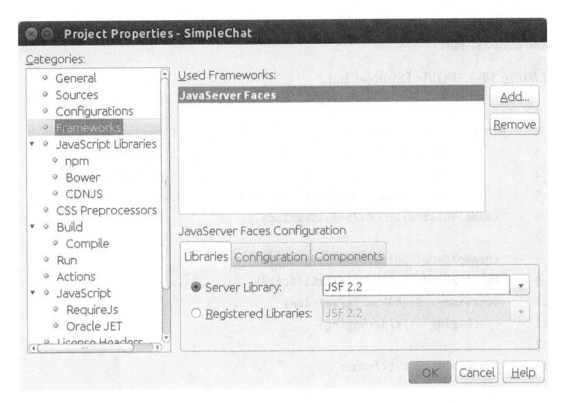

Figure 34-3. *Project Properties*

Click the Configuration tab and enter ***.xhtml** as URL pattern. Close the Properties dialog.

So far, this is like creating any other Java web project with JSF, but this time we'll add a dependency to the Tyrus server. Tyrus is the WebSocket reference implementation, included in GlassFish, WebLogic, and some other servers.

Open the POM and add the dependency shown in Listing 34-3.

Listing 34-3. Tyrus Dependency in the POM File

```
1  <dependency>
2    <groupId>org.glassfish.tyrus</groupId>
3    <artifactId>tyrus-server</artifactId>
4    <version>1.13</version>
5  </dependency>
```

We'll create another version without this dependency on the Tyrus server later in this book. Using Tyrus, the endpoint will be the simplest.

For those who don't use NetBeans, Listing 34-4 shows the complete POM created and edited so far.

Listing 34-4. POM of SimpleChat

```xml
1   <?xml version="1.0" encoding="UTF-8"?>
2   <project xmlns="http://maven.apache.org/POM/4.0.0"
3            xmlns:xsi="http://www.w3.org/2001/XMLSchema-instance"
4            xsi:schemaLocation="http://maven.apache.org/POM/4.0.0
5            http://maven.apache.org/xsd/maven-4.0.0.xsd">
6     <modelVersion>4.0.0</modelVersion>
7
8     <groupId>de.muellerbruehl</groupId>
9     <artifactId>SimpleChat</artifactId>
10    <version>1.0-SNAPSHOT</version>
11    <packaging>war</packaging>
12
13    <name>SimpleChat</name>
14
15    <properties>
16      <endorsed.dir>${project.build.directory}/endorsed</endorsed.dir>
17      <project.build.sourceEncoding>UTF-8</project.build.sourceEncoding>
18    </properties>
19
20    <dependencies>
21      <dependency>
22        <groupId>javax</groupId>
23        <artifactId>javaee-web-api</artifactId>
24        <version>8.0</version>
25        <scope>provided</scope>
26      </dependency>
27      <dependency>
28        <groupId>org.glassfish.tyrus</groupId>
29        <artifactId>tyrus-server</artifactId>
30        <version>1.13</version>
31      </dependency>
32    </dependencies>
```

```
33
34    <build>
35      <plugins>
36        <plugin>
37          <groupId>org.apache.maven.plugins</groupId>
38          <artifactId>maven-compiler-plugin</artifactId>
39          <version>3.1</version>
40          <configuration>
41            <source>1.8</source>
42            <target>1.8</target>
43            <compilerArguments>
44              <endorseddirs>${endorsed.dir}</endorseddirs>
45            </compilerArguments>
46          </configuration>
47        </plugin>
48        <plugin>
49          <groupId>org.apache.maven.plugins</groupId>
50          <artifactId>maven-war-plugin</artifactId>
51          <version>2.3</version>
52          <configuration>
53            <failOnMissingWebXml>false</failOnMissingWebXml>
54          </configuration>
55        </plugin>
56        <plugin>
57          <groupId>org.apache.maven.plugins</groupId>
58          <artifactId>maven-dependency-plugin</artifactId>
59          <version>2.6</version>
60          <executions>
61            <execution>
62              <phase>validate</phase>
63              <goals>
64                <goal>copy</goal>
65              </goals>
66              <configuration>
67                <outputDirectory>${endorsed.dir}</outputDirectory>
```

```
68                    <silent>true</silent>
69                    <artifactItems>
70                      <artifactItem>
71                        <groupId>javax</groupId>
72                        <artifactId>javaee-endorsed-api</artifactId>
73                        <version>8.0</version>
74                        <type>jar</type>
75                      </artifactItem>
76                    </artifactItems>
77                  </configuration>
78                </execution>
79              </executions>
80            </plugin>
81          </plugins>
82        </build>
83
84    </project>
```

The next step is to create a server endpoint, as mentioned earlier. For the name, choose SimpleChat and provide the same name for the package. The endpoint URI will be simplechat.

Next, modify the onMessage method, as shown in Listing 34-5.

Listing 34-5. onMessage Method to Broadcast a Message

```
1    @OnMessage
2    public void onMessage(String message, Session session) {
3      ((TyrusSession) session).broadcast(message);
4    }
```

Now fix the imports (Ctrl+Shift+I).

This method will be invoked every time our endpoint receives a message. All it does is broadcast this message to all clients who have opened a WebSocket connection to this endpoint. Although it seems to be a broadcast, under the hood the server handles individual connections. We'll handle this by ourselves within the Tyrus-less version.

Next, modify the index.xhtml page as shown in Listing 34-6.

Listing 34-6. SimpleChat Page (index.xhtml)

```
1   <?xml version='1.0' encoding='UTF-8' ?>
2   <!DOCTYPE html PUBLIC "-//W3C//DTD XHTML 1.0 Transitional//EN"
3     "http://www.w3.org/TR/xhtml1/DTD/xhtml1-transitional.dtd">
4   <html xmlns="http://www.w3.org/1999/xhtml"
5         xmlns:h="http://xmlns.jcp.org/jsf/html">
6     <h:head>
7       <title>Chat</title>
8       <h:outputScript name="simpleChat.js"/>
9     </h:head>
10    <h:body>
11
12      <h1>Simple chat</h1>
13      <h:form prependId="false">
14
15        <div>
16          Enter message:
17          <h:inputTextarea style="height: 1em;"
18              onkeypress="if (event.keyCode === 13) {
19                acceptValue(this);
20              }"
21          />
22        </div>
23        <h:inputTextarea id="messages"
24          style="width: 100%;
25          min-height: 10em;"/>
26      </h:form>
27    </h:body>
28  </html>
```

This page defines two text areas. One is just a simple one-line input field. I've chosen a text area rather than a simple text field to stay within this field on hitting the Enter key. As you can see in line 18, something happens (calling acceptValue) on pressing Enter.

The second text area is used for the common output. Here we'll display all messages of the users in that chat. The glue code we need is provided in a JavaScript file, simpleChat.js.

In the project's Web Pages, folder, create a new folder, resources, and in that folder the file simpleChat.js. JSF will load this file according to the outputScript tag we have in our page.

Add this content to the script file, as shown in Listing 34-7.

Listing 34-7. The JavaScript Part of SimpleChat

```
1    var websocket;
2
3    window.onload = function () {
4        invokeConnection();
5    }
6
7    function invokeConnection() {
8      websocket = new WebSocket(obtainUri());
9      websocket.onerror = function (evt) {
10        onError(evt)
11      };
12      websocket.onmessage = function (evt) {
13        onMessage(evt)
14      };
15      return true;
16   }
17
18   function obtainUri() {
19      return "ws://" + document.location.host + "/SimpleChat/simplechat";
20   }
21
22   function onError(evt) {
23      writeToScreen('<span style="color: red;">ERROR:</span> ' + evt.data);
24   }
25
26
```

```
27    function onMessage(evt) {
28      element = document.getElementById("messages");
29      if (element.value.length === 0) {
30        element.value = evt.data;
31      } else {
32        oldTexts = element.value.split("\n").slice(-19);
33        element.value = oldTexts.join("\n") + evt.data;
34        element.scrollTop = element.scrollHeight;
35      }
36      return;
37    }
38
39    function acceptValue(element) {
40      websocket.send(element.value);
41      element.value = "";
42      return true;
43    }
```

Our simple chat is ready now. Compile and start the application. Enter some text and press Enter: the text appears in the output area. Open the app in a second browser and enter some more text: it will appear in the output field in all browsers.

Let's talk about how this works. When the page is loaded, invokeConnection is being called. This method establishes a WebSocket communication channel to the server and registers two methods. onMessage is called for regular messages, and onError handles errors. Every time the client receives a message from the server (as sent by the broadcast), it gets the text area we use for the output and appends the message. If a certain maximum is reached, it composes the output of the last few messages.

The method acceptValue is called every time the user hits the Enter key in the input field. The message is sent to the server, and the input field is cleared to accept a fresh value.

So far, we've created a very simple chat application using technologies that have been available since Java EE 7. Java EE 8 added WebSocket for JSF, which I'll talk about at the end of this chapter. In the first version of the simple chat, any message had been broadcasted by a Tyrus session. Next, I'll show how to handle the broadcast by yourself. You'll recognize that in fact this is no broadcast: WebSocket, as I've said, is a full-duplex communication protocol between two peers. To emulate the broadcast, the server needs to send the message to every peer.

An instance of our server endpoint is created every time the URL is opened in your browser. If you stay on that page, you can reuse the existing endpoint. If you want to verify that behavior, simply add a default constructor and report the construction, as shown in Listing 34-8.

Listing 34-8. Observe Object Creation by a Short Constructor Message

```
1   public SimpleChat() {
2       System.out.println("ctor SimpleChat");
3   }
```

Using Glassfish/Payara, the output is logged. You can call the logger instead. Using NetBeans, you may observe this log directly in the output window of the IDE.

For every user, an instance of this class is created. Each object is associated with one client. So if we want to broadcast a message to all clients, then any endpoint needs to know about the others. To do that, each peer session that wants to participate in the chat needs to register itself at a common place. The simplest way to perform this task is to use a static set of peer sessions, as shown in Listing 34-9.

Listing 34-9. HashSet to Hold All Sessions

```
1   private static final Set<Session> peers =
2           Collections.synchronizedSet(new HashSet<Session>());
```

At the beginning and the termination of a session, there's an event we can observe. To connect a method to one of these events, we need to annotate a method either with @OnOpen or @OnClose. These methods need to accept a session argument, which means these methods are the perfect candidates to register and unregister the peer sessions. See Listing 34-10.

Listing 34-10. Methods to Register/Unregister Peers

```
1   @OnOpen
2   public void onOpen(Session peer) {
3       peers.add(peer);
4   }
5
6   @OnClose
```

```
7    public void onClose(Session peer) {
8      peers.remove(peer);
9    }
```

Once we've registered all peers, we just need to iterate them during @OnMessage and send the message to every peer. To do that, we use getBasicRemote() to get a reference to the remote endpoint where we want to send data synchronously, as shown in Listing 34-11. There's a second method, getAsyncRemote(), that can be used to send data asynchronously.

Listing 34-11. Broadcast Message by Sending It to Every Peer

```
1    @OnMessage
2    public void onMessage(String message) {
3      for (Session peer : peers) {
4        try {
5          peer.getBasicRemote().sendObject(message);
6        } catch (IOException | EncodeException ex) {
7          // log, handle, or ingnore exceptions here
8        }
9      }
10   }
```

You may have recognized the different signatures of the onMessage() method. We don't need the session argument, so we can use the overloaded method signature without it.

For your convenience, Listing 34-12 shows the whole endpoint class (without imports).

Listing 34-12. Complete SimpleChat (Imports Omitted)

```
1    @ServerEndpoint("/simplechat")
2    public class SimpleChat {
3
4      private static final Set<Session> peers =
5          Collections.synchronizedSet(new HashSet<Session>());
6
7      @OnMessage
8      public void onMessage(String message) {
9        for (Session peer : peers) {
```

```
10          try {
11              peer.getBasicRemote().sendObject(message);
12          } catch (IOException | EncodeException ex) {
13              // log, handle, or ingnore exceptions here
14          }
15        }
16      }
17
18      @OnOpen
19      public void onOpen(Session peer) {
20        peers.add(peer);
21      }
22
23      @OnClose
24      public void onClose(Session peer) {
25        peers.remove(peer);
26      }
27    }
```

ClassRoom Chat

Let's get back to Alumni. We want to prefix any message with the user who sent it, and we need to handle different chat rooms for different classes.

Pupils grow up and become students. They may change their domicile, school, and university. All in all, over time somebody may belong to different classes, identified by the final class. Once the user is logged in, they may choose a class and enter the dedicated virtual classroom. In each classroom, Alumni offers a blackboard, a calendar of events, and a chat.

We don't want to implement a separate endpoint for each class. Rather, we want to use a single endpoint and distinguish the chat by the final class.

One solution would be to provide information about the classroom with the endpoint URI. Let's assume the classroom is identified by a name. The code might look like the excerpt in Listing 34-13.

Listing 34-13. Pass Parameter via Endpoint URI

```
1   @ServerEndpoint("/classroomchat/{classroom}")
2   public class ClassroomChat {
3
4       @OnOpen
5       public void onOpen(Session peer) {
6           String classroom = peer.getRequestParameterMap().get("classroom").
            get(0);
7           [...]
8       }
9
10      [...]
11
12  }
```

This is quite the style Java EE supports by JAX-RS (Java API for RESTful Web Services): parts of the URI are variable and will be accessible via the request parameter map, as shown in the onOpen method. Really easy, isn't it?

The WebSocket connection is a channel between the client and the server. As an upgrade from HTTP, the first request is initiated by the client. What happens if the user fakes the URI and chooses a different classroom? And we want to include the user in each message. Do you want somebody to spoof the user? Regardless, the approach shown here is really simple, but it might not fit our requirements with regard to matters of security. Why should the client provide information the server already knows?

With these thoughts in mind, Alumni uses a different approach. User and classroom are well known on the server side, so they'll be injected into the endpoint.

Once the user is logged in to Alumni, we store some information within a session scoped object, as shown in Listing 34-14. Here, the user account and the currently selected final class are of note.

Listing 34-14. Session Scoped Object to Hold User Information

```
1   @SessionScoped
2   public class UserController implements Serializable {
3
4       private Account _account;
```

```
5      private FinalYear _finalYear;
6
7      [Getter/Setter and other fields omitted for brevity]
8    }
```

We'll inject an instance of this class into the chat endpoint. The account lets us access the user's name.

INJECTION BY CDI

Remember some characteristics of CDI: you can inject a bean independently from its lifespan. For example, you might inject a request scoped bean into a session scoped bean. Although the session scoped bean is usually alive for more than a request, the injected bean is alive for a single request only. Yet you can access an injected bean during the lifetime of the holding object. Isn't that paradoxical?

CDI accomplishes this trick by injecting a proxy object. This proxy is available during the whole lifetime of the containing bean. Under the hood, this proxy refers to a different object for each request.

Now if we try to prefix every message from the user, like sendObject (_userController.GetAccount().getDisplayName()+ ": " + message), we'll run into an error: albeit injected, _userController resolves to null.

The reason is quite simple: the endpoint will be created within the HTTP request, When the user enters the classroom. The injected user controller contains all the values we expect. CDI doesn't really inject an instance of the class UserController, but a proxy pointing to the active user controller object of the current request. The WebSocket channels are opened by an upgrade from HTTP. The initiating request terminates normally, while the channel remains open. Now if the user enters a message, it's sent via the WebSocket channel. Because there's no HTTP request at that time, the CDI proxy can't refer to any bean, even though the user controller is of session scope. So, the proxy resolves to null.

Even though the user controller is injected as a proxy, it contains the "real" objects. Alumni simply stores these objects within the endpoint, and voilà, we can use them. Besides package and imports, Listing 34-15 shows the complete endpoint class:

Listing 34-15. Classroom Chat of Alumni

```
1   @ServerEndpoint("/classroomchat")
2   public class ClassroomChat {
3
4       private static final Map<Integer, Set<Session>> PEERS = new
         ConcurrentHa\
5   shMap<>();
6       private static final Logger LOGGER = Logger.
         getLogger(ClassroomChat.clas\
7   s.getName());
8
9       private ChatService _chatService;
10      private Account _account;
11      private int _finalYearId;
12
13      @Inject
14      public ClassroomChat(UserController user, ChatService chatService)
   {
15          _account = user.getAccount();
16          _finalYearId = user.getFinalYear().getId();
17          _chatService = chatService;
18      }
19
20      public ClassroomChat() {
21          LOGGER.log(Level.INFO, "ctor ClassroomChat");
22      }
23
24      @OnMessage
25      public void onMessage(String message, Session session) {
26          //String name = session.getUserPrincipal().getName();
27          for (Session peer : PEERS.get(_finalYearId)) {
28              try {
29                  peer.getBasicRemote().sendObject(_account.
                     getDisplayName() +\
30  ": " + message);
```

```
31              } catch (IOException | EncodeException ex) {
32                  // in case of error, log problem and continue
33                  LOGGER.log(Level.SEVERE, null, ex);
34              }
35          }
36      }
37
38      @OnOpen
39      public void onOpen(Session peer) {
40          LOGGER.log(Level.INFO, "onOpen ClassroomChat, user {0}",
41                              _account.getDisplayName());
42          if (!PEERS.containsKey(_finalYearId)){
43            PEERS.put(_finalYearId,
44                              Collections.synchronizedSet(new
                              HashSet<>()));
45          }
46          PEERS.get(_finalYearId).add(peer);
47          sendLatestMessages(peer);
48      }
49
50      private void sendLatestMessages(Session peer) {
51          List<String> messages = _chatService.getLatestMessages
            (_finalYearId);
52          for (String message : messages) {
53              try {
54                  peer.getBasicRemote().sendObject(message);
55              } catch (IOException | EncodeException ex) {
56                  // in case of error, log problem and continue
57                  LOGGER.log(Level.SEVERE, null, ex);
58              }
59
60          }
61      }
62
63      @OnClose
64      public void onClose(Session peer) {
```

```
65          LOGGER.log(Level.INFO, "onClose ClassroomChat, user {0}",
66                              _account.getDisplayName());
67          PEERS.get(_finalYearId).remove(peer);
68      }
69
70  }
```

In lines 13 and 14 we store references to user and final class that have been injected as part of userController. Besides an instance of the UserController, an instance of the ChatService is injected too. And unlike the user controller, this proxy is directly stored within a field (line 15). Will we face the same proxy problem described earlier? A consultant's standard answer would be, "It depends. . . ."

If we define the ChatService as a CDI bean with a short (request) scope, as shown in Listing 34-16, we'll run into a ContextNotActiveException.

Listing 34-16. ChatService as Request Scoped CDI Bean

```
1   @RequestScoped
2   @Transactional
3   public class ChatService extends AbstractService {
4   ...
5   }
```

Extending the scope to session scope doesn't solve this problem: such a scope is stored within the session map of a request, and there may be no request.

There are two possible solutions. You may define the service within the application scope. Or, if you don't want to use a global object with such a long lifespan, you might use a stateless EJB. as shown in Listing 34-17.

Listing 34-17. ChatService as Stateless EJB

```
1   @Stateless
2   public class ChatService extends AbstractService {
3   ...
4   }
```

Comparing this with the simple chat, there are three extensions: Alumni uses a map to held the peers per classroom. Every message is prefixed by the username. And, last but not least, all messages are saved to the database, allowing us to reply to the latest messages on entering the classroom.

Listing 34-18 shows the corresponding part from the service.

Listing 34-18. ChatService (Excerpt)

```
1    @Stateless
2    public class ChatService extends AbstractService {
3
4      public ChatEntry saveChatEntry(ChatEntry chatEntry) {
5        return save(chatEntry);
6      }
7
8      public ChatEntry saveChatEntry(int finalClassId, int accountId,
       String mes\
9    sage) {
10       ChatEntry chatEntry = new ChatEntry(finalClassId, accountId,
         message);
11       return save(chatEntry);
12     }
13
14     /**
15      * retrieves latest 10 messages which are not older than 2 hours
16      *
17      * @param finalYearId
18      * @return
19      */
20     public List<String> getLatestMessages(int finalYearId) {
21       String jpql = "Select concat(a._firstName, ' ', a._lastName, ': ', e._me\
22   ssage) "
23               + "from ChatEntry e "
24               + "join Account a "
25               + "where e._accountId = a._id "
26               + "and e._finalYearId = :finalYearId "
27               + "and e._moment > :refMoment order by e._id desc";
28       TypedQuery<String> query = getEntityManager().createQuery(jpql,
         String.c\
29   lass);
```

```
30        query.setParameter("finalYearId", finalYearId);
31        query.setMaxResults(10);
32        Date refMoment = new Date(new Date().getTime() - 2 * 3600 * 1000);
33        query.setParameter("refMoment", refMoment);
34        List<String> messages = query.getResultList();
35        return Lists.reverse(messages);
36    }
37
38 }
```

JSF 2.3 websocket

One of the highlights of JSF 2.3, as introduced in Java EE 8, has been its support for the WebSocket protocol. Formerly, JSF only used one-way communication from client to server as caused by the HTTP protocol. Sending data from server to client without any client request was a challenge for many years. The WebSocket protocol is one solution to this restriction. It was the main intention to push messages from server to client when the <f:websocket> tag was introduced to JSF 2.3. Currently, this tag doesn't enable the full advantages of this bidirectional protocol. Rather, it establishes one-way communication from server to client. If we need a bidirectional communication with JSF functionality only, we might send data from client to server the traditional way, by using an inputText In conjunction with Ajax. We'll receive data via websocket. Because this workaround only mimics bidirectional communication using different protocols, Alumni's chat doesn't use the new JSF websocket. To sketch for you the principle of this new tag, Listing 34-19 starts with the page.

Listing 34-19. Using websocket in a Page

```
1        <f:websocket channel="events" onmessage="eventListener" />
2
3        <script type="text/javascript">
4          function eventListener(message, channel, event) {
5            document.getElementById("lastEvent").innerHTML += message +
             "<br/>";
6          }
```

```
7          </script>
8
9          <h:outputLabel value="Last event:"/>
10         <h:outputText id="lastEvent" value=""/>
```

In line 1 the websocket tag subscribes to the channel events. This name has to correspond to the channel name you use on the server side. It may be any valid name of your choice. The onmessage attribute refers to a JavaScript function you need to implement for the data handling. In this simple demo code, we use the message to replace the content of the outPutText we declared in line 10.

On the server side, we need a PushContext, which simply can be injected (see line 5 of Listing 34-20). Here we need to provide the channel name. Now we can send messages via this channel to the client (lines 8–10).

Listing 34-20. PushContext as Source for websocket

```
1   @Named
2   @ApplicationScoped
3   public class EventPatcher {
4
5      @Inject @Push(channel = "events")
6      private PushContext _pushContext;
7
8      public void sendMessage(String message){
9         _pushContext.send(message);
10     }
11
12  }
```

When the first client uses this channel, the WebSocket communication will be established. Sending a message is like a broadcast. All clients that have subscribed to this channel will receive the message. The channel automatically closes on application shutdown, so the PushContext needs to be injected into an application scoped bean.

Last but not least, you need to enable the WebSocket endpoint via web.xml.

Listing 34-21. context param as Part of web.xml

```
1    <context-param>
2      <param-name>javax.faces.ENABLE_WEBSOCKET_ENDPOINT</param-name>
3      <param-value>true</param-value>
4    </context-param>
```

Pushing some content to all users is the most common operational area. Because of that, application scope is the default scope for using websocket within JSF. Anyway, you can restrict the channel to session or view. Or you can restrict it to a specified user, which forces the session scope too. (For more information, read the API doc at https:// javaserverfaces.github.io/docs/2.3/vldoc/f/websocket.html).

The JSF websocket tag is great if you want to implement a news ticker or something similar. There's no such requirement for Alumni. Take the explanation given here as starting point for your own experiments.

Summary

This chapter introduced the main aspects of the WebSocket protocol and its use within Alumni. This chat implementation of Alumni is fine with Java EE 8, but it only uses techniques that are available in the former Java EE 7 implementation.

JSF 2.3, which is part of Java EE 8, now directly supports the WebSocket protocol, but Alumni doesn't use it. The primary intent of the current JSF WebSocket implementation is to push messages from the server to the client. This adds unidirectional communication from server to client. Alumni, on the other hand, uses bidirectional communication.

CHAPTER 35

Changing Look and Feel

Sometimes users love to exchange the look and feel of an application, for example by choosing a different theme. The question arises, how can we change the look and feel of an application without changing the program code? If we separated content and layout with CSS, it seems as easy as choosing a different CSS file.

Resource Library

In practice, the layout might depend not only on a single CSS file, but on a couple of CSS files as well as related script files or other resources. Let's recap Chapter 10: JSF is able to group a bundle of resources into a library. In fact, such a library is represented by the content of a folder. If we use the same directory structure for every library, we don't need to provide different names for all the resource files, just the library name.

In the Facelet template `alumniTemplate.xhtml`, we'll retrieve the appropriate library from a backing bean, as shown in Listing 35-1.

Listing 35-1. Get Library from Backing Bean

```
01    <h:outputStylesheet library="#{sessionTools.theme}" name="css/
      alumni.css"/>
02    <h:outputScript library="#{sessionTools.theme}" name="script/alumni.
      js"/>
```

This backing bean is used to hold user-specific information as long as the session lasts. Thus it is session scoped. See Listing 35-2.

Listing 35-2. SessionTools

```
01    @Named
02    @SessionScoped
03    public class SessionTools implements Serializable {
```

415

© Michael Müller 2018
M. Müller, *Practical JSF in Java EE 8*, https://doi.org/10.1007/978-1-4842-3030-5_35

```
04
05     private String _theme = "standard";
06
07     public String getTheme() {
08        return _theme;
09     }
10
11     public void setTheme(String theme) {
12        _theme = theme;
13     }
14
15     ...
16
17   }
```

When the user logs in, we need to read the theme from the appropriate user configuration and set the theme within the backing bean. That's it.

Immediately Change the Look and Feel

Instead of asking a user in a configuration dialog, we may want to enable them to change the look and feel immediately. As a first approach, we'll present two buttons on the screen representing two different themes. If the user clicks a button, we want the look and feel to change instantly.

The solution is quite easy, too. All we need is to set the theme and then to reload the page. If an action of a commandLink or commandButton returns an empty string or nothing (null or void), then JSF reloads the same page. To perform this task, we use setter of the theme as action of the link. See Listing 35-3.

Listing 35-3. Buttons to Switch Theme

```
01     <h:commandLink styleClass="button"
02                            immediate="true"
03                            value="standard"
04                            action="#{sessionTools.setTheme('standard')}"/>
05     <h:commandLink styleClass="button"
06                            immediate="true"
```

```
07                    value="muellerbruehl"
08                    action="#{sessionTools.
                      setTheme('muellerbruehl')}"/>
```

Read from Resources

Increasing the number of buttons in conformity with the number of themes will create an ugly page. A more elegant solution can be achieved by a menu, where the user chooses one of multiple entries. And if we add a theme, then the system should automatically recognize it. For this task, we need to examine the resources. For simplicity's sake, we'll assume that every folder within the `resources` directory containing a CSS file is a resource library. We'll ignore possible versions below that folder.

The method `getThemes` returns a list of strings with all the library folders we've found, as shown in Listing 35-4.

Listing 35-4. Retrieve Themes from Resources

```
01    public List<String> getThemes() throws IOException {
02      String resourcePath = obtainResourcePath();
03      List<String> themes = obtainThemes(resourcePath);
04      return themes;
05    }
06
07    private String obtainResourcePath() {
08      ServletContext context = (ServletContext) FacesContext
09              .getCurrentInstance()
10              .getExternalContext()
11              .getContext();
12      return context.getRealPath("/resources");
13    }
14
15    private List<String> obtainThemes(String resourcePath){
16      List<String> themes = new ArrayList<>();
17      for (File file : new File(resourcePath).listFiles()) {
18        addFilenameIfContainsCss(file, themes);
19      }
```

```
20        return themes;
21    }
22
23    private void addFilenameIfContainsCss(File file, List<String>
      themes) {
24        if (!file.isDirectory()) {
25            return;
26        }
27        try (Stream<Path> paths = Files.walk(Paths.get(file.
          getAbsolutePath())))) {
28            boolean conatinsCss = paths
29                        .filter(Files::isRegularFile)
30                        .anyMatch(f -> f.toString().toLowerCase().endsWith(".
                          css"));
31            if (conatinsCss) {
32                themes.add(file.getName());
33            }
34        } catch (IOException ex) {
35            LOGGER.log(Level.SEVERE, null, ex);
36        }
37    }
```

Figure 35-1 shows an excerpt of the project tree. You'll find a file alumni.css for each theme (muellerbruehl and standard are themes too, but the tree is collapsed here).

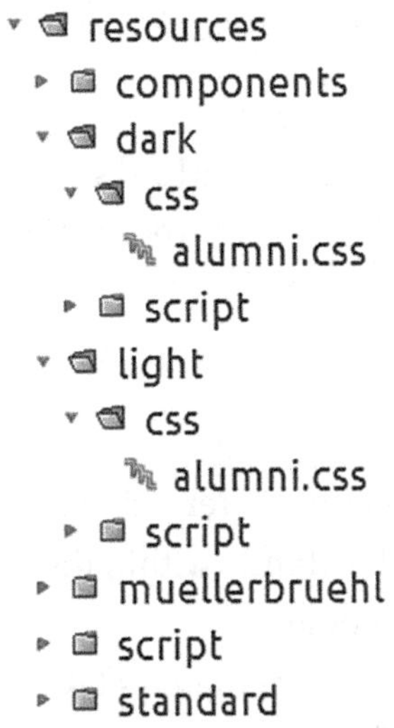

```
▼ ◢ resources
  ▸ ◻ components
  ▼ ◢ dark
    ▼ ◢ css
        ▧ alumni.css
    ▸ ◻ script
  ▼ ◢ light
    ▼ ◢ css
        ▧ alumni.css
    ▸ ◻ script
  ▸ ◻ muellerbruehl
  ▸ ◻ script
  ▸ ◻ standard
```

Figure 35-1. *Resource files for different themes*

Because we don't know where the application resides when it's deployed, we need to figure out the right path. Resources reside in the \resources path. Although it looks like an absolute path from the application's view, it's really a relative path. We need to figure out its parent.

The interesting part of Listing 35-4 is the obtainResourcePath method (lines 7–13). Here we'll retrieve the ServletContext. We can use it to determine a real path. There are many situations in which it's needed to search the resources.

In another project, I needed to create reports. Instead of creating report files from scratch, I added template files that would be completed at runtime. I deployed these files in a resources folder and used the same logic discussed here to retrieve the files' location.

The rest of Listing 35-4 is simple Java code, searching this path for CSS files. If you're not familiar with streams, allow me to recommend my book *Java Lambdas and Parallel Streams* (Apress, 2016) as a good source of information.

Once we figure out the themes, we need to present them to the user in a selectOneMenu, as shown in Listing 35-5.

Listing 35-5. Select Theme (Incomplete)

```
01   <h:form id="theme">
02     <h:selectOneMenu value="#{sessionTools.theme}">
03       <f:selectItems value="#{sessionTools.themes}"/>
04       <f:ajax/>
05     </h:selectOneMenu>
06   </h:form>
```

The preceding listing uses the getter/setter pair we created before. If the user chooses a theme, it will be updated instantly within the backing bean. During the next navigation, JSF will apply the new theme.

But how can we apply the theme immediately? Okay, we can add information to render all: `<f:ajax render="@all"/>`.

Now when the user chooses a different theme, the layout seems to change. But it's not the layout as expected. Only by reloading the page is the expected layout shown. It seems as if @all doesn't really load everything we need.

What if we apply a listener method and add programmatic navigation, as in Listing 35-6?

Listing 35-6. Programmatic Navigation

```
01   public void themeChangeListener(AjaxBehaviorEvent event) {
02     FacesContext facesContext = FacesContext.getCurrentInstance();
03     NavigationHandler navigationHandler = facesContext
04             .getApplication()
05             .getNavigationHandler();
06     navigationHandler.handleNavigation(facesContext, null, "");
07   }
```

In line 6, the third parameter denotes the target page. We'll leave it blank for reloading the current page.

Don't try it. You might use such a fragment for navigation on a request, but not during a partial request. A *partial* request only queries some info to update the current page.

The selectOneMenu isn't intended to trigger any navigation. Some additional libraries—for example, PrimeFaces (www.primefaces.org)—contain extensions for this use case. But, there may be a simple solution to this problem: when the user has chosen a new theme, we need to trigger a page navigation by clicking a commandLink. We use an invisible link and some JavaScript voodoo to perform this task, as you can see in Listing 35-7.

Listing 35-7. Select Theme, Tricking Navigation

```
01   <h:form id="theme">
02     <h:selectOneMenu value="#{sessionTools.theme}"
03         onchange="document.getElementById('theme:refresh').click();">
04       <f:selectItems value="#{sessionTools.themes}"/>
05       <f:ajax/>
06     </h:selectOneMenu>
07
08     <h:commandLink id="refresh" immediate="true"/>
09   </h:form>
```

In line 3, we define some code that gets processed during the click event. It simply searches for the invisible link and performs a click on it.

But how does JSF perform a page navigation when the user clicks a link? Surprise—under the hood it also uses JavaScript! And if we use the same functionality, we really add navigation capability to the menu. See Listing 35-8 and Figures 35-2 and 35-3.

Listing 35-8. Select Theme (Final)

```
01   <h:form id="theme">
02     <h:selectOneMenu value="#{sessionTools.theme}"
03                       onchange="mojarra.jsfcljs(document.
                          getElementById('theme'),
04                          {'theme':'theme'},'');return false;">
05       <f:selectItems value="#{sessionTools.themes}"/>
06       <f:ajax />
07     </h:selectOneMenu>
08   </h:form>
```

Figures 35-2 and 35-3 show two different themes. On the top left you see the drop-down menu box that enables the user to change the menu. Both figures show the German version (you could see that for yourself, right?).

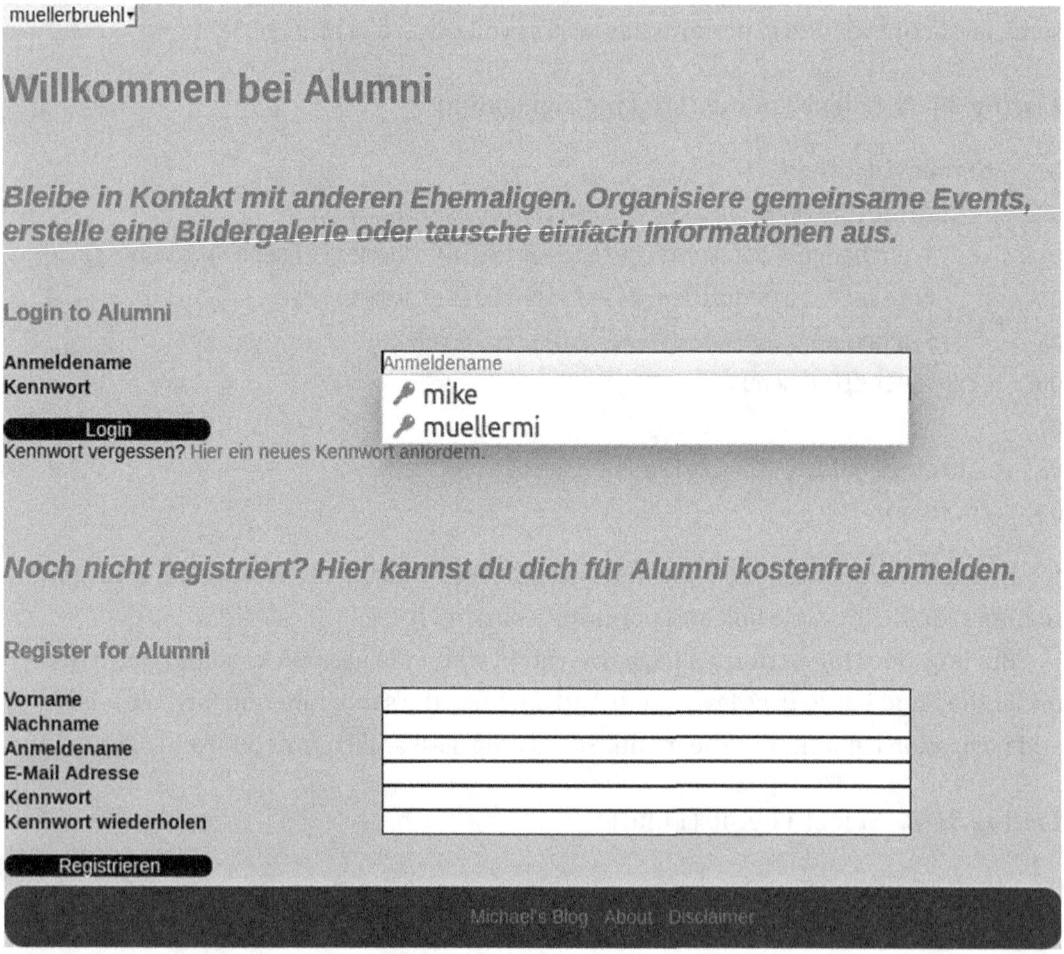

Figure 35-2. *Example of muellerbruehl theme*

dark ⌄

Willkommen bei Alumni

Bleibe in Kontakt mit anderen Ehemaligen. Organisiere gemeinsame Events, erstelle eine Bildergalerie oder tausche einfach Informationen aus.

Login to Alumni

Anmeldename   Anmeldename
Kennwort   Kennwort

Login

Kennwort vergessen? Hier ein neues Kennwort anfordern.

Noch nicht registriert? Hier kannst du dich für Alumni kostenfrei anmelden.

Register for Alumni

Vorname
Nachname
Anmeldename
E-Mail Adresse
Kennwort
Kennwort wiederholen

Registrieren

Figure 35-3. *Example with dark theme*

Summary

Changing the look and feel of an application is as simple as changing the resource library. To apply such a change at once, we need to trick the system a bit. This chapter also showed you how to find files in the application server file system during runtime. Last but not least, it demonstrated how JSF assigns the navigation capabilities to HTML elements.

CHAPTER 36

Handling Constants

JSF 2.3 introduced the ability to import constants for use within the Expression Language (EL).

Navigation by Strings

JSF supports internal as well as external navigation. Internal navigation is defined in the source code, whereas external navigation is described by an external XML file.

Let's take a look at a simple internal navigation first in Listing 36-1.

Listing 36-1. Direct Navigation by String

```
1    <h:commandLink styleClass="button"
2                          value="#{msg.btnWelcome}"
3                          action="/user/welcome.xhtml"/>
```

In line 3 we define the navigation target. This is quite easy but can be error-prone. If you have a typo in the action, JSF may display the page properly, but clicking the link doesn't perform any action. And if you want to move or rename the welcome page, you have to update all occurrences within your code. It's easy to forget one of them. That's why some developers prefer external navigation. Personally, I don't like to define my navigation in an XML file. For the Books application, I used a different strategy to mitigate this problem.

In the page, we call a navigation method that uses an enum. For the page we use a logical string that's automatically converted to an instance of the enum when calling that method, as shown in Listing 36-2.

© Michael Müller 2018
M. Müller, *Practical JSF in Java EE 8*, https://doi.org/10.1007/978-1-4842-3030-5_36

Listing 36-2. Self-Made enum Navigation

```
1    <h:commandLink styleClass="button"
2                        value="#{msg.btnWelcome}"
3                        action="/#{sessionTools.
                         navigate('UserWelcome')}"/>
```

Listing 36-3 shows a shortened excerpt of the Books navigation, and Listing 36-4 shows an excerpt of the enum.

Listing 36-3. Navigation Method (as Part of the Backing Bean)

```
1    public String navigate(Page page) {
2      return page.getRedirectUrl();
3    }
```

Listing 36-4. Excerpt of the enum Page

```
1    public enum Page {
2
3      UserTemplate("/user/booksTemplate"),
4      <other pages here>
5      ;
6
7      private Page(String url) {
8        _url = url;
9      }
10     private final String _url;
11
12     public String getUrl() {
13       return _url + ".xhtml";
14     }
15
16     public String getRedirectUrl() {
17       return _url + ".xhtml?faces-redirect=true";
18     }
19     ...
20   }
```

Now if we have a typo in the page declaration we'll get an error immediately when the page is displayed. Such an obvious error helps discover problems. And the main advantage of this approach is the use of a logical name. If we want to relocate or rename the page, we only need to update the enum, keeping all pages unchanged.

Importing Constants

With the current version of Java EE 8/JSF 2.3, we can do even better—and this is what we use for Alumni's navigation. For example, we pick the forgot password link, as in Listing 36-5.

Listing 36-5. Navigation Using an enum

```
1    <div>
2      #{msg.lblForgotPassword}
3      <h:link value="#{msg.lblRequestPassword}"
4                   outcome="#{Page.RequestPassword.url()}"/>
5    </div>
```

Take a look at line 4. Here the outcome is directly composed by the enum's `url`. We just use the enum as we do in a Java source file. As a prerequisite, we need to tell the EL about our enum. That's where the new `importConstants` tag comes into play. Within the metadata, we need to declare this tag in conjunction with the full class name, as shown in Listing 36-6.

Listing 36-6. Import Constants for Use in the EL

```
1    <f:metadata>
2      <f:importConstants type="de.muellerbruehl.alumni.gui.enums.Page"/>
3    </f:metadata>
```

Although Alumni only imports enums, you can use the `importConstants` tag for any kinds of constants.

Summary

JSF 2.3 introduced a new tag `importConstants`. As its name suggests, this tag is used to import constants that can be used in the EL afterwards. In Alumni this feature is used, among others, for easy, configurable internal page navigation.

HTML

The HyperText Markup Language is used to describe the contents of a web page. Like XML, HTML is a member of the Standard Generalized Markup Language (SGML).

I assume at least a basic knowledge of XML. Thus, this book won't go into detail about how to build an XML document. An HTML document has to consider similar rules, but sometimes is less strict. Unlike XML, where you define your own tags, HTML comes with a set of predefined tags. The most common tags are briefly described in the following sections.

HTML Structure

An HTML document starts with a document type, followed by an <html> tag, which is comparable to the document root of an XML document. Within that, a tag for header and body might be included. In the case of XHTML, which is HTML built with strict XLM rules, the doctype is preceded by the XML version.

This basic structure is shown in Listing A-1.

Listing A-1. Basic HTML File

```
1   <?xml version='1.0' encoding='UTF-8' ?>
2   <!DOCTYPE html>
3   <html>
4       <head>
5           <!-- header content -->
6       </head>
7       <body>
8           <!-- body content -->
9       </body>
10  </html>
```

429

© Michael Müller 2018
M. Müller, *Practical JSF in Java EE 8*, https://doi.org/10.1007/978-1-4842-3030-5

As of HTML5, the doctype is nothing more than the simple `<!DOCTYPE html>`, which is supported by all of today's important browsers. In older HTML versions, there were different doctypes, using strict, transitional, or frameset mode, such as `<!DOCTYPE HTML PUBLIC "-//W3C//DTD HTML 4.01 Transitional//EN">`.

HTML Header

Tag Name	Description
`base`	Base address (URI) of this page. Relative paths will be prefixed by this. This binds all paths to a special URI. Don't use this if you want to keep your page portable.
`link`	Describes the relation from the current document to others. Used to point to files that should be loaded together with the page, like a CSS file.
`meta`	Metainformation for the current document, often including author, keywords (for search engines), forwarding information, and more.
`style`	Internal Cascading Style Sheet. If used in conjunction with an external style sheet, it will overwrite styles defined for the same path.
`title`	Title of this page. Displayed by most browsers within the heading or tab control.

HTML Body

For the body, many more tags are defined. Associated tags are grouped together. These tables list only commonly used elements.

Page and Text Structure, Linking

Tag Name	Description
h1	Semantic decoration of heading 1. Without any style, it would be displayed using a bigger font size. Thus, HTML doesn't just assign a semantic meaning. Lower level headings range from h2–h6.
div	Used to divide the text into sections, a container element for other elements. It should be used only if no other tag with a more specific semantic meaning is available.
p	Indicates a paragraph, used to split longer texts into single paragraphs. Developing a web application, you usually don't have that much text.
hr	Horizontal ruler, used for a thematic break. Unless overwritten by CSS, it draws a horizontal line.
ol	Ordered list, a container for list items. Unless overwritten by CSS, the contained items are numbered.
ul	Unordered list, a container for list items. Unless overwritten by CSS, the contained items are displayed with a bullet point.
li	List item.
a	Anchor, defines a hyperlink.

Other semantic structure tags include nav (navigation), aside, main, section, article, footer, address, and more.

Forms and Input

Tag Name	Description
form	Defines an HTML form, which acts as a container for input elements, buttons, and so on. Form values might be submitted by an appropriate element.
input	A generic input element. The attribute `type="..."` specifies the characteristic of this element, such as `text` (text field), `radio` (radio button), `checkbox`, `submit` (button).
textarea	A multi-line text field.
button	A clickable button. This element can be defined more flexibly than `input type="submit"`. The drawback is that it doesn't submit any value. Thus, a script handler is needed to perform an action.
select	A selectable list. It can be parameterized for a single or multi select.
label	Defines a label that might be assigned to an input element.

The HTML page in Listing A-2 shows a simple form.

Listing A-2. HTML Page with a Form

```
1    <?xml version='1.0' encoding='UTF-8' ?>
2    <!DOCTYPE html>
3    <html>
4        <head>
5            <title>form demo</title>
6        </head>
7        <body>
8            <form>
9                <label for="txtName">Name:</label>
10               <input type="text" id="txtName"/>
```

```
11                <br/>
12                Nationality
13                <select>
14                    <option>English</option>
15                    <option>French</option>
16                    <option>German</option>
17                </select>
18                <br/>
19                <input type="submit" value="send"/>
20            </form>
21        </body>
22    </html>
```

Literal text within the tags, such as Name: or Nationality, shown in Figure A-1, is displayed as is.

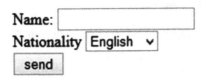

Figure A-1. *Output of form demo*

Other tags in this category include fieldset, legend, datalist, optgroup, option, textarea, keygen, output, progress, and meter.

Tables

Tag Name	Description
table	An HTML table element.
caption	Table caption.
thead	Table header. Optional semantic decoration.
tbody	Table body. Optional semantic decoration. A table might contain more than one body section.
tfoot	Table footer. Optional semantic decoration.
tr	Table row. Nested directly into table or in one of the three sub-parts. Optional, if there's only one row.
th	Column header. Content of a header cell. Displayed in bold, if any style is omitted.
td	Table data. Value of a table cell.
colgroup	Optional column group. Container for column definitions, for example to define styles for the columns.
col	One column.

Listing A-3 shows an HTML table in action.

Listing A-3. HTML Page with a Table

```
1    <?xml version='1.0' encoding='UTF-8' ?>
2    <!DOCTYPE html>
3    <html>
4        <head>
5            <title>Table demo</title>
6        </head>
7        <body>
8            <table>
9                <caption>Invoice</caption>
10               <colgroup>
11               <!-- if used, you'll find attributes for each col -->
12                   <col/>
13                   <col/>
```

```
14                     <col/>
15              </colgroup>
16              <thead>
17                 <tr>
18                     <th>Amount</th>
19                     <th>Description</th>
20                     <th>Price</th>
21                 </tr>
22              </thead>
23              <tbody>
24                 <tr>
25                     <td>1</td>
26                     <td>Personal Computer</td>
27                     <td>500</td>
28                 </tr>
29                 <tr>
30                     <td>1</td>
31                     <td>Laser printer</td>
32                     <td>300</td>
33                 </tr>
34              </tbody>
35              <tfoot>
36                 <tr>
37                     <td></td>
38                     <td>Total</td>
39                     <td>800</td>
40                 </tr>
41              </tfoot>
42          </table>
43      </body>
44  </html>
```

Using the full decoration, as Listing A-3 does, is unusual. Omitting optional elements, you'll get a more commonly used table definition, as shown in Listing A-4.

Listing A-4. HTML Page with a Table, Simplified

```
1    <?xml version='1.0' encoding='UTF-8' ?>
2    <!DOCTYPE html>
3    <html>
4        <head>
5            <title>Table demo</title>
6        </head>
7        <body>
8            <table>
9                <caption>Invoice</caption>
10               <th>Amount</th>
11               <th>Description</th>
12               <th>Price</th>
13               <tr>
14                   <td>1</td>
15                   <td>Personal Computer</td>
16                   <td>500</td>
17               </tr>
18               <tr>
19                   <td>1</td>
20                   <td>Laser printer</td>
21                   <td>300</td>
22               </tr>
23               <tr>
24                   <td></td>
25                   <td>Total</td>
26                   <td>800</td>
27               </tr>
28           </table>
29       </body>
30   </html>
```

Both versions produce a page like Figure A-2.

Amount	Invoice	
	Description	Price
	Personal Computer	500
1		
	Laser printer	300
1		
	Total	800

Figure A-2. *Output of HTML table*

Using appropriate attributes—or even better, using CSS—you can style a table with borders and other decoration.

Tag Completion/Tag Guessing

Consider the simple input tag `<input type="text" id="txtName"/>`. The tag is correctly closed by a slash /. Using HTML5, it can omit this slash: `<input type="text" id="txtName">`. Although in older versions, `<br>`, could be used instead of the correct `<br/>`.

Here are some formatting elements:

```
This text is <b> bold, <i> bold and italics, </b> italics only.
```

Most browsers will render "This text is **bold, *bold and italics,* *italics only.***" In XML, that code wouldn't be valid. You can't overlap tags, and for every opening tag, a closing counterpart is required.

This would be correct within XML:

```
This text is <b> bold, <i> bold and italics, </i></b> <i>italics only.</i>
```

Tip   Remember that HTML should be used for content only—formatting should be performed by CSS. So, don't use these elements in a real HTML page. In the sloppy version, if some text follows the missing italics end tag, it will be displayed in italics.

As these examples show, browsers *try* to interpret sloppy HTML pages. Some people revel in this feature of browsers. Some love to omit everything a browser tries to complete by itself to reduce load time. But really, if you omit such a small fraction of characters, less than 1 percent, *you* might be able to measure a shortened load time, but the user would never notice it.

In his book *Tangled Web* (No Starch Press, 2011), Michal Zelewski shows which flaws might occur by this attempted tag completion, which often amounts to simply tag *guessing*. For security reasons, all tags should be valid in the sense of XML. This can be enforced by using XHTML, which is HTML refined as valid XML code.

For those programmers new to web development, who have never used HTML before, this appendix is only a very basic introduction. For learning HTML, lots of good books are available on the market, and you can find lots of online tutorials on the Internet.

Tip   W3schools offers some nice tutorials into different web technologies, including HTML. You can check it out at `www.w3schools.com/html`.

APPENDIX B

Cascading Style Sheets

CSS is a language to add styling information to HTML, XML, or other kinds of documents. It's designed to support the separation of content (HTML) and style (CSS). For example, there's no need to use old styling elements of HTML like <i> and <b> because all styling can be applied better with CSS.

In short, CSS addresses an HTML (or XML) element with a *selector* (a kind of path) and applies a group of one or more styles to it. Different selectors may refer to the same element. CSS resolves the so-called *cascade* and applies all styles to the element. If the same style element will be applied, CSS determines the most specific selector, or if still ambiguous, the last definition.

CSS can be included within the style tag of the HTML page. We'll use this here for demonstration purpose only. In real applications (like Books and Alumni, described in this book), all CSS statements are placed into a separate file as described by these apps. This allows the reuse of the same definition for different pages and applies a consistent look and feel.

Listing B-1 shows a small example, and Figure B-1 shows the output.

Listing B-1. HTML Page with Embedded CSS

```
1    <?xml version='1.0' encoding='UTF-8' ?>
2    <!DOCTYPE html>
3    <html>
4        <head>
5            <title>CSS demo</title>
6        </head>
7
8        <style type="text/css">
9            label {
```

© Michael Müller 2018
M. Müller, *Practical JSF in Java EE 8*, https://doi.org/10.1007/978-1-4842-3030-5

```
10                    font-weight: bold;
11                    font-size: 2em;
12              }
13          form label {
14                color: red;
15                font-size: 1em;
16              }
17        </style>
18
19        <body>
20            <label>Enter your name</label>
21            <br/>
22            <form>
23                <label for="txtName">Name:</label>
24                <input type="text" id="txtName"/>
25                <input type="submit" value="send"/>
26            </form>
27        </body>
28    </html>
```

Enter your name

Name: [   ] send

Figure B-1. *CSS applied*

label is an element selector. It simply selects an HTML element. Other kinds of selectors include id selectors and class selectors (discussed shortly). Following this selector, the styles are specified within curly braces. The styles in this example are self-explanatory. The unit of the font size is a relative unit: 2em doubles the size within the current context.

form label is a composite element selector, addressing labels nested within a form element. As you can see, the color style is added to the bold style, while the font-size is overwritten, because the selector is more specific than the standalone label selector. If you exchange the order, the result will be the same.

But if you use a selector which is as specific as a selector specified earlier in this file, it will overwrite the style, as shown in Listing B-2. Figure B-2 shows the output. Because the font-size in line 13 refers to label with the same specifity as in line 5, the font-size will be set to this size, overwriting (or simply ignoring) the format made in line 5.

Listing B-2. Example of CSS Overwriting Former Instruction

```
1   ...
2       <style type="text/css">
3           label {
4               font-weight: bold;
5               font-size: 2em;
6           }
7           form label {
8               color: red;
9               font-size: 1em;
10          }
11          label {
12              font-weight: normal;
13              font-size: 1em;
14          }
15      </style>
16  ...
```

Enter your name
Name: [   ] send

Figure B-2. *CSS applied*

Line breaks and spacing as used in the examples are optional. This

```
1   form label {
2       color: red;
3       font-size: 1em;
4   }
```

is equivalent to this:

```
1   form label {color: red; font-size: 1em;}
```

Multiple elements might be declared at the same time, using a comma as separator. The following

```
1   label {font-size: 1em;}
2   input {font-size: 1em;}
```

441

is equivalent to this:

```
1    label, input {font-size: 1em;}
```

Selectors

Any CSS instruction is applied to the element(s) addressed by a selector. In the former examples the element names had been used as such a selector. CSS knows various kinds of selectors.

Type Selector

All selectors discussed so far have been *type* selectors, sometimes known as *element* selectors. The elements are addressed by their tag names.

Id Selector

Here an element is addressed by its id. Id selectors start with a hash sign (#). Here's an example:

```
1    #txtName {color: red;}
```

Class Selector

Here an element is addressed by its class name. Class selectors start with a dot (.), as shown in Listing B-3.

Listing B-3. CSS class

```
1    ...
2        <style type="text/css">
3            .requiredInput {background-color: yellow;}
4        </style>
5    ...
6        <input type="text" id="txtName" class="requiredInput"/>
7    ...
```

Attribute Selector

The *attribute* of an element and its value are indicated by square brackets. Listing B-4 illustrates.

Listing B-4. CSS Instruction for an Element Type

```
1    ...
2        <style type="text/css">
3            [type="text"] {background-color: yellow;}
4        </style>
5    ...
6        <input type="text" id="txtName"/>
7    ...
```

Nesting Selector

One selector to address nested structures was used in the introductory example: tagname1 tagname2 refers to an element of type tagname2, which is nested into an element of type tagname1. tagname2 might be nested anywhere within tagname1.

Note that the > addresses elements that are immediately nested, as shown in line 17 of Listing B-5 (Figure B-3 shows the output).

Listing B-5. CSS Nesting Selector (Line 17)

```
1    <?xml version='1.0' encoding='UTF-8' ?>
2    <!DOCTYPE html>
3    <html>
4        <head>
5            <title>CSS demo</title>
6        </head>
7
8        <style type="text/css">
9            label {
10               font-weight: bold;
11               font-size: 2em;
12           }
```

```
13          form label {
14              color: red;
15              font-size: 1em;
16          }
17          form > label {
18              color: blue;
19          }
20      </style>
21
22      <body>
23          <label>Personal information</label>
24          <br/>
25          <form>
26              <label>Enter your name</label>
27              <br/>
28              <div>
29                  <label for="txtFirstName">Last name:</label>
30                  <input type="text" id="txtFirstName"/>
31              </div>
32              <div>
33                  <label for="txtLasrName">First name:</label>
34                  <input type="text" id="txtLastName"/>
35              </div>
36                  <input type="submit" value="send"/>
37          </form>
38      </body>
39  </html>
```

Personal information

Enter your name
Last name: [   ]
First name: [   ]
[send]

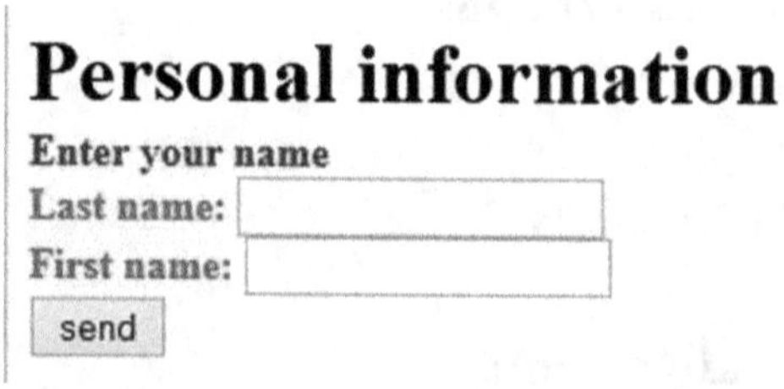

Figure B-3. *CSS nesting example*

Only Enter your name is displayed in blue. Using the > operator, the labels for entering last or first name could have been addressed by form > div > label, because this includes the missing div in the path.

Sibling Selector

The tilde (~) selects all the following siblings of an element. A *sibling* is an element on the same nesting level. The plus sign (+) selects the neighbor sibling element. Listing B-6 illustrates, and Figure B-4 displays the output.

Listing B-6. Sibling Selector Example

```
1    <?xml version='1.0' encoding='UTF-8' ?>
2    <!DOCTYPE html>
3    <html>
4        <head>
5            <title>CSS demo</title>
6        </head>
7
8        <style type="text/css">
9            label {
10                font-weight: bold;
11            }
12            label ~ label {
13                color: green;
14            }
15            label + label {
16                font-size: 2em;
17            }
18        </style>
19
20        <body>
21            <label>first label</label>
22            <label>second label</label>
23            <br/>
24            <label>third label</label>
25        <body>
26    </html>
```

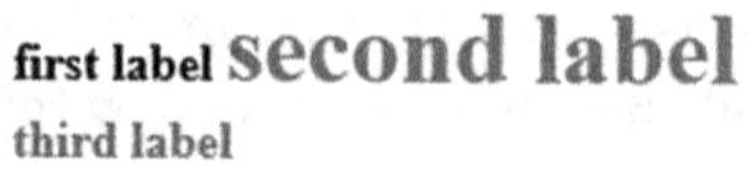

first label second label

third label

Figure B-4. *CSS sibling example*

`label ~ label` is used to select the second and third labels, which both are siblings of the first label. `label + label` selects only the second label, which immediately follows the first label, whereas the third is separated by a `<br/>` tag.

Box Model

Each element uses a space, which is determined by its display style and its content.

Text elements like `label` or `input` are of display type `inline`. The width of an element is determined by its content. Each element is arranged right of the previous one. Depending on browser window size, line breaks may be inserted.

Elements like `div` are `block` elements. These elements can have a width attribute to define their width. Otherwise, the full width of the browser window is used. `block` elements are arranged vertically.

With CSS, it's possible to define a display type `inline-block`. (Valid values for the `property` display are `none`, `inline`, `block`, and `inline-block`.) Such elements are arranged horizontally like `inline`, but it's possible to define a width independently from its content. For example, consider a `label`, which usually ends where the text finishes, regardless of a width declaration. If you use `display: inline-block;` you may assign a width of your choice to that label.

The height of an element is usually determined by its content.

In a *box model*, each element has a width determined by its content, or in the case of a `block` (including `inline-block`) element, by a `width` attribute. The height is usually determined automatically. Surrounding the element is a `padding` of a defined size, which might be 0. Outside this padding, a `border` may be defined. And beyond the border there is a `margin`.

Listing B-7 demonstrates this model, and its output is shown in Figure B-5. To make the padding visible, each `div` element has its own background color that surrounds the inner `label`. The `margin`'s background is transparent. It simply defines the gap between browser the elements as well as the distance to the browser's border. To make it visible in this book, the background color of the whole HTML document is set to gray.

Listing B-7. CSS Box Model

```
1    <?xml version='1.0' encoding='UTF-8' ?>
2    <!DOCTYPE html>
3    <html>
4        <style type="text/css">
5            html {
6                background-color: lightgray;
7            }
8            div {
9                display: inline-block;
10               width: 60px;
11               padding: 10px;
12               border-style: solid;
13               border-color: blue;
14               border-width: 10px;
15               margin: 20px;
16               background-color: red;
17           }
18           div + div {
19               background-color: orange;
20           }
21           br + div {
22               width: 200px;
23               background-color: green;
24           }
25           label{
26               background-color: white;
27           }
28           div + div > label{
29               display: inline-block;
30               width: 60px;
31           }
32       </style>
33
34       <body>
```

447

```
35          <div><label>content<label></div>
36          <div><label>content<label></div>
37          <br/>
38          <div><label>content<label></div>
39       <body>
40    </html>
```

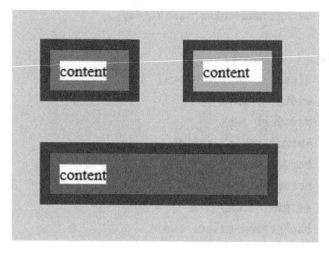

Figure B-5. *CSS box model example*

The boxes in the first line both have a width of 60 pixels. This is more than the width of the label contained in this div. For the second div, the label display is re-defined as inline-block. This allows defining a width for this label. As you can see, the label (white background) gets wider, but the width of the div (which is of the same width) doesn't change.

The two elements of the first line seems to have the same width as the third box. But 2*60 is not equal to 200!

Characteristic of the box model is that it defines the content size, not the whole display size. So we have to add padding, border, and margin, both on the left and right side. 2*(60+2*padding+2*border+2*margin) = 2*(60+20+20+40) = 280, and this equals the second line, 200+20+20+40 = 280.

The understanding of this box model is essential for calculating a layout. With CSS3, it's possible to change this default model by box-sizing: border-box;. Applying border-box, the width determines the width including padding and border.

Note   To enable a simple calculation, the example for the box model uses a fixed size, given in pixels. For real applications, relative sizes like em (as used in the other examples) or percent should be preferred. Relative sizes simply allow changing the size globally and are essential for a responsive design.

Enhanced Styling

With CSS, it's possible to reorder the content. Or to add text or images. Or to change the design depending on the display size. This appendix merely introduced the basics of CSS.

The applications in this book sometimes use such enhanced styling features, such as pseudo elements, divers positioning, background, media queries, and more. They're described in the appropriate chapters.

Note   If you want to learn CSS, lots of good books are available on the market, and plenty of good online tutorials are on the Internet. W3schools's CSS tutorial is worth a look: `www.w3schools.com/css`.

APPENDIX C

Tag Libraries

When developing a web application, you always have to create some HTML pages to be displayed in the browser. One approach is to hide the HTML handling and fully generate the pages. The other extreme is to mix the application code into a HTML page.

But the most common solution is to separate page from code. To do that, some instructions are placed into the page that invoke your code. Technically, these instructions are HTML/XML tags or attributes, although some may call them something else. For example, AngularJS instructions are HTML attributes, but they call them *directives*. "Traditional" JSF apps are usually built with tags, but since JSF 2.2, you can waive some tags and use pass-through elements instead.

All those tags are grouped together and are available using different namespaces. Table C-1 provides an overview about these namespaces.

Table C-1. *Namespaces*

URI	Prefix	Description
`http://xmlns.jcp.org/jsf`	`jsf:`	Pass-through elements
`http://xmlns.jcp.org/jsf/core`	`f:`	JSF core library
`http://xmlns.jcp.org/jsf/html`	`h:`	JSF HTML library
`http://xmlns.jcp.org/jsf/facelets/`	`ui:`	Facelet Templating tag library
`http://xmlns.jcp.org/jsf/composite`	`cc:`	Composite Component tag library
`http://xmlns.jcp.org/jsf/passthrough`	`p:`	Pass-through attributes
`http://xmlns.jcp.org/jsp/jstl/core`	`c:`	JSP Standard Tag Library (JSTL)
`http://xmlns.jcp.org/jsp/jstl/ functions`	`fn:`	JSTL functions

© Michael Müller 2018
M. Müller, *Practical JSF in Java EE 8*, https://doi.org/10.1007/978-1-4842-3030-5

This appendix gives a brief overview of and quick reference to tags from the Standard JSF Component Library and JSP Standard Tag Library. Full references are available online (https://javaserverfaces.github.io/docs/2.3/index.html), or check out *JavaServer Faces 2.0* by Ed Burns and Chris Schalk (McGraw-Hill, 2010). Note that although that book was written for JSF 2.0, it's still useful for JSF 2.3.

The tags are grouped by library and listed alphabetically. Additionally, some common attributes are described.

Pass-through Elements

This is only a marker namespace. JSF tries to detect components, which are marked by jsf: (or whatever alias you've chosen with the namespace declaration). Known components are added to the component tree as if defined in one of the other libraries. Unknown components are added as pass-through elements.

JSF Core Library

Elements of the JSF core library are usually prefixed with f:, but you can change that during the declaration of the namespace. The tags (as well as those of the other libraries) are listed in Table C-2 without any prefix.

Table C-2. Namespaces

Tag Name	Description
actionListener	Declarative registers an ActionListener to the closest parent UIComponent.
ajax	Declarative adds an AjaxBehavior to the parent UIComponent or to its child UIComponents.
attribute	Adds an attribute to the surrounding UI component.
attributes	Adds attributes to a map for the surrounding UI component.
convertDateTime	Registers a DateTimeConverter for a UIcomponent.
converter	Registers a named (self-written) converter for a UIcomponent.

(continued)

Table C-2. (*continued*)

Tag Name	Description
convertNumber	Registers a `NumberConverter` for a `UIcomponent`.
event	Registers a `ComponentSystemEventListener` for a `UIComponent`.
facet	Registers a named facet for a `UIComponent`.
importConstants	Imports constants so they can be used within the EL.
loadBundle	Loads a localized resource bundle if available, otherwise the default resource bundle.
metadata	Declares metadata for a Facelets view. Using Facelets, a view corresponds to a (HTML) page, if not specified by the optional `f:view`.
param	Adds a parameter to the closest parent `UIComponent`.
passThroughAttribute	Defines a pass-through attribute. Such an attribute would be passed to a browser without interpretation by JSF.
passThroughAttributes	Pass through a group of parameters delivered by EL as a `Map<String, Object>`.
phaseListener	Adds a listener to phase events.
resetValues	Resets the values of the components declared in the render attribute, for example to clear input fields of a form.
selectItem	Adds an item to a select box, or combo box.
selectItems	Adds multiple items provided by an EL expression to a select box.
setPropertyActionListener	Registers an action listener to the closest parent `UIComponent`.
subview	Defines a subview component for pages with JSP. Has no purpose on modern Facelets pages.
validateBean	Causes the closest parent `UIComponent` or all nested `UIComponents` to be validated by bean validation.

(*continued*)

Table C-2. (*continued*)

Tag Name	Description
validateDoubleRange	Validates a range (minimum to maximum, both optional) of values of an inputText component with a backing field of type double.
validateLength	Validates the length of the closest parent UIComponent.
validateLongRange	Same as validateDoubleRange, but for a Long.
validateRegex	Validates the input against a regular expression.
validateRequired	Declares the closest parent UIComponent being required. Same effect as the required="true" attribute.
validator	Registers a validator for the closest parent EditableValueHolder, for example input text.
valueChangeListener	Registers a listener to the valueChange event of the closest parent UIComponent.
verbatim	Registers a child UIOutput element for JSP. No purpose for modern Facelets pages.
view	The container for all JSF components. Using Facelets, the view is implicitly declared, so there is no need for an explicit view tag. But you might use it to pass additional information like language and so on.
viewAction	Register an action (method) to be invoked in a given phase. To be used within the metadata tag.
viewParam	Retrieve a parameter (id and value) from a get request. To be used within the metadata tag.
websocket	Registers a websocket connection that receives push messages sent by the server.

JSF HTML Library

The HTML library contains tags that are rendered to HTML elements. HTML elements are not only rendered, JSF-specific features are added too. The common namespace is h (prefix h:). Table C-3 lists these tags.

Table C-3. *JSF HTML Library*

Tag name	Description
body	Counterpart to HTML body tag. It also offers resource relocation, for example for JavaScript or CSS files.
button	Renders an HTML input element of type submit. This is used to perform a navigation by an HTTP GET to the URL specified by the outcome attribute.
column	Represents the column of a dataTable. The content of the column as well as its header are defined within suitable sub-elements.
commandButton	Renders an HTML input element of type submit, reset, or image. It may perform an action and/or a navigation.
commandLink	Renders an HTML link (<a href=...> and may perform an action on click.
dataTable	Renders an HTML table with as many rows as provided by the collection or other suitable data structure.
doctype	Renders a doctype declaration.
form	Renders an HTML form and adds it to the JSF component tree. When the form is submitted, all the JSF components within that tag will be processed. A couple of JSF elements, including commandLink, need to be nested in a JSF form for proper function.
graphicImage	Renders an image that's provided in a resource folder.
head	Not only renders a HTML head element, but is used as parent element when using resource relocation, for example to load a script or CSS file from one of the resource folders.

(*continued*)

Table C-3. (*continued*)

Tag name	Description
inputFile	Used to browse for and upload a file.
inputHidden	Renders an HTML input field of type hidden. Like the other input elements, a value from a backing bean may be assigned too.
inputSecret	Renders an HTML input field of type password. All input characters will be displayed as asterisks.
inputText	Renders an HTML input field of type text. This tag is the workhorse for most forms.
inputTextarea	Renders an HTML textarea. Like the inputText, this might be used to display and query some text. It might contain multi-line text, which covers a bigger area on the screen. Most modern browsers allow the user to resize this element.
link	Renders an HTML link (<a href=...> that can be used for bookmarkable navigation.
message	Used to display the first Faces message that is queued for an (input) element to which the message element refers.
messages	Able to display all messages that are not displayed by a certain message tag or that will be displayed globally.
outputFormat	Renders an HTML spam element to display the text bound to this component by the binding attribute or value. This element might be parameterized by param subcomponents and will be formatted by a MessageFormat.format() method.
outputLabel	Renders an HTML label. It might be assigned to an input element through its for attribute.
outputLink	Renders an HTML link (<a href=...>, which is mostly used to navigate outside the app.
outputScript	Used to include a script file via resource relocation.
outputStylesheet	As before, but for a CSS file.

(*continued*)

Table C-3. (*continued*)

Tag name	Description
outputText	Renders its value as text within the page. By default, the < will be escaped as < to prevent HTML injection.
panelGrid	This component renders an HTML table. Its child components become cell content of that table.
panelGroup	This tag is rendered as an HTML span element containing all its child elements. It can be used to place a couple of elements somewhere only one element is expected, for example into one cell of a table.
selectBooleanCheckbox	Renders an HTML input element of type checkbox.
selectManyCheckbox	Renders an HTML table with a set of checkboxes, either in one row or one column, depending on the direction of the layout.
selectManyListbox	Renders a listbox (HTML select element) where the user may choose from multiple entries.
selectManyMenu	Renders an HTML select element with a height of 1. The user may open it like a drop-down list and choose multiple elements.
selectOneListbox	Renders a listbox (HTML select element) where the user may choose from one entry.
selectOneMenu	Renders an HTML select element with a height of 1, which acts as a drop-down list to select one element.
selectOneRadio	Renders a set of radio buttons. Like the buttons on old car radios, the user may choose exactly one of them.

Common Attributes

This section describes some attributes which are widely used in many tags described before. Table C-4 lists these tags.

Table C-4. *Attributes*

Tag Name	Description
disabled	If true (default is false), the element will be rendered "grayed," indicating no input or other action is possible.
id	Provides an id to the element. An element may be accessed by its id, which needs to be unique within its scope.
for	Takes the id of another element the element containing this attribute refers to. Used for labels or messages.
readonly	The component will be rendered as usual, but input is impossible.
rendered	Defines a condition to render the component. The default is true. An element without this attribute will be rendered.
styleClass	Defines the CSS class used for this element. Renders to the HTML class attribute.

Facelet Templating Tag Library

The Standard Facelets Templating Library is available for the Facelets UI language, but not JSP. I recommended preferring Facelets over JSP because lots of new features are only available for this view declaration language. This library is declared by the "http://xmlns.jcp.org/jsf/facelets" namespace and is prefixed with a default prefix of ui. Table C-5 lists these tags.

Table C-5. *Facelets Tags*

Tag Name	Description
component	Former version of composition as used for Facelets prior to JSF 2.0. Unlike composition, this can't specify a template.
composition	This defines a composition of elements (part of a page) that can be included by include into other pages or compositions. A composition may define a template where it's used from. In such a case, navigating to the composition will render the whole template. All markup outside composition will be ignored.
debug	Provides some internal information for debugging purposes, like the component tree. Will be invoked by pressing Ctrl+Shift+D by default, or another hotkey if defined.
decorate	A reusable fragment of a page, similar to composition. Unlike composition, any markup outside this element will be used too.
define	Defines the part of a composition that will be inserted in the Facelets template at the place of an insert tag that defines the same name you provide the define tag.
fragment	Defines a reusable part of a page, like component. Unlike component, any markup outside fragment is recognized too.
include	Includes the file that's defined by the src attribute into the current Facelets view.
insert	Inserts content into a template. (See composition.)
param	Used within the include tag, param is able to pass a parameter (key + value) into the included composition or other appropriate tag.
remove	Removes the included markup at compile time. Might be used for comments, which won't be rendered to the client.
repeat	Iterates over a collection. For each iteration, a copy of all of its child elements will be included into the component tree. Used to repeat elements without the need for rendering a table. If a table is needed, prefer dataTable.

Composite Component Tag Library

JSF 2.0 and later supports composite components built up by using the VDL.
A component consists of two main parts: the interface and the implementation. The Composite Component tag library offers tags for both, as well as tags for other properties to modify the behavior of a component. Table C-6 lists these tags.

Table C-6. *Composite Component Tags*

Tag Name	Description
ActionSource	Defines a part of the composite component that can have an actionListener attached.
attribute	Within the interface it defines an attribute (parameter) that can be passed from the using component into the composite component.
clientBehavior	Defines a client behavior. Usually an event of a subcomponent that can be subscribed by the calling (using) component.
editableValueHolder	Defines one or more subcomponents that can have a converter tag or valueChangeListener attached.
extension	Can be used to pass design time metadata to the composite component according to JSR 276. JSR 276 is in "dormant" status.
facet	This can be used within the interface to declare a named facet, which can be passed from the using component to a facet declaration within the implementation.
implementation	This tag encapsulates the implementation of the component. Within the tag, arbitrary components can be arranged that define the component.
insertChildren	Defines an insertion point to insert one or more components that have been nested into the using component.
insertFacet	Defines the place where a named facet (as defined within the interface section) will be inserted.
interface	Defines the interface of the component.
renderFacet	Inserts a named facet into the implementation part of the composite component.
valueHolder	Defines one or more subcomponents that can have a converter tag attached.

Pass-through Attributes

This is a marker namespace only. As mentioned in the JSF spec, it might be declared as
`xmlns:p="http://xmlns.jcp.org/jsf/passthrough"`.

If JSF detects an attribute marked by `p:` (or whatever alias you've chosen by the namespace declaration) it will render this attribute without modification.

Before pass-through attributes became live with JSF 2.2, the `p:` alias commonly had been used for the PrimeFaces library, so you might choose `pt:` instead.

JSP Standard Tag Library (JSTL)

Before JSF 2.0, JSP was the only view definition language (VDL). Now Facelets is the preferred VDL, and the major enhancements are available for Facelets only. For backward compatibility, JSP is still supported and thus the JSTL. Most of these tags might be replaced by Facelet tags. But in some special situations, it might be appropriate to use a tag handler instead of a UI component, for example `forEach` in place of `repeat`. The following table shows only that excerpt of the JST which is offered by NetBeans autocompletion. Table C-7 lists these tags.

Table C-7. *JSTL Attributes*

Tag Name	Description
catch	Can be used as a parent tag to catch all exceptions thrown by the handling of its subtags.
choose	Parent tag for a cascade of when(s) and otherwise. Similar to the Java `switch` statement.
forEach	Iterates over a collection or range of values.
if	Test for a condition. Handles all its nested elements only if the test results to true.
otherwise	Child of `choose`. Similar to `default` of a Java `switch`.
set	Sets the value of a variable. Usually the result of an EL expression (or JSTL function).
when	Child of `choose`. Similar to `case` of a Java `switch`.

JSTL Functions

These functions likewise exist for backward compatibility. Usually they can be fully replaced by the EL. They're listed here for the sake of completeness, but I don't discuss them in this book. Table C-8 lists these tags.

Table C-8. *JSTL Functions*

Tag Name	Description
contains(dataString, search)	Produces true if search is contained in dataString.
containsIgnoreCase(dataString, searchString)	Same as before, but case insensitive.
endsWith(string, subString)	Tests whether string ends with subString.
escapeXml(string)	Replaces character which that be interpreted as XML markup by XML entities, for example < becomes &lt.
indexOf(string, subString)	Returns the index of subString within string.
join(stringArray, delimiter)	Concatenates all elements of the array with delimiter in between.
length(string)	Returns the length of string.
replace(string, find, replace)	Replaces all occurrences of find by replace within string.
split(string, delimiter)	Splits string by delimiter into an array of strings.
startsWith(string, subString)	Tests whether string starts with subString.
substring(string, start, end)	Returns a part (substring) of string as defined by the index start and end (excluded).
substringAfter(string, subString)	Returns the part of string after subString.
substringBefore(string, subString)	Returns the part of string before subString.
toLowerCase(string)	Returns string converted to lowercase.
toUpperCase(string)	Returns string converted to uppercase.
trim(string)	Returns string without leading or trailing white space.

APPENDIX D

Programming Style

As you may have noticed, I always use an underscore to prefix fields. Oracle recommends against starting a variable with an underscore or a dollar sign (you can read this recommendation for yourself at `http://docs.oracle.com/javase/tutorial/java/nutsandbolts/variables.html`), although it says that the practice is technically legal. One of my technical reviewers requested that I strictly follow the Java naming conventions, arguing that this is a book for novices and should follow convention.

But this is not a book for programming novices. It's for experienced Java developers who are new to JSF and, perhaps, to web development. A naming convention is not a law, and anyway, the convention in question is just a recommendation in a tutorial. If you take a look at the Java naming convention site (`www.oracle.com/technetwork/java/codeconventions-135099.html`), you'll can see that it's not maintained anymore: "This page is not being actively maintained. . . . The last revision to this document was made on April 20, 1999." So, it's quite old.

I have some reasons to prefix fields, which I'm going to explain. I don't want to start a discussion about the pros and cons. I just to explain why I do it this way. As an experienced Java developer, you should be able to transform my source code into a different style. Using a modern IDE, that would involve nothing more than a small rename.

Let's go back a few years in history, to when the so-called *Hungarian notation* was useful and popular. Using this notation, every variable is prefixed by its type, for example `intNumber`, which should indicate that the underlying type is an integer. This had been very helpful for languages that aren't strongly typed. `intNumber = 3.142` might be a valid assignment. In such a case, the prefix should remind the programmer to use integer values only.

For Java, with its strong type system, there's no need to use this Hungarian notation. if you declare `int number`, the compiler would reject `number = 3.142`.

© Michael Müller 2018

M. Müller, *Practical JSF in Java EE 8*, https://doi.org/10.1007/978-1-4842-3030-5

Similarly, a second prefix was used to indicate a broader scope of a variable. For example, a prefix mb_ indicated a *member variable*, which we call a *field*. No question, mb_intNumber is a really ugly variable name. So let's throw away these old-fashioned prefixes. For a modern programming language, there is no need for them.

But what happens to properties? If we have a field number and we want to assign a new value with a getter? Because of variable hiding, you can't do it this way:

```
1   private int number;
2   public void setNumber(int number){
3      number = number;
4   }
```

To distinguish field and local variables, you need different names. This is the C# way, translated into Java:

```
1   private int number;
2   public void setNumber(int value){
3      number = value;
4   }
```

Now, the method signature always contains value, which might be meaningless. Next approach:

```
1   private int fNumber;
2   public void setNumber(int number){
3      fNumber = number;
4   }
```

Now we have different names for field and local variables, but it's harder to read. And according to the "rules" of camelCase, the variable name becomes uppercase. Let's try the underscore:

```
1   private int _number;
2   public void setNumber(int number){
3      _number = number;
4   }
```

The underscore is less disturbing than any other prefix. The field name will be written in lowercase as usual. The only drawback is that it doesn't follow the full naming convention.

There's another common solution to this problem: using `this`:

```
1   private int number;
2   public void setNumber(int number){
3     this.number = number;
4   }
```

In my opinion, that fits the naming convention but is a misuse of `this`. `this` refers to the object itself (other languages use `self`). It's very useful if an object needs to pass itself to some method or create a fluent interface (such as a builder) to return itself. But here it's simply (mis)used to distinguish a field from a variable, which could be better done by choosing a different name.

Let's take a look at copying a file within a folder:

```
copy file1 file2
```

If you need to copy the folder, you might use a dot:

```
copy .\otherFolder
```

Although it's technically possible to use the dot for a file in the current directory, you usually won't use

```
copy .\file1 .\file2
```

or `cp ./file1 ./file2` the UNIX way.

That looks strange and ugly—like `this.field` looks strange and ugly to me.

And if you're a polyglot programmer, using C# too, you may know that this prefix is very common in this Java sibling (both are C-like languages). In rare cases, there might be a need to edit the source outside an IDE using a simple editor without syntax coloring. As a side effect, the underscore is very helpful in identifying a field in such situations.

Now you know why I'm using the underscore prefix for fields in all my projects, including this book. But you are welcome to change it in your version of the downloaded sources.

APPENDIX E

Bibliography

Title	Author(s)	Publisher and Year
Java EE 7	Arun Gupta	O'Reilly, 2013
Mastering JSF 2.2	Anghel Leonard	Packt Publishing, 2014
Continuous Enterprise Development in Java	Andrew Lee Rubinger, Aslak Knutsen	O'Reilly, 2014
JavaServer Faces 2.0	Ed Burns, Chris Schalk	McGraw-Hill, 2010
Design Patterns: Elements of Reusable Object-Oriented Software	Erich Gamma, Richard Helm, Ralph Johnson, John Vlissides	Addison-Wesley, 1994
The Tangled Web: A Guide to Securing Modern Web Applications	Michal Zalewski	No Starch Press, 2011
Selenium WebDriver Practical Guide	Satya Avasarala	Packt Publishing, 2014

You'll find more, including lots of German titles, at `http://it-rezension.de/Books`.

© Michael Müller 2018
M. Müller, *Practical JSF in Java EE 8*, https://doi.org/10.1007/978-1-4842-3030-5

Afterword

Although we just started with Alumni, the goal is not to describe the whole application but interesting aspects with respect to JSF. Creating a final class for example is similar to entering data as we did for Books. The principle is the same, just the content is different.

Of course, there might be more JSF stuff to instruct. For example, JSF 2.2 introduced the flow scope.[1] This kind of scope has defined entry and exit points. It is really good if you like to define a series of logically coupled pages like a wizard. Neither of my application uses such a feature. They are designed in a way that the user might navigate to any page at any time, improperly for the flow scope.

Instead of focusing on every JSF feature, this book focused on practical development by real applications. You did not suffer every JSF detail, but you learned (I hope you did) a lot of related Java EE technologies. These are the foundations for you to create your own applications. I predict, enhancing your knowledge will be relatively easily once you start developing with JSF. If you need more than we covered within this book, please refer to the JSF and Java EE reference.

I'm going to finish this book before it gets oversized and boring. I hope you enjoyed reading and found value in it.

Follow my blog at `https://blog.mueller-bruehl.de`. And maybe you can leave a comment there about this book.

Stay tuned!

—Michael

---

[1]`https://javaserverfaces.github.io/docs/2.3/javadocs/javax/faces/flow/FlowScoped.html`

469

© Michael Müller 2018
M. Müller, *Practical JSF in Java EE 8*, https://doi.org/10.1007/978-1-4842-3030-5

Index

© Michael Müller 2018
M. Müller, *Practical JSF in Java EE 8*, https://doi.org/10.1007/978-1-4842-3030-5